Interpersonal Essentials

Melanie Booth-Butterfield

West Virginia University

D1366303

Allyn and Bacon

Boston ∎ London ∎ Toronto ∎ Sydney ∎ Tokyo ∎ Singapore

Editor in Chief: Karen Hanson
Series Editor: Karon Bowers
Marketing Manager: Mandee Eckersley
Editorial-Production Service: Matrix Productions Inc.
Composition and Prepress Buyer: Linda Cox
Manufacturing Buyer: Julie McNeill
Cover Administrator: Kristina Mose-Libon
Electronic Composition: Cabot Computer Services

Between the time Website information is gathered and then published, it is not
unusual for some sites to have closed. Also, the transcription of URLs can result
in unintended typographical errors. The publisher would appreciate notification
where these occur so that they may be corrected in subsequent editions.

Library of Congress Cataloging-in-Publication Data

Booth-Butterfield, Melanie.
    Interpersonal essentials / by Melanie Booth-Butterfield.
      p. cm.
    Includes bibliographical references and index.
    ISBN 0-205-31721-9
      1. Interpersonal communication.   I. Title.

BF637.C45 B6545 2002
158.1—dc21   2001045137

Printed in the United States of America

10   9   8   7   6   5   4   3   2   1   06   05   04   03   02   01

CONTENTS

Preface   ix

PART ONE   Beginning Interpersonal
Relationships: Understanding Yourself
in Interpersonal Communication   1

1 Interpersonal Communication in Relationships   1

Interpersonal Communication: What Is It Anyway?   2

Relationships of Choice   5

Principles of Interpersonal Communication   5

Communication Competence   7

Interpersonal Relationships and Cultural Background   9

2 Self-Concept and Self-Esteem   13

How Self-Esteem Influences
Interpersonal Communication   14

Origin of the Self   16

Three Types of Self-Concept   17

Interdependent versus Independent Self-Images   18

Falling in Love and Your Self-Concept   19

3 Perceptions and Impression Management   24

Importance of Initial Perceptions   25

Three Major Perceptions:
Character, Competence, and Composure   27

Perceptions of Attractiveness in Interpersonal Interactions   28

Similarities in Relational Perceptions   30

Why Similarities Are Attractive in Relationships   32

Managing the Impressions of Others: Communication   34

4 Interpersonal Needs and Trust   39

Interpersonal versus Physical Needs   40

Inclusion, Affection, and Control   42

Complementary versus Symmetrical
Needs in Relationships   44

Interpersonal Trust   46

5 Personality Traits in
Interpersonal Communication   56

Description of Traits   57

Link to Communication Process   58

Traits Operating in Communication Interactions   59

When Personality Traits Will Have the Most Influence   65

6 Shyness, Communication Apprehension,
and Avoidance   69

Shyness   70

Communication Apprehension   72

Willingness to Communicate   74

PART TWO   Relational Interactions:
Understanding the Interactive Nature
of Interpersonal Communication   82

7 Pattern of Relational Stages:
Coming Together and Falling Apart   82

Stages of Coming Together   83

Stages of Falling Apart   87

8 Expectations, Affinity, and Immediacy   94

Making Contact   95

Short-Term Relational Expectations   96

Affinity Seeking   96

Immediacy   102

**9 Nonverbal Messages in
Interpersonal Relationships   108**

Nonverbal Cues Early versus Later in a Relationship   109

Interpretation of *My* Nonverbal Messages
versus *Your* Nonverbal Messages   110

Forms of Nonverbal Messages in Relationships   111

How the Use of Time Communicates in Relationships   121

Nonverbal Sensitivity   123

Increasing Your Nonverbal Sensitivity   123

10 Saying It Right: The Impact of Words   126

Words Have Intentional and
Not-So-Intentional Meanings   128

Word Selection   129

Situations Affecting Verbal Communication   134

Verbal Communication:
A Requirement for Interpersonal Relationships   135

Verbal Communication Reflects Relationship Processes   136

11 Self-Disclosure   141

What Is Self-Disclosure?   142

Functions of Self-Disclosure   142

Levels of Self-Disclosure   144

Valence   144

Risk   145

When Is Self-Disclosing Appropriate?   146

Male and Female Differences in Disclosure Patterns   147

What Happens When You
Don't Disclose in Relationships?   148

Relational Implications   149

12 Listening and Understanding in Interpersonal Communication   153

Functions of Listening   154

Listening = Attention + Reception + Perception   156

Problems with Listening: Barriers We Construct   159

Behaviors Associated with Listening Competence   162

Perception Checking   164

Why Paraphrasing Works   165

Nonverbal Sensitivity as a Form of Listening   166

13 Understanding and Communicating Emotions   171

Components of Emotions   172

Characteristics of Emotions   173

Affective Orientation   175

Effective Communication of Emotions:
Own It, Name It, Locate It   176

A Specific Emotion: *Jealousy*   178

PART THREE Communication and Decisions to Maintain Relationships **186**

14 Making Decisions about Relationships: Resources and Social Exchange **186**

Resources **187**

Social Exchange **190**

Exchange versus Communal Orientation **193**

15 Relationships at Work: Just Friends, Flirting, or Harassment? **198**

Why Interpersonal Relationships Develop in Work Settings **199**

Differences between Work and Social Communication **200**

Just Friends: Platonic Relationships at Work **201**

What Is Flirting? **203**

What Is Sexual Harassment? **203**

Distinguishing between Flirting and Harassment **206**

Communication Strategies to Deal with Harassment **207**

16 Influence and Assertive Communication **212**

Dominance as Influence **213**

Assertive Communication **217**

What Assertiveness Can Do for You **220**

Verbal and Nonverbal Components of Assertiveness **222**

17 Conflict Management: How to "Fight Fair" **229**

What Constitutes Conflict? **230**

Sources of Interpersonal Conflict   230

Toxic Conflict Strategies   232

Interpersonal Problem Solving: Attitudes   234

"Rules" for Fair Fighting: Communication Skills   235

18 When All Else Fails: Making the Best of Termination   242

Dissatisfaction Phase   243

Reasons for Relational Termination   245

Communication during the Relational Termination Stage   246

Terminating So We "Can Still Be Friends"   248

You've Been Terminated . . .   250

Summary of Response to Relational Termination   253

Putting It All Together   253

Index   257

PREFACE

Whether you are students, professors, or out-of-school, lifelong learners, welcome to *Interpersonal Essentials*! This is a book for people who probably have never had a formal class on interpersonal communication in relationships. This doesn't mean that you haven't had relationships before. You no doubt have. You may have a great deal of "hands on," real-world experience with people. But you may never have had a course with organized instruction in this area. You will find that it *is* possible to maximize your relationships by learning better ways of communicating. You don't have to learn everything through trial and error.

A central philosophy in this book is that you can make your relationships better by working on your communication, understanding it, and improving your skills. This is true whether the relationships deal with platonic friendship or romance, are just beginning, or have been ongoing for years. Don't just let relationships flow and think, "Whatever happens happens." Or, "If it's meant to be, it will work out." You wouldn't have that attitude with your career. You wouldn't do that with raising children. Why would you think and act that way with your most important relationships? Interpersonal relationships take attention and effort.

A cautionary note about interpersonal communication: *All* answers are not *correct* answers. Keep in mind that *all* responses and ways of thinking and behaving are not equally competent ways of thinking and behaving in relationships. It is sometimes easy for people to shrug and say about their communication style, "Well, it works for me," when in reality there are well-understood ways that our communication can actually improve relationships.

In an area of study such as interpersonal communication, people may tend to believe that their own relationships and ways of communicating are standard and functional. After all, that's what you've grown up with. That has been the model. Many students think all answers about relationship communication are equally valid. "This is the way it happens in my relationships, so it must be true." While we would be unlikely to engage in this type of thinking with Chemistry, History, or Math, interpersonal communication elicits defensive responses. "When I disclose, I never think of it that way," or, "When I broke up with my significant other, it was. . . ." Such applications, if they are perceived as "truth," where *all* answers are valid answers, can undermine learning and progress.

This doesn't mean that we should not explore our own lives and our own individuality as we're reading *Interpersonal Essentials*. But we need to recognize potentially unproductive patterns of communication and understand that our experience may not have been typical or easy to generalize. We can check our own experiences with the research-based information to analyze how we can improve.

Orientation of *Interpersonal Essentials*

This might be the only scholarship-based interpersonal communication book you ever read. Or, if the ideas resonate with you, it might be the first of *many* interpersonal books you pick up and study. In any event, *Interpersonal Essentials* is intended to be a first step in helping you to improve your communication interactions and understanding in relationships.

With this in mind, the concepts and ideas we will be discussing are basic, straightforward, and absolutely necessary in relationships. They are appropriately labeled "Interpersonal Essentials." Trusting. Listening. Communicating with emotions. Understanding nonverbal communication. Dealing effectively with conflict. All of these concepts are crucial to the success of interpersonal communication in relationships.

But don't let the straightforward nature of the concepts and conversational style fool you. All of the concepts and patterns discussed are firmly based on current social scientific research. I don't make this stuff up! You can look at these studies in their original journals. There is a reference list provided, and I would love it if you actually looked up the books and articles to do more in-depth reading in the area.

I would also love it if you threw this book in your bag, or the back of the car, and took it to the beach with you. Or take it on the plane, train, or subway as you travel somewhere. A bit of water, sand, or even the hot sauce from your lunch won't hurt it. This book is yours. Mark it up. Highlight parts that are important to you. Make notes in the margins. Just don't stick it on a shelf and forget about it. The important thing is to read *Interpersonal Essentials*, talk about it, and think about the concepts and ideas presented. Discuss the interpersonal communication concepts with your friends, family, and romantic partners. They are involved in these relationships too.

The writing style of the book is intended to be casual and conversational. It's not particularly formal. Instead, it is intentionally informal. (Although I have to admit, it is probably for the best that all of my idiosyncratic ways of expressing things and grammatical atrocities didn't make it through the editorial process). I want this book to read as if we were face-to-face, discussing communication in interpersonal relationships.

Organization of the Book

Interpersonal Essentials is organized into three major sections, reflecting the specific focus and various stages of development in interpersonal relationships. As you can see, Part One contains six chapters dealing with communication basics and you, as an individual, in relationships. My assumption here is that people need to understand who they are—their self-concept and their interpersonal needs—in order to know what will be satisfying or what may be an obstacle for them as they develop interpersonal relationships. Chapter 1 sets forth some guiding communication principles and orientations followed in the book. The other five chapters focus on how you as a unique communicator might view the world and your relationships. They examine your perceptions of yourself and others, how your needs affect your communication motives, and various personality traits that influence how you feel and act in communicating.

But you can't just look at one person in a relationship. Part Two contains seven chapters that all deal with cognitive patterns and skills we need to develop in order to be effective in our relationships. This part discusses how communication is a progression of complex interactions and interactive elements, as we move toward greater intimacy or move further apart. Importantly, these chapters explain communicative behaviors and skills you can develop to improve your chances of making an interpersonal relationship "work" and heighten relational satisfaction. For example, Chapters 10 and 13 examine how the very words you choose to express your emotions can influence outcomes in your relationships.

Part Three focuses on more complex skills and decision making in ongoing relationships. These five chapters concentrate on features of relationships that we may find are more difficult to handle in relationships. How do we deal with complicated friend/work relationships? How do we persuade our relationship partners to go along with us? What should we do when there is serious disagreement and relational conflict? What happens when we do not want a relationship to terminate, but our partner wants to terminate? How do we communicate at the end of relationships? Although difficult, some of these concepts may be the most crucial, because they can have the most devastating outcomes for how we see ourselves and for the maintenance of our relationships.

I won't try to tell you that "good communication" will solve all the problems in your life. It won't. And I won't tell you all communicators will play by fair rules in relationships, will try to cooperate and do what is honestly best for all involved. They won't. People unfortunately sometimes play vicious games—either knowingly or because they aren't aware of better ways of communicating. However, if you can understand, analyze, and enact the essentials of interpersonal communication, you can put things in perspective, enhancing your relational potential. You will be better prepared for communication in relationships throughout your life.

Acknowledgments

Finally, I want to acknowledge some people who have made *Interpersonal Essentials* possible. Karon Bowers, my editor at Allyn and Bacon, has been incredibly encouraging and invariably optimistic throughout this process. I would also like to thank the following reviewers for their thoughtful comments and helpful suggestions: Mary Helen Brown, Auburn University; Kelby Halone, Clemson University; Tina Harris, University of Georgia; Mark Morman, Baylor University; and Scott Paynton, Humboldt State University.

I have wonderful families—both born into and married into. I appreciate them every day, even though I don't tell them often enough. They have never set traditional expectations for me, or told me what I *shouldn't* do. And they have always been supportive of Steve and me.

Of course, my center and inspiration in *Interpersonal Essentials*, as well as the actual originator of several of the book's best ideas, is my husband, Steve. We really do try to use all of this interpersonal communication knowledge in our twenty-two-year marriage. We haven't got it perfect yet, but we're still having a great time practicing.

I hope you find the study of interpersonal communication as intriguing as we have. Read on!

Melanie Booth-Butterfield

1 Interpersonal Communication in Relationships

OBJECTIVES

Here is what to look for in this chapter to make sure you've understood the ideas. Can you do these things? It's even better if you can accomplish them without having to look back through the chapter.

1. Define interpersonal communication.

2. Tell the difference between achieved and ascribed roles.

3. Distinguish between rules and roles, giving an example of each.

4. Distinguish between explicit and implicit rules, giving an example of each.

5. Explain "relationships of choice" and why interpersonal communication is so important in them, then compare the communication to that in nonchoice relationships.

6. Recognize and correctly categorize an illustration of each of the principles of interpersonal communication.

7. Give a real-life example of each principle of interpersonal communication.

8. Use an example to distinguish among knowledge, skill, and motivation in communication competence.

9. Explain the difference between content and relational information in interpersonal communication.

CHAPTER OUTLINE

Interpersonal Communication: What Is It Anyway?

Definitions
Relationship of Rules to Roles

Relationships of Choice

Principles of Interpersonal Communication

Communication Competence

Interpersonal Relationships and Cultural Background

People want to have relationships. We may differ on the type, frequency, intensity, and so forth, of those relationships, but human beings want to have interpersonal relationships in their lives. We want some form of connectedness and support. We want to be understood and to feel extremely important to at least one other person. It may be that we feel we have a lot of love that we want to share and give away. Or it may be as immediate as that we want someone to give us that really special, perfect Christmas present, or to be the one person we could call, no matter what time or where, if our car won't start.

The problem is that, while we really *want* relationships like that, we often don't know how to go about *achieving* such close, important relationships. That's where interpersonal communication comes in. You have to be self-aware and adept at interpersonal communication in order to form (and maintain) relationships.

That's what this book is about. "How can I go from being a stranger or acquaintance with someone I find attractive to creating a real relationship with that person?" And, "Once we have built a good relationship, how do I keep from letting it drift away?" "I want to be a good partner in my relationship, but I'm not sure how to do that."

Interpersonal Communication: What Is It Anyway?

Many people throw the term "interpersonal communication" around without really knowing what it is. We're always saying that we want to have an interpersonal relationship, that we are communicating interpersonally. But what does it really mean?

Definitions

Is interpersonal communication just "two people talking"? Not really. If that were the case, whenever you talk to the guy behind the counter as you're paying for your cup of coffee, or when a lawyer is asking you questions, it would be interpersonal communication. Those two situations are really more business communication than interpersonal. The definition of "two people talking" is too broad, and more appropriately pertains to what is termed "dyadic communication." A dyad is two people talking to each other.

Does "interpersonal" mean "romantic"? Not necessarily. Although we may think of many romantic relational illustrations of interpersonal interactions, we can communicate interpersonally with a wide variety of people in a wide variety of settings—neighbors, roommates, old or new friends, co-workers, other members of social groups, and lovers. Both platonic and romantic relationships engage in interpersonal interactions.

So, does interpersonal communication mean that you are sharing deep, dark secrets? Maybe. In part. When we engage in interpersonal communication we *may* be sharing secrets, but that is not required. We often share some intimate thoughts in the context of a close interpersonal relationship, but interpersonal communication has a much wider range than simply intimate disclosures.

Interpersonal communication is when we interact on an individual-to-individual basis with someone, and we get beyond the roles in the situation. But what are "roles"? We all play varying roles in our lives. Some roles are ascribed to us by birth; for example, we are born male or female, of a certain race, and on a specific date. We are born into a given cultural or ethnic group. These are roles that we do nothing to achieve and cannot control. For better or for worse certain ascribed roles are largely unchangeable. What we are talking about with interpersonal communication is getting beyond the roles that are *achieved*, those that we work to attain in some way. Often this is a career role. We play the role of student to another person's role of teacher; we are in the roles of "leader," doctor–patient, lawyer–client, and so on. These are social and situational roles that guide our communicative behavior.

When we get into a situation in which we are "interpersonally communicating," the societal roles don't control our behavior. We are no longer talking just as customer–salesperson, but rather as two interested (or not interested) individuals. To illustrate, if you are communicating in your salesperson role you must be very polite to customers even if they're rude. But if this were an interpersonal interaction, you might decide to be just as abrupt and rude as the other person. (Of course, none of *you* would ever act like this!) Conversely, if you are engaged in your job role, you may not be able to communicate your interest as openly, and flirt or have extended conversations with a customer you find attractive.

Another aspect of interpersonal communication is that as an interpersonal relationship builds, it will be characterized by increased *psychological and/or emotional closeness*. Role-bound relationships do not become more close and emotional. They may become more efficient as you learn to work effectively with each other or predict the other's desires, but they are not really close. (Alternatively, this means that when interpersonal relationships go bad, there will tend to be more intense negative emotion than in role-bound relationships.)

Relationship of Rules to Roles

We should also make a distinction between roles and rules. *Roles* are comprised of relatively clear-cut patterns of rules, typically imposed on you by an external entity such as your workplace or your family. If you are communicating within a particular role, you follow those rules. Rules don't tend to change within a specifically defined role. That means that when you are in your "church member" role, you will follow the expectations for that type of interaction by avoiding profanity, acting respectful, dressing appropriately, and so on.

Rules are operating in every interaction, but the rules that guide you will differ depending on the societal role or situation you are in at the time. *Rules* are the set of guidelines that tell us what communicative behavior is expected, normative, or prohibited in a situation. In interpersonal relationships we tend to develop or create our own rules. Patterns of behavior evolve—sometimes positive and sometimes negative. But they are ours, and they tend to be unique to our own interactions.

Rules can also be explicit or implicit. *Explicit* rules are ones that are clearly and openly stated. "You must stop at the stop sign." "You have to come home by 11 P.M." "Now that we're seeing each other seriously, you're *not* dating your ex, right?"

Implicit rules often give us more trouble. They are not clearly stated, but they are "assumed." They are implied by the relationship. We expect others to follow those implicit rules, yet we may never talk about them until after they are broken. "I thought you knew I was going to Florida over break." "I didn't know you counted on me for a ride home every night." "You mean I *can't* have this kitten in the apartment?"

In instructional contexts, explicit rules are usually communicated through a syllabus. That way everyone is clear about expectations, schedules, assignments, and so on. (Most students are not happy if a class is full of implicit rules they are expected to follow for their grades.) In the corporate world explicit rules are communicated via contracts, handbooks, and legal restrictions.

In interpersonal relationships, however, there are more implicit than explicit rules. Few people give their friends a list of the "expected rules" for the friendship. To even talk about it seems absurd. And this lack of explicit rules can cause problems. Sometimes we don't even realize that a rule existed until it is violated in the relationship. That's why it is a good idea to talk about what you and your partner expect in the relationship—really think about the rules and what is important in your interactions.

Relationships of Choice

In this book we will focus on *relationships of choice*. Those are interpersonal relationships that you choose to focus on and work on, but that you also may leave if they become dysfunctional or unproductive for you. Compare this to family relationships. In families we don't choose who we live with, interact with, or are related to. We can't decide where we're going to be born and grow up. We typically can't divorce our family. We typically cannot terminate the relationship, just as we did not *choose* to start the relationship. Families are not relationships of choice.

Now this is not to say that families do not communicate interpersonally, but the pattern tends to be very different. It is very difficult to get beyond your role of son or daughter when interacting with your parents. You have years of background and teaching that you did not create. That's why there are entire courses of study that examine family and sibling communication as a separate area of investigation.

Principles of Interpersonal Communication

There are several principles of communication that will apply to all your interpersonal interactions.

1. *Communication is not only central to the relationship, communication* is *the relationship.* Very simply, you will not form interpersonal relationships without communication. And you have to keep on communicating once the relationship is started. Relationships in which people stop talking openly to each other become empty shells and eventually deteriorate.

2. *You cannot* not *communicate.* As long as you are in the presence of another person, you will be communicating. You can't help it! The messages are sent and received; however, they may not always be processed consciously. Notice that this principle does not mean that the messages have to be *accurate*. Many times what we communicate to others is not what we had intended. (You think you're communicating that you are nervous and shy, but people around you think you're stuck-up.) So our goal is to communicate in such a way that our message will be received as we intended it to be.

3. *Meanings are in people.* We can say this about any communicative interaction, but it is especially true in interpersonal interactions. How we interpret what people say to us and how they act toward us is a function of our past experiences and how we view the current situation. The meaning is not in the words or gestures, but rather how we perceive them.

For example, the word "dog" probably brings up the image of a furry, four-legged animal to most of you—but not to everyone. Some people envision a small fluffy dog, while others imagine a large Rottweiller. We probably envision the "dog" related to dogs we have known. Some people may even interpret a "dog" as a form of human being. So even with a relatively simple concept such as this, you can see how messages may be misinterpreted.

How much *more* misunderstanding could there be about an interpersonal term such as "love"? Or "commitment"? Or "independence"? These are words that are much more difficult to specify, yet we may think that our partner understands them as we do. We have to be aware that people will interpret messages according to what is in their experience, rather than what we intend.

4. *Communication is irreversible.* How many times have you thought, "I wish I hadn't said that"? How many times has your mouth worked faster than your brain and you wanted to "take something back"? Obviously, it can't be done. Communication is irreversible. Once a message has registered with a receiver, it cannot be undone. We can say we're sorry, or that we didn't mean our words to sound that way. But we cannot reverse and erase the message.

So what's the lesson here? Think before you communicate. Some circumstances make thinking before you talk less likely. Fast-paced communication allows for little thought. Highly emotional times, such as when you lose your temper or when you are blinded by "love," tend to overwhelm rational interaction. And, of course, if you are under the influence of alcohol or other drugs, your thought processes will be disrupted. We need to think about the outcomes of our communication, because that process is irreversible.

5. *Messages contain both content and relational information.* Every message that you communicate contains information on at least two different levels. The content level is the actual information you want to get across and is carried primarily in the words you say. You may be discussing going to a concert with a friend. The particulars of when, where, and how are the content level. But your excitement and happiness at this upcoming event illustrates the relational level.

The relational level communicates how you want the receiver to interpret the message in the context of your relationship. This part of the message is transmitted primarily through nonverbal cues—*how* we say what we say. When we say to our friends, "I hate my history class," this statement may tell them that we need comforting, that we are angry and just blowing off steam, or that we really are afraid of doing poorly.

Humor is very telling at the relational level. Some people could kid you about your nickname, and you would get angry, whereas other people could say the same things and it's all right. This illustrates the difference between the content and relational aspects of messages.

6. *Communication is a learned skill, not an innate ability.* Some people believe that either they are "born communicators" or they are not. Not true, but we may think that communication is innate because we have grown up with it. Of course, just because we do it every day doesn't mean that we are effective at communicating.

If people were born communicators there would be no need for a book such as this. But the reality is that we need to learn to be better at communication in relationships. (Keep in mind all the people around you who are really bad at relationships. They have *learned* unproductive patterns that will persist in their interpersonal interactions unless they *relearn* more productive ways of communicating.)

7. *Communication is a tool. The outcome depends on how you use it.* Communication, like guns and hammers, can be used either for positive outcomes or negative outcomes. Have you ever used words to hurt someone? Or to comfort someone? Sometimes people say "we just don't communicate enough." Wrong. Of course you have to have *some* interaction. But it's really not a matter of how much communication; it's what type of communication and how you use your messages that predicts whether a relationship will go or not.

8. *More communication is not necessarily better communication.* Some people talk a lot but they don't really say anything. Some marriage partners insist their relationship broke up because they stopped communicating. These are two examples of how wrong communication can be. Just because you are interacting does not mean that you are doing it well. You may be offending people, boring them, or obsessing about a topic that has been overdone.

Of course, you have to have some minimal level of communication to be competent and develop relationships. But the quality and skill of your communication is important for the success of your interactions.

Communication Competence

Our ultimate goal is to achieve competence at our interpersonal communication efforts, so that we can build productive relationships with friends, coworkers, lovers, and family members. This is easier said than done! Communicative competence is composed of three distinct factors: *knowledge, skill,* and *motivation.* You will not be able to maximize your interpersonal communication potential without all three (Rubin & Morreale, 1996; Spitzberg, 1983).

Knowledge is the information you need to understand in order to become a better communicator. This often includes understanding why something occurs as it does, or recognizing pitfalls of poor communication, or simply the patterns of communication that will be the most effective. Knowledge is the content component. Knowledge often means that you can respond correctly on a test. You "know" what the best form of communication is. But that isn't enough. You also need to have the skill to actually enact the correct responses.

The *skill* component of communication competence is being able to put the knowledge to work through behaviors. Not only do you know what self-disclosure is, but you can actually *do* it. Just because you can answer questions correctly on a written test does not mean that you are a competent interpersonal communicator. You have to be able to enact the appropriate communicative messages at appropriate times. (Think of taking a lifesaving class. You might be able to select the right answers or develop explanations on an exam to get your certificate, but do you have the skills to go into the water, drag someone out, and apply mouth-to-mouth to revive them?)

The third component for interpersonal competence is *motivation*, the desire and the will to enact the appropriate skills. You understand what self-disclosure is (knowledge), you have the behavioral skill to engage in self-disclosing (skill), but do you want to do it (motivation)? Without the motivation to be a good interpersonal communicator, the knowledge and skill will not make a difference. (To go back to the lifesaving example, without motivation to put those skills to use, you would let the person drown.)

All three components must be present to be competent at interpersonal communication. We have all known people who wanted to do the right thing: They tried hard, but they simply didn't have the skills to be relationally effective. On the other hand, we have also known people who had all the skill in the world, knew exactly what should be done in a situation, but lacked the desire to be a good partner and therefore were not competent by choice.

Finally, we have to realize that it takes two to make relationships work. No matter how competent you become at communicating interpersonally, there will still be problems. Your partner may want to play relational games, whereas you want openness and honesty. Situational factors such as job demands, timing, or other friends of your partner may interfere with your relationship, even if both of you want to make it work. However, learning to be competent at interpersonal communication—acquiring the knowledge, behavioral skills, and motivation—is your best bet for developing productive, successful, and fun relationships.

Of course, this brief explanation of communication competence in interpersonal interactions is an oversimplification of the process. Interpersonal competence is extremely complex and can include verbal and nonverbal elements, timing of messages, adaptations to your receivers, and more. But this is a beginning to give you an idea of where we are going throughout this book.

Interpersonal Relationships and Cultural Background

The desire and need for interpersonal relationships appears to be pan-cultural. People everywhere want to have relationships that are special to them, in which they feel close and appropriately connected to others, and to have interpersonal contexts in which they feel totally accepted and "understood." How we go about this process, our priorities, and what the relationship eventually looks like may differ depending on whether you are Native American, Asian American, or Hispanic, but the fundamental concepts remain the same. People disclose information to others, they listen, they express feelings, they have an awareness of themselves, they make decisions about relational behavior, they have conflict.

This is certainly not to say that cultural background does not shape our view of relationships, personality, attributional processes, or how we view conflict or loss of a relationship. Numerous intercultural scholars have focused on such facets as attachment in relationships, saving face, individual versus group concerns, the role of silence and respect, resource allocation, and an entire range of interpersonally related topics (see Markus, Kitayama, & Heiman, 1996, for a review). Nevertheless, we can say that all groups of people strive to create and succeed in interpersonal relationships. Specific norms for how these are accomplished and what is expected may vary based on ethnicity, gender orientation, age, parentage, country of birth, and so on, but basically we're more similar than we are different in wanting positive relationships. So, as you read these chapters, you might apply and adapt the concepts to your own ethnic or societal background, at the same time recognizing expectations of others from differing backgrounds. Communication in relationships may operate in different ways, but the results are amazingly similar.

Summarizing and Looking Ahead

As you can see, this book is divided into three major parts (1) understanding ourselves as communicators, (2) understanding the interactive nature of relationships, and, (3) communication and decisions to maintain relationships. These don't represent hard-and-fast lines, but rather suggestions for understanding yourself, others, and communication concepts operating in relationships. The chapters in the first part explore understanding of ourselves as communicators in dyadic relationships. For example, this chapter has explained principles underlying interpersonal communication (e.g., communication is a tool), how interpersonal communication differs from other forms of interactions (e.g., you have to get beyond the roles to form interpersonal relationships) and the nature of communication competence that we would like to build.

The chapters in the second part address how relationships may grow as a function of our communicative behaviors—that is, what I do affects how you communicate, and vice versa. So this part looks at skills that can be used to develop and maintain interpersonal relationships.

The chapters in the final part deal with decision making about whether or not to work at maintaining relationships, as well as additional skills needed to do this communicative work once a relationship is started. Not all relationships last forever. And maybe it is best if some of our relationships terminate. But we want to be able to maximize our chances of succeeding in the most productive relationships, in the relationships we value the most. How do we do this? We first have to understand ourselves.

REFERENCES AND RECOMMENDED READINGS

Buss, D. (1996). The evolutionary psychology of human social strategies. In E. T. Higgins & A. Kruglanski (Eds.), *Social psychology handbook of basic principles* (pp. 3–38). New York: Guilford Press.

Harvey, J., & Omarzu, J. (1997). Minding the close relationship. *Personality and Social Psychology Review, 1,* 224–240.

Knapp, M., & Miller, G. R. (1985). Introduction: Background and current trends in the study of interpersonal communication. In M. Knapp & G. Miller (Eds.), *Handbook of interpersonal communication* (pp. 7–24). Beverly Hills, CA: Sage.

Langer, E. (1992). Interpersonal mindlessness and language. *Communication Monographs, 59,* 324–327.

Markus, J., Kitayama, S., & Heiman, R. (1996). Culture and "basic" psychological principles. In E. T. Higgins & A. Kruglanski (Eds.), *Social psychology handbook of basic principles* (pp. 857–913). New York: Guilford Press.

Morisaki, S., & Gudykunst, W. (1994). Face in Japan and the United States. In S. Ting-Toomey (Ed.), *The challenge of facework* (pp. 47–93). Albany: State University of New York Press.

Motley, M. (1992). Mindfulness in solving communicators' dilemmas. *Communication Monographs, 59,* 306–314.

Pavitt, C., & Haight, L. (1986). Implicit theories of communication competence: Situational and competence level differences in judgements of prototype and target. *Communication Monographs, 53,* 221–235.

Rubin, R., & Morreale, S. (1996). Setting expectations for speech communication and learning. In E. Jones (Ed.), *Preparing competent college graduates: Setting new and higher expectations for student learning* (pp. 19–29). San Francisco: Jossey-Bass.

Spitzberg, B. (1983). Communication competence as knowledge, skill, and impression. *Communication Education, 32,* 323–329.

Watzlawick, P., Beavin, J., & Jackson, D. (1967). *Pragmatics of human communication.* New York: Norton.

STRUCTURED INTERACTION

Choose someone from class that you don't already know. That means not your roommate, a friend from high school, or boyfriend/girlfriend. Sit close together, face each other, and take turns responding to the following statements. Each person should complete all statements.

1. My name is _____. My major is _____.

2. When I'm not studying for classes one of my favorite activities is _____.

3. When something surprises me I feel _____.

4. I think most people perceive me as _____.

5. When I'm in groups _____.

6. I worry about _____.

7. My parents _____.

8. A characteristic that I think is one of my strengths is _____.

9. My impressions of you are _____.

     Take hold of your partner's hand, look at him or her, and complete the following statement:

10. Right now I'm feeling _____.

     Release hands and go on.

11. This communication experience has been _____.

RULES IN YOUR RELATIONSHIPS

Individually, write down four rules you have developed in your interpersonal relationships. These should be rules that are important to *you*, and that are not necessarily societal rules. They can be for either romantic relationships, good friends, or roommates.

Rule example: Be on time when you say you're going to meet me, or else call.

1.

2.

3.

4.

Now get into groups of 3–5 people to discuss those rules. Are they shared? Are you the only one who feels that way? Is there an order of importance? Why are these rules important to you?

2 Self-Concept and Self-Esteem

OBJECTIVES

This chapter deals with how self-concept and self-esteem are related to interpersonal communication. You need to know these aspects and it's best if you write them out.

1. Define self-concept and explain how it is different from self-esteem.

2. Describe at least three ways our self-concept affects interpersonal communication.

3. Define self-serving bias and explain how it interacts with self-esteem to influence our interpretation of communication.

4. Differentiate among three types of self-concept (public, real, ideal) and give an example of each.

5. Explain how someone with an *independent* self-image might communicate in relationships. Give examples.

6. Explain how someone with an *interdependent* self-image might communicate in relationships. Give examples.

7. Draw a diagram of how your self-concept acts to filter your communication messages, both their production and their reception.

CHAPTER OUTLINE

How Self-Esteem Influences Interpersonal Communication

Origin of the Self

Three Types of Self-Concept

Interdependent versus Independent Self-Images

Falling in Love and Your Self-Concept

Why should we be talking about "self-concept" in a communication class? Isn't this more appropriate for a psychology class? The truth is that you need to be aware of and understand your self-concept, because it influences both how you send messages and how you interpret messages coming to you.

Your *self-concept* is the image you have of yourself. How do you define yourself on a general basis? Self-concept includes all the personality traits that characterize us. For example, we might describe ourselves as a stable, happy, hardworking person. In contrast, we might have a self-concept that includes depression and anger, but intelligence as well.

Self-esteem is slightly different. *Self-esteem* entails the positive or negative evaluations we have of ourselves. Thus it is the evaluative component that rates our personal characteristics. We all have days when we feel pretty confident about ourselves, and other days when we don't like ourselves as much. But our self-esteem is how we truly feel about ourselves most of the time.

Think of your self-esteem as a protective glass shield around your core, inner self. All messages that are communicated to you pass through this glass shield, and all messages that you communicate to others must also pass through the protective glass shield. The better your self-esteem, the higher the quality of the glass shield.

If this glass is high quality, the messages will pass through the shield with greater clarity and accuracy. You will be able to clearly communicate messages, confident that your encoding will remain pure and not be distorted as it passes through the glass. In addition, the clear glass shield gives you an accurate perception of those who are sending you messages and the intent they are trying to communicate.

However, if your self-esteem is low and you feel inferior in many ways, it is as though the glass shield is of poor quality. It may be discolored or have flaws or air bubbles in the glass. This glass may even have cracks or be uneven in thickness and wavy like an old window. When messages pass through this type of self-esteem/shield, they tend to be distorted. The discoloration makes the messages appear different than they were intended. The cracks send messages slanting off at odd, misshapen angles. Therefore the poor self-esteem biases and distorts messages we both send and receive.

How Self-Esteem Influences Interpersonal Communication

Have you ever tried to compliment someone who has low self-esteem? "Your hair looks really nice like that." "I want you on my work team because you have the abilities we need." "You're really a great guy." It's likely that in some way your compliment was rejected or turned back. Why?

Because such positive messages are inconsistent with how the person perceives himself—or inconsistent with his self-concept.

As in the protective glass metaphor used above, all of our communication messages must pass through the self-concept. If we have a positive self-concept, we will tend to put forth confident, more objective, realistic messages. But if we have a poor self-concept, the messages we both send and receive become distorted by it. We won't present messages of strength because we don't feel strong or confident. Often our messages will be falsely optimistic, but fragile because we don't really believe them. If our self-esteem is poor, we will tend to believe anything negative or critical that people may say of us—regardless of their ability to evaluate that aspect.

In comparison, when we have a well-rounded self-concept and healthy self-esteem, we tend to be more realistic about how we interpret what people say to us. If they are critical, we may look to see if they are valid judges. If they are too complimentary, we may doubt that too. An important point here is that people with high self-esteem are *not* egocentric and think they are superior. They don't interpret all messages as positive. Instead, they are simply better judges of the messages because they can perceive messages and situations more clearly.

In addition, because people with good self-esteem tend to like themselves and think they are pretty OK people, they are more likely to be able to take even negative feedback and make productive use of it. They don't dwell on their hurt feelings. They don't become paranoid and rejecting when facing criticism or failure. People with good self-esteem can examine even critical messages and see how they could improve their interactions. They try again.

Unfortunately, we see a difference by gender in self-esteem. Women in our society tend to have lower self-esteem than men do, with the largest differences appearing in adolescence and declining with age. Gender differences in self-esteem are not large, may not affect everyone, and are not as consistent in African American samples. But such advantages for males have been consistently found in research involving over 97,000 subjects (Kling, Hyde, Showers, & Buswell, 1999). It isn't clear why this is true, but somehow our society rewards and builds boys' esteem more strongly than girls'.

In comparison, recent studies tell us that African American adolescents and young adults have slightly higher self-esteem than white Americans (Gray-Little & Hafdahl, 2000). African American young people today appear to have a clear sense of self and feel positive about it. This pattern is somewhat stronger for females than for males. These findings certainly have implications for communication in interpersonal relationships.

One illustration of how your self-concept and self-esteem may bend or filter messages is called the self-serving bias. The *self-serving bias* means that we tend to perceive success as our doing and failure as due to someone or

FIGURE 2.1   How Self-Esteem Affects Our Attributions about Why
Outcomes Occured

	How Self-Esteem Affects Our Attributions	
	Positive Event	Negative Event
High Self-Esteem	"I did a good job."	"I need to work harder."
Low Self-Esteem	"Must have gotten lucky!"	"I'm just a loser, no good at this."

something else. In that way, our perception of ourselves as capable, successful individuals is upheld. However, it has been found that this self-serving
bias does not hold true for everyone. Sometimes in people with low self-
esteem we see just the opposite. They attribute failures to themselves and
successes to something external to them. Can you see how that "protects"
their image of themselves? If their self-concept and self-esteem says they are
inefficient, incompetent jerks, then failure is entirely consistent with how
they see themselves. But triumph or success would be inconsistent with
their self-image. On the whole, while all of us use this sometimes, the self-
serving bias is most predictive of people with a positive self-concept in realistic situations.

Origin of the Self

Where do we get our self-esteem, and how does our self-concept develop?
Why do some people seem confident right from the start, whereas other
people are full of self-doubt and negative self-image?

Self-concept, or the set of traits that make up our personality, appears
to be both inherited and developed through interaction. Some parts of ourselves, such as extraversion, inhibition, or aggressiveness, appear to be with
us at birth. Although there is flexibility in how much they will be exhibited
as we mature, the basic traits seem to be inherited or possibly genetic.

Other aspects of our self-concept develop as we age and become more
self-aware. Many are modeled from others around us—for example, courte-
ous behavior or leadership traits. So the descriptors that make up our self-
concept come from both inborn traits and traits that are built as we observe
and communicate with others.

The best bet about where our self-esteem originates is in very early
childhood messages. Children who are repeatedly told (either directly or
indirectly) that they are no good or worthless come to believe that at a very
core level. Probably those sources are early childhood caregivers. Parents or

other close family members who subtly communicate that the child doesn't count, isn't important, is a bother, or is stupid, create negative expectations that may be ingrained for life.

Similarly, early childhood experiences with other children, or even subtle societal messages, may add to that negative or positive self-image. Children who are teased mercilessly, who experience violence against them, or have many frightening things happen to them grow up with low self-esteem. They may feel as though they cannot control their lives or achieve something they set out to do, or don't deserve to feel good about themselves.

In contrast, children who have difficult times but overcome them or achieve despite the odds tend to feel better about themselves. Thus, positive self-esteem doesn't just mean you had a great childhood with fantastic, caring parents. It also develops from how you are taught to deal with life and whether you are communicated with in such a way that positive patterns about *yourself* develop.

It should also be noted that some children seem to be born more confident and optimistic than others. They may be born with certain traits that are positively valued by most of the people around them. This does not mean that there is a "self-concept gene." It means that optimism and positive affect seem to be trait-based and somewhat innate. That is, some people will tend to orient more positively, with a "can do" attitude and positive emotionality almost from birth. This may well give them a step-up in developing that positive self-esteem.

Whether inborn or developed early in life, we know that a person's *self* is very difficult to alter. Once it is set, it may be set for life because it is at the very core of our understanding of ourselves. Any significant change after childhood will probably be very gradual and not happen overnight. That is why it is so very important for young children to be in a supportive, caring, self-enhancing environment from birth.

Three Types of Self-Concept

Everyone has three types of self-concept that may be in operation at different times: public self, real self, and ideal self.

The *public self* is how you want others to perceive you—the image you portray in public. We may want to *seem* confident and outgoing, even if we aren't. Or, we may want others to think we are more modest about our accomplishments than we actually feel. So, to some extent, the public self-concept is the image we communicate to others.

The *real self* is how you actually view yourself when you examine yourself and are realistic about who you are. This is as close to "real" and honest as you can get. Maybe you don't think you are as competent as others think you are. Maybe you really understand that you are an extremely ambitious person. You may or may not let others see this view of yourself, but typically in close interpersonal relationships you will share this with your partner—let him or her understand how you really see yourself.

The third type of self-concept is your *ideal self*—the person you would like to be. This is the image that you believe you want to work toward. Probably the ideal will be "better" in some ways than your real self-concept. For example, your ideal self may be an Olympic-class gymnast, an expert guitar player, or a truly dedicated family member. Some aspects of your ideal self may be more attainable than others. Of course it's good to have goals to strive for, but on the other hand, you don't want to have an ideal self that is so unrealistic and relentlessly driving you that you hate your real self. Many people with eating disorders have a body self-image that they strive for which is unrealistic and unhealthy (e.g., being 5 foot 8 inches tall and weighing 104 pounds).

How do all of these types of self-concept fit together? Well, if they *don't* fit together and coordinate fairly well, it can make us very unhappy. The closer the three types are, the more comfortable we will be. To illustrate, if your public self is quite different from how you actually are, you may find yourself "playing roles" all the time. This is often reported by people who perceive themselves as gay, but don't feel safe having a gay public persona. They may communicate in a "straight" or heterosexual manner even though that is not their real self-image. Or it may pertain to a teacher in a small town who is far more liberal than that role allows. He or she may communicate a more conservative public self in dress, attitudes, and conversation than he or she really feels.

Similarly, if your ideal is too different from your real self-image, that can be problematic as well. You may not have the physical body type to be a professional basketball player. You may not have the temperament to be extremely outgoing and a life-of-the-party person. If we don't recognize these real versus ideal images, we may constantly feel we are falling short of where we "should" be. Yes, we always want to improve ourselves and have goals to strive for, objectives to attain. But it is best for our emotional and mental health if we coordinate these three self-images and understand how to bring them realistically closer together.

Interdependent versus Independent Self-Images

An interesting extension of self-concept work is the division between interdependent and independent self-images. People with *interdependent self-images* see themselves as integral parts of relational systems. In part, they define themselves by how they interact with others, and they envision the world as a cooperative place where people coordinate and interact together. In comparison, people with *independent self-images* see themselves operating predominantly as individuals, orienting with competition more than cooperation. Independent people see themselves as acting upon the world, whereas the interdependent people see themselves as acting within the world.

People who have a strongly independent self-image may have more difficulty integrating into relationships. This is not to say that they don't have close relationships, but it means that they don't define themselves through relationships. Thus, cooperative, other-oriented communication may not be their first impulse. Some researchers say this pattern is typical of more traditionally masculine people in our society (Cross, Bacon, & Morris, 2000; Cross & Madsen, 1997).

On the other hand, people with a strongly interdependent self-image are mightily concerned with other people, very other-oriented. They may do well in supporting relationships, but may not compete well in other areas because they are quite concerned about others' feelings and cooperating with people around them. This pattern has been likened to more feminine individuals in our culture (Cross & Madsen, 1997).

Clearly, both types of self-images have their advantages. Also, it is important to remember that the self-image doesn't mean that individuals *cannot* communicate in the opposite manner, or that they don't have elements of both depending on the situation. It means that when they examine their own motivations and how they see themselves, the first impulse will be to follow either the interdependent or the independent pattern.

Falling in Love and Your Self-Concept

Interestingly, although we may not be able to clearly define "falling in love," the experience of it seems to be positive for your self-concept. Most people enjoy the excitement and experience of falling in love, and at least one study has shown that it's also good for you (Aron, Paris, & Aron, 1995). This study found that both male and female college students were equally likely to fall in love and that younger students were more likely to fall head-over-heels than older students.

The main point of the study, however, was that people experienced more diversity of domains in their self-concept after falling in love. They felt more confident. They broadened their horizons. They also reported higher self-esteem and greater feelings of being able to accomplish goals (or confident about doing what they set out to do) after falling in love.

Falling in love is not the equivalent of staying in love or keeping the relationship from falling apart. But interpersonal communication competence can help, and the process rounds out your self-concept.

Conclusions

In this chapter we have taken a first step in analyzing how our self-esteem (positive or negative evaluations of self) and our self-concept (descriptive information about facets that make up who we are) influence our interpersonal communication. Our self-esteem acts as a filter on both communicative enactments and interpretations. We tend to communicate consistently with how we see ourselves, as illustrated by the public, real, and ideal self-concepts. It is also important to remember that everyone is not exactly alike in how connected they feel to others. People may feel interdependent or independent, and these self-images no doubt impact how they lead their own lives and what they expect from others in relationships.

The next step is to examine how we perceive others, both in early stages of acquaintance and as judgments made later on as we get to know others.

REFERENCES AND RECOMMENDED READINGS

Aron, A., Paris, M., & Aron, E. (1995). Falling in love: Prospective studies of self-concept change. *Journal of Personality and Social Psychology, 69*, 1102–1112.

Buss, A. (1997). Evolutionary perspectives on personality traits. In R. Hogan, J. Johnson, & S. Briggs (Eds.) *Handbook of personality psychology* (pp. 345–366). New York: Academic Press.

Cross, S., Bacon, P., & Morris, M. (2000). The relational-interdependent self-construal and relationships. *Journal of Personality and Social Psychology, 78*, 791–808.

Cross, S., & Madson, L. (1997). Models of the self: Self-construals and gender. *Psychological Bulletin, 122*, 5–37.

Gray-Little, B., & Hafdahl, A. (2000). Factors influencing racial comparisons of self-esteem: A quantitative review. *Psychological Bulletin, 126*, 26–54.

Kling, K., Hyde, J., Showers, C., & Buswell, B. (1999). Gender differences in self-esteem: A meta-analysis. *Psychological Bulletin, 125*, 470–500.

Kling, K., Ryff, C., & Essex, M. (1997). Adaptive changes in the self-concept during a life transition. *Personality and Social Psychology Bulletin, 23*, 981–990.

Robins, R., & John, O. (1997). The quest for self-insight: Theory and research on accuracy and bias in self-perception. In R. Hogan, J. Johnson, & S. Briggs (Eds.), *Handbook of personality psychology* (pp. 649–679). New York: Academic Press.

PUTTING THE PIECES TOGETHER: COMMUNICATION AND SELF-CONCEPT

List several aspects of yourself that are a part of your self-concept. They describe who you are. Then describe how each of these influences your interpersonal communication. Be specific and use examples.

1.

2.

3.

4.

5.

6.

7.

8.

9.

10.

IMAGE OF YOUR SELF-CONCEPT

Your self-concept is not a smooth and round bubble around you. It is composed of layers of your self-image that relate to different aspects of your life and values. It all surrounds you and serves to screen certain outgoing messages and modify certain incoming messages. Draw an image that represents how you see *your* self-concept working around you.

Example: athletic ability, family, church, intelligence, popularity, responsibility, fun loving, good-person/not-good-person, creative, loving, shy, sociable, attractive-unattractive.

THOUGHTS AND COGNITIONS ABOUT WHO YOU ARE AND YOUR LIFE (A SELF-ESTEEM EXERCISE)

What is good about my life is . . .

1.

2.

3.

4.

5.

6.

7.

8.

9.

10.

What is positive and good about *me* is . . .

1.

2.

3.

4.

5.

6.

7.

8.

9.

10.

CHAPTER

3 Perceptions and Impression Management

OBJECTIVES

This chapter deals with how our perceptions affect our communication and the impression management concerns we have. To assure that you have understood the content, can you do all of these?

1. Provide at least three reasons why initial perceptions are so important at the beginning of relationships and how communication is involved.

2. Three major evaluations we make of others are about their character, composure, and competence. What is each and how is the *lack* of each related to communication in relationships?

3. Describe three major types of attractiveness. Use examples to explain how different levels of each may occur in the same person (e.g., person is highly physically attractive, but not socially attractive).

4. Define homophily and use it in a coherent sentence.

5. What is the danger involved in the liking–similarity relationship?

6. Give an example of each of the three types of perceived similarity: demographic, background, and attitude/values.

7. Explain the statement "Perceived similarity allows us to reduce uncertainty in relationships." Then apply it to a relationship of your own.

8. Explain why similarity with your partner is reinforcing.

9. Describe the relationship "work" or effort that being similar with your partner lessens.

10. Describe the personality trait of self-monitoring from a communication perspective.

CHAPTER OUTLINE

Importance of Initial Perceptions

Three Major Perceptions: Character, Competence, and Composure
   Character
   Competence
   Composure

Perceptions of Attractiveness in Interpersonal Interactions
   Physical Attractiveness
   Social Attractiveness
   Task Attractiveness

Similarities in Relational Perceptions

   Demographic Similarity
   Background Similarity
   Attitudes, Beliefs, and Values
     Similarity

Why Similarities Are Attractive in Relationships
   Uncertainty Reduction
   Reinforcement
   Increasing Rewards by Decreasing
     Relational Work

Managing the Impressions of Others: Communication

"I am what I think you think I am."

Although we may reject the idea that we actually *are* what others think us to be, our perceptions of people around us generally drive our communication (or avoidance of communication) with them. We interact with people based on images we have of who they are, what they're like, and what their attitudes and opinions seem to be. If they seem likable, open to interaction with us, reasonably attractive, and nonthreatening, we may be more likely to begin a relationship with them.

But specifically, what are these perceptions based on? What kind of information is valued? How is it interpreted? What types of perceptions are likely to lead to more interpersonal interaction? That is the focus of this unit.

Importance of Initial Perceptions

First impressions are incredibly important (and not just in job interviews or with the parents of your friends). The initial impressions or perceptions we form of others tend to be the core around which other impressions are built. Numerous social psychological and person perception experiments have shown that merely by changing one word in a description or one aspect of someone's image, the entire perception of that individual alters. This means that one feature of your clothing, appearance, or conversation early in your acquaintance can alter how people view you.

In addition, those initial impressions can form even before you actually come into contact with the other person. It doesn't matter that the information is hear-say, rumor, no longer true, or an outright falsehood. The earliest information a perceiver encounters will shape and influence later impressions and communication when you actually meet.

Now, you may be sputtering at this point. You may think that such importance placed on first impressions sounds terribly superficial. After all, people should get to know the "real you." Yes, I agree. But in the real world it often does not happen that way, so it's beneficial to be aware of the impact of early perceptions.

Here are three major concepts to keep in mind about how initial perceptions work in our thinking and communicating processes.

1. *Perceivers tend to make the pieces fit.* This means that once people have a certain image of you, any information coming later tends to be interpreted to be congruent with it. For example, let's say you wear a substantial amount of gold jewelry and come from the East Coast. Some people may view that as a sign that you're from a big city, are thoroughly interested in commercialized city activities, and don't like outdoor activities. In reality, these perceptions may be inaccurate, but from now on when those people encounter information about you, they will try to make it fit their initial impressions. The puzzle pieces may be wrong, but they still try to make them fit. Changing that impression may be difficult. This leads to the second factor.

2. *Humans tailor their communication to fit their perceptions.* When we communicate with someone, especially if we don't know the person well, we tend to direct our conversation into topics that are consistent with the view we hold of him or her. Thus, if we believe Person A is into "city things," we may ask questions about city life, club scenes, traffic, shopping, and so on. We may avoid discussing nature trails, backpacking, and the best types of footwear for hiking, because we believe that this person would be uninterested in such topics. We're well-intentioned and we are just trying to be good conversationalists.

After the interaction, we think to ourselves, "Well it just goes to show that my first impression was accurate. All we talked about what how exciting and fast-paced things are on the East Coast." We probably don't realize that Person A was never given an opportunity to talk about other topics. Those avenues of conversation would be inconsistent. We don't realize that we directed the talk and interpreted the interaction along the lines of our preconceived impressions.

An additional point to consider here is that negative information is more heavily weighed than positive information. It seems to be human nature that we incorporate positive information into our overall view of an individual, but when we perceive something negative we really focus on that. "Yes, Chris is an overall great person, but I noticed that he is a cheap tipper." Such negative information may stay with the perceiver and be over-estimated when making assessments about the other person.

3. *Change is "work," so we are unlikely to do it.* We are unlikely to change those first impressions unless there is a compelling need to do so. Change requires thoughtful, cognitive effort. We have to rethink our impressions. It's "work" and we don't like that. Instead, it is easier to simply maintain the first perception of the individual unless there is some strong reason to change (e.g., we're going to be interacting with this person regularly be-cause she or he is our new roommate, boss, advisor). Often it's easier just to avoid the person instead of altering the image you hold. When that hap-pens, people never get the opportunity to change or correct an initial im-pression because there is not a second chance.

Three Major Perceptions: Character, Competence, Composure

The perceptions of character, competence, and composure are important central points around which we evaluate and describe others (Burgoon, Buller, Hale, & deTurck, 1984; Burgoon & Hale, 1987; McCroskey & Teven, 1999). We may not use these exact words. In fact, low competence may translate to "loser" and low character could be expressed as a "sleaze" fac-tor. But they mean similar things. These concepts have been shown to be separate dimensions that predict different kinds of behavior, and each can be described ranging from high levels to low levels.

Character

Is this person trustworthy? In the field of psychology, this is called conscien-tiousness and relates to whether you can depend on this person to do what is "right" rather than just what suits his or her own needs in the situation. People of high character don't betray you. They are dependable and don't lie, cheat, steal, or do other interpersonally damaging behaviors. In compari-son, people of low character are always looking out for themselves and will do whatever it takes for them to get ahead, or what is easier for them to do at the time.

People with high levels of character are reliable, conscientious, and not self-centered. However, we must typically observe the person over time to clarify this perception. High character is not easy to observe, and low character is often not immediately apparent. You may not realize this characteristic until the individual is put into a competitive situation, is under pressure, or in some other way has the opportunity to fail to show high character.

Competence

Competence perceptions may be more easily observable than character because competence relates to skill—how skilled or effective someone is at a task. You might observe that someone is a very competent listener, or public speaker, or salesperson. In relationships, some people are highly skilled at keeping conversations flowing smoothly or at getting acquainted with new people. Highly competent people also tend to be attractive socially and for specific tasks at hand.

However, just because someone is competent does not mean that he or she has high character. In other words, people may be *able* to do something well, but may not do it if it doesn't benefit them. Ideally in relationships, our partners will be both competent and of high character.

Composure

Composure is the perception of being poised and in control (or said another way, *not* being out-of-control). Communicators who are perceived as having low levels of composure are often viewed as emotionally volatile. That means they may show their impatience or let their tempers out when under pressure. Or they may become flustered and frequently be seen as ill at ease and uncomfortable.

Very nervous people are perceived to have low composure, whereas "cool," laid-back people are viewed as composed. One warning here: Extremes in composure in either direction may be negatively perceived. Sure, we don't want to be perceived as high-strung, nervous and tense. But on the other hand, we don't want to be so "composed" as to appear comatose. People who are overly composed are sometimes perceived to be conceited, aloof and distant, or uncaring. Hence, effective communicators understand when to communicate relaxation and when to communicate appropriate animation and excitement (Burgoon, Buller, Hale, & deTurck, 1984).

Perceptions of Attractiveness in Interpersonal Interactions

Perceived attractiveness is important in interpersonal communication because it predicts who we want to move closer to, who we would like to be with. Am I attracted to Tyra Banks, the model, or to Bill Gates of Microsoft fame? Perceptions of attractiveness are not unidimensional. There are three attractiveness dimensions that can influence interpersonal behaviors: physical, social, and task.

Physical Attractiveness

Whenever we first think of attractiveness, we probably think of the outward appearance of people: how handsome, beautiful, or clean-cut they look. That perception is of *physical attractiveness,* and in our culture there is no doubt that it has a major impact on various areas of our lives (see Chapter 4). Physical attraction also plays a role in our interpersonal relationships, especially in early stages. Physical attractiveness and proximity are two major predictors of friendship and romance relationship development. For instance, we're more likely to begin relationships with reasonably attractive people who live or work or attend classes with us. We tend to like and want to be associated with physically attractive people. We tend to self-disclose more to them and think they are well-adjusted, highly competent people (Langlois et al., 2000).

Although physical attractiveness may be a matter of individual taste to some extent, (note the popularity of Marilyn Manson, Taye Diggs, and Pamela Anderson), there is also widespread agreement on what we consider physically attractive in our culture, and even across cultures (Langlois et al., 2000). For example, people with symmetrical or well-balanced facial features tend to be perceived as more physically attractive. So do people with wide-set eyes. Our culture's ideal also tends to be an athletic and fit-looking body type, along with a lower waist-to-hip ratio for women (that means her waist is considerably smaller than her hips). It has even been found that babies look longer at pictures of "attractive" faces than of "unattractive" faces.

Social Attractiveness

We may be initially attracted to how someone looks, but that visual impact tends to fade as the relationship progresses and we get better acquainted with the person. Unfortunately, we sometimes find out that an individual is not as socially attractive as he or she is physically attractive. (That spectacular-looking dancer is truly dumb.) *Social attractiveness* refers to how much you want to spend time with someone. This is the person who is fun to be with, good at conversations, and makes you feel good when you interact. Socially attractive people are rewarding to be around. We may be particularly socially attracted to individuals we perceive to be similar to us.

You can increase your own social attractiveness by improving your social communicative skills. Socially attractive people orient toward others, are fairly optimistic and agreeable about life, and tend to be easy to be around. Socially attractive people tend to provide more rewards than costs to people with whom they interact. They may tell interesting stories and be sympathetic, attentive listeners. An important consideration here is that socially attractive people communicate an interest in *us*. They remember us, and they ask questions about our interests, rather than always talking about themselves. Nervous, shy people often have lower social attractiveness ratings because they make their partners do most of the interaction "work." They don't carry their part of the conversation.

Task Attractiveness

The third type of attractiveness is *task attractiveness*, that is, how much you want to work with a person, how much you want to be with him or her for a specific job or assignment. Certainly task attractiveness is related to competence, and may vary from situation to situation depending on what is required in the task. You might want to work with someone who has strong math skills for an accounting project, but if the project involves food preparation, you will probably find a chef more task attractive.

Obviously it would be a great relationship combination if your partner had all three types of attractiveness. (He or she is great looking, enjoyable to be with, and highly competent.) But this combination is not often the case. People we have a blast with and laugh our heads off with may not be the best work partners. Sometimes people we like the most are not the most physically attractive, and conversely someone who is extremely good-looking could turn out to be incredibly conceited. So it is important to be aware of each form of attractiveness and not confuse the functions each fulfills in interpersonal communication.

Similarities in Relational Perceptions

When we view and perceive others, a basic feature is how similar or dissimilar we are to them. This perception of *homophily* refers to how similar we perceive ourselves to be with other communicators and occurs at several levels: demographic, background, and attitudes/beliefs. In general, the more similar we perceive other people to be, the more we view them positively and the greater the likelihood that we will want to pursue a relationship with them.

Demographic Similarity

Demographic similarity includes factual information about people that they cannot easily modify: their age, sex, nationality, job type, year in school, and so on. To build relationships, we tend to gravitate toward people who are somewhat similar demographically to us. This doesn't mean identical. We don't want clones of ourselves. But homophily in these areas tends to make the relationship easier.

If you think about it, probably most of your closest friends are within five to seven years of your age and are current or recent college students. In many ways, this makes sense because you can share activities, problems, and so on. In fact, if you're honest with yourself, when you see close friends with a large difference in their ages (he's 60 and she's 23, or she's 60 and he's 23), you may wonder what they see in each other. What can those two have in common? We often find relationships between people of widely differing demographics to be curious. Right or wrong, we seem to *expect* relationships to build among individuals with demographic similarities.

Background Similarity

Background similarities consist of being alike in upbringing, where you came from, social "status" (however that may be defined), life experience, and other environmental areas. Homophily in the area of background gives you a similar worldview or perspective on life. For example, if you grew up in a very rural area, the activities you learned might include horseback riding, hunting and fishing, and socializing mostly with people familiar to you. On the other hand, if you grew up in a more urban environment, you may have more experience with using mass transit systems, different types of night life, and swimming in pools rather than lakes, creeks, or other natural bodies of water.

Does dissimilarity mean that you will not befriend someone who does not share your background? No. But it means that you may perceive that you have less in common with that other person, and not try to build a friendship with him or her. One of the functions of university life is to get people acquainted and provide opportunities to interact with and understand people with very different backgrounds from yours. Check out someone *different* from you. You might learn some things.

Attitudes, Beliefs, and Values Similarity

Attitudes, beliefs, and values form the core of our perceptual evaluation of others. Perceptions of similarity or dissimilarity in these areas strongly impact relationship potential. We especially find it easier to be with and form relationships with people we agree with. Notice that, unlike demographic perceptions, these perceptions will be less immediately apparent. After all, we don't go around with a list of our attitudes posted on us like name tags. (However, some people might argue here that the T-shirts and tattoos people display *do* communicate their attitudes.)

Generally we have to interact and get to know people before we understand their opinions and beliefs. Unfortunately, that doesn't stop people from stereotyping others and thinking that because you are from a certain age group, gender, racial or ethnic background you hold specific beliefs. Such leaps of perception can erect barriers in relationships and are difficult to alter for reasons discussed earlier.

When we perceive that someone holds the same opinions we do, whether the view concerns traditional family values, university policies, or Garth Brooks, we tend to find that person more attractive. At least when people agree with our opinions, we believe they have good taste!

Similarities on attitudes and beliefs seem to form the foundation of ongoing relationships. Many people find that they can accommodate or work around dissimilarities in background (you're a Texan and I'm from New England) or demographics (we can be close friends even if you're a Native American and I'm African American). But large differences in core values are difficult to overcome in maintaining relationships.

Word of warning here: Just as we tend to be attracted to people who share similarities with us, we also tend to perceive people we *like* as being similar to us, perhaps more similar than they actually are. ("I think dogs are great, and I'm sure she loves dogs too.") Conversely, if we do *not* like someone, we will tend to believe that person is more different from us than he or she really is. Such biases in our perceptions can lead to surprises and misunderstandings in relationships.

Why Similarities Are Attractive in Relationships

Why is it that we're more likely to develop relationships with people we perceive as similar to us in certain important ways? Yes, the old saying that "opposites attract" may be true initially. We find differences exciting. Challenging. We may also find differences attractive if they are differences on characteristics that we perceive as negative in ourselves. (For example, "I'm disorganized and that's bad. You're organized and that's good.") But differences in others can also be tiring and even annoying. That's why, overall, similarities are more motivating and functional in long-term relationships.

There are several reasons why similarities are attractive to us in relationships. They center on reducing the uncertainty in a relationship, reinforcement of attitudes and behaviors, and making relational life easier.

Uncertainty Reduction

First, human beings don't like high uncertainty—in classes or in interpersonal relationships (Berger & Calabrese, 1975). Uncertainty, or not knowing, makes us edgy and anxious as we try to avoid negative surprises. Therefore, it is easier to be around folks who are similar to us. We feel as though we know them better and understand their perspective. Our *uncertainty is reduced*. (In Chapter 5 we will describe how some individuals have a higher tolerance for uncertainty than others do, a trait called "tolerance for ambiguity." So there may be differences in your preferences depending on your personality characteristics.)

This uncertainty reduction function of similarities allows us to accomplish two things in our interactions: *prediction and explanation* of communicative actions. First, as we get to know people, or *think* we know them based on similarities, we can predict what they will do or how they will react in various situations. Think of trying to buy a birthday gift for someone you hardly know. There is much uncertainty because you don't have any idea what the person might like (so let's just get him a pair of gloves). In contrast, when buying a gift for someone you know well and are similar to, you can imagine what you would like to receive. In that way, you can predict the person's response to the gift. (I'd like a new soccer ball, so I'll bet he would too.) Such predictions of communicative behavior could extend to situations such as reacting to stress, meeting new people, calls from parents, or experiencing cheating in a romantic relationship. You may be able to avoid troubles if you can predict how a friend will act.

The second function of similarities in reducing our uncertainty is being able to explain why people acted the way they did after the fact. If we perceive them as similar we might think, "I know how I'd react if someone insulted me about how I was dressed, so I'm sure she was angry too." If you have ever been clueless about why someone behaved in a certain way, you know that it's not a pleasant feeling. You just can't imagine what made the person communicate in that manner. Therefore, perceived similarities in relationships help us to feel as though we understand our partner better.

Reinforcement

Perceived similarities are also *reinforcing*. If another person is similar to us, especially in attitudes and feelings, then our own attitudes and feelings seem more legitimate, they're more OK. For example, I'm a gay or bisexual college student. If others around me think those orientations are odd or weird, I may question myself. It may hurt my self-esteem. However, if I am around other gay and bisexual college students the attitudes and behaviors are reinforced. It's all right and understandable to feel that way. The same would hold true for other interests: patriotism, wanting to have children, the importance of making money to support a certain lifestyle, the value of "independence." Similarities on any of these can reinforce your own opinions and beliefs.

This reinforcement function of similarity is a primary reason why social groups tend to have similar political attitudes, opinions about how to live, goals, ideas about what is "fun," and so on. This is also why we may feel uncomfortable if we find ourselves in a class or work situation with people who are very different than we perceive ourselves to be.

Increasing Rewards by Decreasing Relational Work

The third reason why perceived similarities lead to more relational potential is that it is simply less work to be around someone with attitudes, tastes, and background similar to ours. It's just easier. We're similar so we like the same types of activities, and we have to spend less time hassling over them. For instance, we both enjoy classic comic books, so let's spend some time in that store. We both love to shop and enjoy Asian food, so there's no problem about what to do with our Saturday. We don't argue over what CDs to play because hip-hop is both of our favorites. We're of a similar age, so are less likely to disagree on attitudes about the government.

When we perceive ourselves as similar to our friend, there is less to negotiate and argue about. We don't have to try as hard to make the other person understand our perspective. That's relational "work." However, remember that we tend to believe that people we like are similar to us— perhaps more similar than they actually are. Because we believe ourselves to be "just alike," we may neglect to listen to and check out the other person, thinking that he or she will react just as we do. Even if we are quite symmetrical about ideas and tastes, it is still a good idea to check with our friend or lover, just to make sure we don't jump to the wrong conclusions.

Managing the Impressions of Others: Communication

The final aspect we're going to discuss concerning interpersonal perceptions is impression management. Sometimes you may want others to perceive you in a specific way (party animal, scholar, upwardly mobile businesslike person), and you actively try to manipulate those impressions through your verbal and nonverbal communication. This is *impression management.*

Let's say you would like someone you just met to have an impression of you as an adult who is fairly well traveled and sophisticated. You might be selective about what you tell this person. You mention travel to Washington, D.C., and how interesting the "street life" is in New York City. You may not add that the D.C. trip was a sixth-grade field trip in a big yellow bus, or that the New York City experience was a family vacation with your little brother and sister. However, you have created a certain impression in the mind of your receiver.

Sometimes managing impressions is simply letting another's perceptions stand. For example, he thinks you're older than you are and you don't correct him because that is a positive perception for you. You allow that inaccurate perception to persist.

We all engage in impression management sometimes and to some extent. Be honest. Hardly anyone is entirely authentic and shows their real self-concept to everyone. It probably wouldn't be possible anyway, given that meanings are in the minds of receivers and therefore not entirely in our control. But we do alter our communication at times to try to create a certain image with an audience. When you go for a job interview or an interview to get into graduate school, you probably select clothing that will communicate a specific impression of you.

Although we all engage in impression management sometimes, some individuals are more conscious and aware of the perceptions they're creating than others are. So they do it more often. *Self-monitoring* refers to people who are very aware of how they are coming across to others and who adapt their communication to fit the image they want to achieve. High self-monitors adapt a lot, and low self-monitors are relatively unaware or uncaring of the perceptions created, and hence are less likely to change to fit the situation.

It is important to note that impression management is *not* telling bold-faced lies that create a false image. It's more subtle than that. Given what we have discussed about perceptions of attractiveness, competence, similarities, and so on, you understand how they work to foster relationships. Then *you* make the decisions about what aspects of yourself to emphasize or de-emphasize in communicating. And impression management could work to discourage relationships as well as encourage them. For instance, someone shows extreme interest in you, but you don't reciprocate that interest. So when you talk you don't mention similarities between you.

As communicators, we probably engage in less impression management communication after we develop a relationship than we do at the beginning of a relationship. After someone gets to know us better, we may feel safer letting them see the real "us"—scary as that may be!

Conclusions

This entire chapter deals with perceptions others form about us and how those perceptions affect relationship development. We make assessments of potential partners' competence, character, and composure, remembering that first impressions are very difficult to change. We recognize that there are different types of attractiveness depending on the needs of the situation. We understand the roles of similarity, whether it be demographic, background, or attitudes and values, in relationships, and why perceptions of similarities are functional in interpersonal communication. Perceptions *are* in the minds of the receivers, but if we understand these processes, then we can use communication to maximize our relational potential.

REFERENCES AND RECOMMENDED READINGS

Berger, C., & Calabrese, R. (1975). Some explorations in initial interaction and beyond: Toward a developmental theory of interpersonal communication. *Human Communication Research, 1,* 99–112.

Berry, D., & Landry, J. (1997) Facial maturity and daily social interaction. *Journal of Personality and Social Psychology, 72,* 570–580.

Burgoon, J., Buller, D., Hale, J., & deTurck, M. (1984). Relational messages associated with nonverbal behaviors. *Human Communication Research, 10,* 351–378.

Burgoon, J., & Hale, J. (1987). Validation and measurement of the fundamental themes of relational communication. *Communication Monographs, 54,* 19–41.

Burleson, B., & Denton, W. (1992). A new look at similarity and attraction in marriage: Similarities in social-cognitive and communication skills as predictors of attraction and satisfaction. *Communication Monographs, 59,* 268–287.

Duck, S. (1977). *The study of attraction.* Farnborough: Saxon House.

Langlois, J., Kalakanis, L., Rubenstein, A., Larson, A., Hallam, M., & Smoot, M. (2000). Maxims or myths of beauty? A meta-analytic and theoretical review. *Psychological Bulletin, 126,* 390–423.

McCroskey, J., & Teven, J. (1999). Goodwill: A reexamination of the construct and its measurement. *Communication Monographs, 66,* 90–103.

Shackelford, T., & Larsen, R. (1997). Facial asymmetry as an indicator of psychological, emotional, and physiological distress. *Journal of Personality and Social Psychology, 72,* 456–466.

Singh, D. (1995). Female judgment of male attractiveness and desirability for relationships: Role of waist-to-hip ratio and financial status. *Journal of Personality and Social Psychology, 69,* 1089–1101.

Swann, W., & Gill, M. (1997). Confidence and accuracy in person perception: Do we know what we think we know about our relationship partners? *Journal of Personality and Social Psychology, 73,* 747–757.

Thornhill, R., & Gangestad, S. (1994). Fluctuating asymmetry and human sexual behavior. *Psychological Science, 5,* 297–302.

APPLYING ATTRACTIVENESS AND SIMILARITY CONCEPTS

1. Think of someone you know quite well and consider to be a good friend. Describe how that person is (1) physically attractive, (2) socially attractive, and (3) task attractive to you.

2. Describe how someone who has a different cultural background than you do may prove to be more challenging because of lack of similarities.

3. What similarities are most important to you in choosing a romantic partner? A roommate?

EXERCISE IN SELF-PRESENTATION

The following are some situations in which you want to create a certain image of yourself with other people. Think about and then describe how you communicate to achieve that perception of yourself. Try to be specific and provide details.

1. You are meeting your new colleagues at work on your internship for the first time.

2. You run into an old friend from high school while you're at a social gathering.

3. Your boyfriend/girlfriend takes you to meet his or her parents on Parents Day at college.

4. You are interacting with your communication professor, whom you want to be your official advisor.

5. You find yourself on a committee with someone you actively dislike. This person has betrayed you in the past.

6. You are at home in your apartment, getting ready for your new potential roommate to arrive so you can get acquainted.

7. You have gotten a speeding ticket and are interacting with the judge about the fine.

8. You're out some night and meet someone you find *really* attractive. You want to encourage and impress this person.

4 Interpersonal Needs and Trust

OBJECTIVES

After studying and discussing this chapter you should be able to do the following things.

1. Explain four ways interpersonal needs differ from physical needs and include an illustration of each.

2. Define inclusion, affection, and control as interpersonal needs.

3. Describe relational communication outcomes of partners who are (a) high versus low on affection, (b) high versus low on inclusion, (c) both high on control, and (d) both low on control needs.

4. Describe relational solutions (other than termination) that could realistically meet individuals' interpersonal needs in each of the four situations in objective 3.

5. Distinguish between complementary and symmetrical needs in relationships.

6. Give the definition of interpersonal trust.

7. List and explain the four components of interpersonal trust.

8. Explain the process of building versus destroying trust.

9. Describe at least four outcomes of low trusters in relationships.

10. Recognize the difference between trusting and gullibility when given a scenario.

CHAPTER OUTLINE

Interpersonal versus Physical Needs

Inclusion, Affection, and Control

Complementary versus Symmetrical Needs in Relationships

Interpersonal Trust

Components of Interpersonal Trust
Building versus Destroying Trust
Reciprocation Wariness
Trust versus Gullibility
Benefits of Trusting

Nathan is an attractive college sophomore who tries hard to be everyone's friend. He wants to be included in everybody's group, all social activities, and clubs, but he does not want to do activities by himself. He overexerts himself in these areas.

Sharell is an alert, intelligent, caring 21-year-old. But she seems stubborn and resists any attempts to do things other than "her way." She also tries to tell others what to do, which doesn't always sit well with her friends.

Maria is a good-natured, socially skilled person, but she seems insecure and needs more affection and reassurance than most people you know. People sometimes take advantage of her need to be loved.

You probably recognize these people, or ones very much like them. Each individual has a distinct communication pattern that can cause problems for her or him in the instructional environment—even though the problematic patterns have nothing to do with a lack of intelligence, ability, or academic motivation. The communication patterns just described are motivated by a desire to satisfy each person's interpersonal needs.

Simply put, *interpersonal needs* means that people need other people in order to feel happy and satisfied (Schutz, 1966). We all have these needs. Apparently they are within us from the time we were born. Some people have more of one form of need than another, and differing levels of each, but we all have them and they motivate us to communicate in ways to get them fulfilled. If we aren't getting our interpersonal needs met, we will tend to be frustrated and unhappy. The difficulty is that we may not recognize what it is that's making us react in a certain manner. Interpersonal needs aren't obvious and clearly observable like our physical needs are.

Interpersonal versus Physical Needs

Let's look at how interpersonal needs are different from our physical needs such as the need for water, food, or air. Interpersonal and physical needs can be distinguished in four major ways: (1) the directness of their impact, (2) their predictability, (3) their flexibility, and (4) their requirements for interaction.

First, our physical needs are easily recognizable because they have a very *direct* and immediate impact on our well-being. Our body tells us when we're cold, hungry, or thirsty. There are direct and observable consequences if our physical needs are not met. Without air we die. Without food and water we soon become sick and will shortly die if we don't meet those physical needs. Interpersonal needs are not so clear-cut. If we aren't given enough recognition and love we suffer, but we don't necessarily die. Just because we aren't allowed to take control of something or have personal autonomy, we don't immediately become ill, but we will be upset and frustrated. You see, we can *live* without getting our interpersonal needs met, but we can't live *well*. Sometimes the drive to meet the needs, or the frustration of those needs, does result in sickness. People get depressed and are more likely to suffer stress-related illnesses, turn to drugs, even commit suicide. So the consequences of unfulfilled interpersonal needs are not inconsiderable—but they are *less direct* and obvious than unmet physical needs. In the classroom, unmet interpersonal needs often results in disruptions in the instructional process. In relationships unfulfilled interpersonal needs often translate to dissatisfaction and difficulty in keeping the relationship together.

A second way interpersonal and physical needs differ is in their *predictability*. We can predict fairly accurately how much water a person weighing 160 pounds needs in a given temperature, for a given time period, at a given activity level. (For example, football players need more liquid than their coaches of the same size who pace the sidelines.) But we cannot easily predict how much affection Chris needs to feel happy and secure. We can't assess exactly how much attention and recognition each of our acquaintances will need each day. Individuals differ in the amount of interpersonal needs they have, and what is sufficient affection for one person may be inadequate for another. Body size and activity level make no difference here.

A third way interpersonal needs are different from physical needs is in the *flexibility* with which they can be satisfied. If you are hungry, the only real way you can satisfy that hunger is with food, and everyone can satisfy the physical need of hunger by eating. That's not true of interpersonal needs. They can be met in various ways. If I can't get my socializing needs met with my particular group of friends, I can join a fitness club, I can go shopping at the mall, or I can dial a conversation line on the phone or enter a chat room on the Internet. Your affection needs can be met by your significant other or by your family members, children, close friends, or even your pets. Many people lavish great amounts of affection on their dogs and cats and receive love from them in return.

Thus people can be very creative about meeting their interpersonal needs because there are so many channels that can be used. This is very important to remember because we often put an unfair burden on one individual in our life when we expect her or him to satisfy *all* of our needs. This aspect will be discussed more fully later in this chapter.

The final way interpersonal and physical needs differ is in their *requirement for interaction*. When you're thirsty, you can get a drink by yourself. You don't need companionship to make use of the air you breathe. But the satisfaction of interpersonal needs requires interaction. In order to fulfill your need to be a leader, you must have followers. To meet your attention and recognition needs, you have to have an audience there to listen, laugh, and applaud. If you feel the need for love and affection, someone has to interact with you to provide it. Interpersonal needs cannot be met in isolation. They require communication and interaction to be satisfied.

Sometimes we may postpone fulfillment of a need through solitary activity. For instance, if people are lonely they might stay very busy with physical work or keep their minds active with other things, but that simply distracts them from the current feeling. It helps, but it doesn't satisfy the real need for affection or companionship. One of the reasons it may be difficult to tell if your partner has unfulfilled needs is that we can postpone gratification of interpersonal needs in a way we cannot with water or food. So it may *seem* that people around you don't need anything. Close attention is needed to be able to tell what people really need in their relationships.

Inclusion, Affection, and Control

Now that we know that interpersonal needs are different from physical needs, let's examine more closely what those needs are and how they influence communication. The three basic interpersonal needs are inclusion, affection, and control. All other labels we have for our needs can be subsumed into these three central categories (Schutz, 1966).

Inclusion is the need to be included, to socialize with and be interesting to others. It is the need to feel that you fit in or belong with groups of individuals. Meeting our inclusion needs doesn't require deep, extended, personally revealing, "quality" communication, but may simply be "hanging out." Individuals who prefer to engage in numerous social activities, enjoy being "on the go," and like to have people around them most of the time have high inclusion needs. In contrast, those who enjoy a great deal of "alone time" or prefer more solitary activities, avoiding larger group activities and focusing time with only one other person, probably have lower inclusion needs.

In comparison, if people have very low inclusion needs they may dislike all the social activity and group interaction that is so much a part of this society. These folks may look for ways to "escape" the constant participation demands by going off by themselves frequently, not attending social functions, or showing a strong interest in individualized education, such as reading or computer work.

The second basic category of interpersonal needs is the need to give and receive *affection*. We all need to feel loved and cared for to some extent, but some people have a greater need than others. The affection need, unlike inclusion, is typically satisfied in one-to-one interaction and may involve deeper communication levels. It also takes on a strongly nonverbal component because many of the ways we demonstrate liking and affection are through our gestures, touching, interaction distances, and facial expressions. Students with high affection needs may also be more overt in their verbal declarations of affection and want others to tell them they like them.

People whose affection needs are unfulfilled may find others taking advantage of them if they can't get these needs met in their regular relationships. They trade off efforts or favors for affection. Unfortunately, some people mistake sexual interactions for affection, and may find themselves in unproductive relationships hoping to find "love."

The need for *control* is the third basic interpersonal need. This is the need to make decisions and take on responsibility—sometimes for ourselves and sometimes for others. People who are high on certain kinds of control needs want to make the choices and decisions that govern interactions or control their lives. They tend to be perceived as "independent" and have an opinion on every issue. If people are low on the need for control, they want other people to take the lead or guide decision making. When you ask them what movie they want to see, they answer, "I don't care, you decide," and they really mean it! We may interpret someone's low control needs as "lacking initiative," being overreliant on others, or simply as being easygoing.

Most children are used to having adults make decisions for them, so in earlier years this may not be a problem. But difficulties may be evident when they get older. Adolescents might experience more difficulties. Adolescence is a time of heightened control needs as students reach an age when they expect and attempt to make choices for themselves. This can also be seen when 18-year-olds leave for college. They have an increased need to make decisions and have autonomy in their own lives. But this can sometimes create conflict with parents who are used to making decisions and exerting "control" over their kids.

To summarize, affection, inclusion, and control are needs that each of us has to different degrees. Because so much of our communication is oriented toward fulfilling those needs, it is important that we recognize them and channel the communication appropriately. But human needs are more complex than a simple three-category system. Not only do we have all three needs, but each need is further divided into the need *to give* affection, inclusion, or control, and the need *to receive* affection, inclusion, and control.

Now that we understand what each need is and what communication associated with it may indicate, we'll look at the difference between the need to give each and to receive each. This distinction relates to who does the initiating of the communication messages. If you are high on the need to give inclusion, it means you want to ask others to be with you, to invite friends to join you in activities. If you are high on the need to receive inclusion, you want other people to invite you, to be interested in you. You want friends to choose you for the team, fraternity, or church committee. In other words, you have a stronger need for others to initiate the inclusion.

In contrast, if you are low on the giving end of inclusion, you are un-likely to issue invitations, ask others to go with you to a movie, or start up a social club. People who are low on the need to get inclusion won't care if others don't include them and won't be bothered if friends don't call them on the phone to initiate interactions. Remember, people low in inclusion needs overall prefer to work alone and may view group interactions as a waste of time.

If people are high on the need to give affection they will probably be very demonstrative, "touchy" people. They may freely tell you what a great person you are. When people are high in the need to receive affection, they will want affection shown to them. They may seek out situations where af-fection is overtly communicated and will expect overt shows of affection from relationship partners. They may be very unhappy if their boyfriend or girlfriend doesn't reassure them directly of the value of the relationship.

Sometimes though, people are low in the need to give affection and they will not desire to initiate affectionate communication. In relationships they may not demonstrate the caring they feel, and may seem "cool and dis-tant" to their partners. They may also be low on the need to receive affec-tion. That is, they don't care much whether a parent, friend, or teacher tells them how much they care for them. They may not expect nonverbal shows of affection and when such demonstrations come, even in private, they often feel embarrassed and overwhelmed.

The giving and receiving of control needs is a bit more complicated. If someone has a high need to give control, he or she will want to initiate deci-sions that affect other people. This person will actively seek leadership roles and supervisory positions so that her or his own decisions will be enacted. These are people who become department chairs, organizational presidents, or high-level managers.

If people are low in the need to give control, they don't care much about power and aren't concerned that they control or guide others. They will not try to take the lead, not because they want to follow, but because they just don't feel the need to direct other people. When people are low on the need to receive control, however, they don't want others to make deci-sions for *them*. They may seem fiercely independent and reject attempts from others to control their actions. Remember a low need to *get* control is not the same as a high need to *give* it, but they may go together.

Complementary versus Symmetrical Needs in Relationships

Thus far we have been discussing interpersonal needs only from the perspective of the individual who feels the need. But interpersonal relationships are made up of two individuals, each with her or his own set of needs. Each partner in a friendship has needs. Husbands and wives both have needs. What happens if they don't fit nicely together? What are the best patterns of "relational fit"?

Needs of people in relationships can be complementary or symmetrical. *Complementary* needs are those based on differences in needs that are balanced off by your relational partner. A person with a high need to give affection is in a relationship with a person with a high need to get affection. Someone high in the need to get control is in a relationship with one who is high in the need to give control, resulting in a perfect leader–follower relationship.

Symmetrical needs are based on similarity of needs between the partners. When both partners have high inclusion needs, they may have friends over to their home or go on group outings frequently. Because symmetrical partners are similar in their interpersonal needs, they may tend to understand and empathize more fully with each other than do complementary partners.

But both symmetrical and complementary patterns can lead to interaction problems. What happens when one person has a high need to give and get affection and the other has a low need? The first partner tends to feel disappointed, not appreciated, and unloved, while at the same time the other may feel pressured and "smothered." Or consider the example of Deb and Mike. She has higher inclusion needs and would like to attend community activities such as local arts festivals, or have friends over to their apartment regularly, but Michael prefers to be alone with her or spend time playing his computer games or reading. He thinks she's a "social butterfly" and she thinks he's in a "rut." Clearly, complementarity has its disadvantages.

However, symmetrical relationships can be problematic too. If both people are high in the need to give control there may be quarreling over who does what, how things are done, whose schedule is correct, and even the appropriate way to wash the car. When both partners have high control needs, they always have an opinion on everything because they want to make the "best" decision (translated as "their" decision).

The situation might be just as difficult if each had high needs to get control. Then neither person would want to make the choice and take the lead, so there might be frequent drifting, or waiting for some external circumstance to determine the direction they should take.

So how can relationships survive such difficulties with interpersonal needs? A quick answer would be to compromise. But compromise isn't the best solution in this case because it means that neither partner is having the needs fully met. Such a course may result in dissatisfaction down the road.

The key lies in the *flexibility* of interpersonal needs satisfaction. Recall that interpersonal needs can be satisfied in a variety of ways. This means that one relationship partner does not have to be the source of satisfaction for all the other partner's needs. This is particularly important if one has very high needs levels. In other words, if you have affection needs that aren't being met, your primary partner doesn't have to bear the sole responsibility. Love and affection can also be received from other family members, close friends, even your pets, as well as your significant other.

Similarly, inclusion doesn't necessarily mean your partner has to be included all the time. People with high inclusion needs, like Deborah, can join clubs without their partners. They can go out to dinner with groups of friends, have extensive interaction at their workplace, or participate in church or civic activities in which the partner is not necessarily active. This results in the inclusion needs of one partner being met without stressing the other partner by forcing group interaction.

Control needs can also be creatively handled. High-control partners often experience dissension because they are trying to direct each other in the relationship. But we can satisfy our control needs by other means too. Often people get their control needs met in their jobs. Administrators make managerial and personnel decisions every day.

Unfortunately, some people have jobs where it is impossible to satisfy their control needs: factory assembly-line work, unskilled labor, entry-level positions where others tell you what to do. In such cases, additional avenues need to be explored to avoid being domineering at home. If you can't satisfy your control needs at work you might become a social group leader, captain of the hockey team or bowling league, chair of a community task force, or student government representative.

Sometimes hobbies offer opportunities to satisfy control needs. Animal trainers, artists, and even car- or motorcycle-racing enthusiasts experience a sense of control in making decisions that influence external circumstances. Find a hobby that allows you to make detailed and independent choices: rock climbing, windsurfing, fashion design, songwriting, skateboarding.

The important thing is to meet your own control needs so you can be contented and satisfied. You can do this without ruining close interpersonal relationships with friends and family by being overcontrolling or "bossy." But you must be aware of your own interpersonal needs and their consequences, recognize how you could meet the needs without overburdening your friends and partners, and be willing to communicate to get the needs of inclusion, control, and affection met.

Interpersonal Trust

"Trust me." Oh yeah, right! Has anyone ever said this to you? The phrase "trust me" has almost become a cliché in our society. But we do know that people who can "trust"—can believe in someone—tend to do better in relationships. After all, how can you have a close relationship with someone you don't trust? So interpersonal trust is an essential part of developing a relationship.

In discussing interpersonal trust we'll consider what components make up a trusting situation, how trust can be productive for a relationship, and how lack of trust can cause relationships to deteriorate. First let's define interpersonal trust. *Interpersonal trust* is an individual's characteristic belief that the sincerity, benevolence, or truthfulness of others can generally be relied on. What does this mean? First of all, trust is attitudinal, a belief system, and not always behavioral. You *feel* trust, and then you may act upon that trust. So trust itself is not necessarily behavioral, but the outcomes of trust are.

Second, when you have interpersonal trust for someone, you believe that they will not knowingly do you harm. Note that the definition says that the people "can generally be relied on." This suggests that even people we trust greatly may not be the best ones to trust with cooking a dinner for us or investing our money. But if we trust them generally, we will tend to believe them and think they are honest and will not go behind our back, disrespect us, or undermine our goals.

Components of Interpersonal Trust

When we think of trusting someone, we need to apply four criteria. That is, four components make up a truly trusting interpersonal situation. If you don't see all four operating in your case, perhaps you aren't trusting the other person. You can check for yourself whether you are involved in a trusting relationship.

1. *One Person Is Relying on Another for Some Outcome.* Interpersonal trust assumes some interdependence between people, rather than total self-reliance. In other words, if you always do everything for yourself, and you are completely independent, you don't need to "trust." But such total independence is probably unlikely and not feasible, especially in relationships. On a societal level for instance, we trust that food served in restaurants and products sold in stores are not contaminated. We rely on that. (Note that when such trust is betrayed, consumers win huge lawsuits.)

Interpersonally, we may trust our roommates to lock the door when they leave for the weekend. We rely on them in this case. Relationally, we trust that friends will tell us the truth when we ask about our new hairstyle, college class choice, or what they saw our significant other doing last

Saturday night. Again, interpersonal trust implies that you are relying on someone else for something you cannot accomplish by yourself.

2. *The person who is trusting the other is risking some loss.* "If you never risk, you never lose." That's some people's motto. Maybe they've been burned in relationships. They are low trusters. If you really trust someone, you put the person in charge of something important to you, whether it be your car, your clothing, your unlisted phone number, or your self-confidence. Parents make trusting decisions when they select godparents for their children.

It isn't unusual to hear people say they would trust another with some aspect of their lives, but not another. An example might be, "I'd never trust him with my bank account number," or "I wouldn't leave my house with her." If you say that you "trust" someone, but the aspect you trust the person with is of minimal importance, easily replaceable, or doesn't matter to you, then you haven't fully trusted. You know that a relationship is truly meaningful when someone trusts you with his or her most important assets—new car, children, ATM card, or Labrador retriever. When you trust, you risk some loss.

3. *The outcome is viewed as uncertain.*   You are not absolutely sure your friend will meet you at the designated time. You can't be 100 percent certain that the potentially embarrassing information you just disclosed to your roommate won't go any further. It can't be called "trust" if the outcome is certain.

For example, you aren't really trusting that the sun will rise tomorrow, or that the Internal Revenue Service will be a part of your life. Those are certainties. Trust implies that at some point you don't *know* what will happen, but you take a "leap of faith." You give up the control and just believe. Interpersonal trust occurs when you think someone will uphold what he or she says, that the person will fulfill the trust, but you cannot be sure. Trusting involves uncertainty.

4. *The potential loss to the truster if the trust is violated is greater than the potential gain if the trust is fulfilled.* This may be the most important, yet subtle, component of interpersonal trust. Simply put, if I trust you and you do not uphold that trust, I will be hurt more than I will benefit if you *do* uphold the trust. If I rely on you to catch me when I fall, and you don't catch me, I get hurt. But if you *do* catch me, what do I gain? Yes, I trust you more, but I already had some level of trust for you to begin with. Any gain is small by comparison.

We face these trade-offs every day when we drive in traffic. If a car coming toward us has the turn signal on, we trust that means the driver is going to turn. However, if we trust the signal, pull out into the road, and the driver *doesn't* turn and the car rams into us, the trust has been violated. The damage to us in this case (trust violation) is more extensive than the gain we would obtain if the driver had just followed the turn signal as indicated (trust fulfilled).

Let's look at a second, more interpersonal example. Someone you know verbally offers you a job. You quit your current job, terminate your lease, and prepare to move out of state before you receive the formal, official job offer from the company. That is trust. Unless your current life is miserable anyway, you stand to lose more if that job offer doesn't come through than you gain if trust is fulfilled.

Relationally, we see examples of trust operating all the time. Let's say you believe/trust your partner to be free of STDs when you have sexual interaction. If he or she is truthful with you and trustworthy, you won't catch an STD and you may feel closer. On the other hand, if this partner betrays your trust by having sexual contact when he or she knows about an infection, you're in trouble. You have received more harm (infection, angry feelings) than you would gain if this person had been honest and had upheld the trust you felt.

To summarize, in interpersonal trust situations all four components of trust are operating. If any component is absent, check it out because you're probably not really trusting.

Building versus Destroying Trust

A final point here. Building interpersonal trust tends to be an incremental process. We do it a step at a time. For example, we test people by sharing minor information, finding out if they can handle it, and then perhaps trusting them with more. Creating trust between people tends to take time. It truly is descriptive to say that trust *grows*.

However, betrayal of trust hits like an avalanche. It tends to happen quickly and often with devastating results. Betrayal of trust is the most-cited reason for anger in close relationships. It is a huge violation of expectations we hold for our close partners. We may destroy the trust someone has in us with one action. We carelessly let a secret slip out, we drink too much and hook up with someone other than our significant other, we say words we wish we could take back. But once trust is destroyed in a relationship it is difficult, if not impossible, to get it back.

The main point to learn here is to avoid betraying someone's trust. Don't play games with this one. Trying to regain trust will take monumentally more effort, time, and care than it took you to develop the trust with that person in the first place. If someone really trusts you, take care of that trust and guard it gently.

Reciprocation Wariness

Not everyone is *able* to trust others easily. They may have had bad experiences in which they felt betrayed. They may be fiercely independent and not want to let anyone too close, or have to depend on others. These experiences may lead them to being a low truster. One factor associated with low trust is a concept termed reciprocation wariness (Cotterell, Eisenberger, & Speicher, 1992). *Reciprocation wariness* is a deep fear of being exploited in relationships leading to disinclination to accept aid, return aid, or contribute a great deal to social relationships. The person does not give back, or reciprocate, resources in the relationship and often declines resources others may offer because they don't want to be "in debt."

It's very difficult to build a close relationship with someone who is reciprocation wary. People may be wary of the normal give-and-take of friendships for fear of commitment or entanglement in a relationship—even though they would *like* to have a long-term relationship.

Reciprocation-wary people have also been found to be less cooperative on negotiated tasks, and to have more negative responses to uncooperative communication from others. (Imagine being this person's roommate!)

Even friends and roomates tend to evaluate high-wary people as unsympathetic and inconsiderate, and to view them as manipulative. They're always playing the angle, looking for the time when others are going to take advantage of them. In residence hall settings, students who were supervised by high-wary resident assistants evaluated them as unapproachable, hesitant to develop close relationships, and unresponsive to student needs. Overall, it stands out that being reciprocation wary appears to be unproductive for relationship development.

Trust versus Gullibility

Just because you tend to be trusting doesn't mean you're a fool. People who are high in trust are not necessarily more gullible. *Gullibility* implies acting with knowledge that the other person is untrustworthy. In other words, if you believe that a friend will stand you up for an appointment because he has done it before, he has done it to other people, and you still rely on appointments with him—you're gullible. You're gullible if you know that someone can't keep a secret—she tells you all sorts of private information about other people—and yet you self-disclose private information to her. If everything tells you that an individual will betray your trust, but you go ahead and trust the person anyway, that's being gullible.

Gullibility seems to relate more to dependency than to high trust. People who are highly dependent and not very self-reliant tend to get taken advantage of, that is, be gullible. Just because you are a high truster does not mean that you've left your brain behind.

Benefits of Trusting

Simply put, trust is good for a relationship. Lack of trust puts obstacles in the way of deepening a relationship. Several studies have also shown that high trusters have fewer interpersonal difficulties in all types of relationships, compared to low trusters.

People who do not fear trusting others can be interdependent in relationships. They can open up, feel safer, and truly get to know and understand their partners, as well as help their partners understand them.

In addition, doesn't it feel good to know that someone trusts you? When someone trusts you, you feel important and warm. In contrast, think about how you feel when someone communicates to you that he or she does *not* trust you. The person thinks you are untrustworthy. Whether this person is your boss, your parent, a police officer, or your lover, lack of trust doesn't exactly make you feel positive toward him or her, does it. So the fact that your friend trusts you tends to add something beneficial to the relationship, and may even encourage you to uphold that trust.

Low trusters have been found to experience more envy, competitiveness when it's not warranted, resentfulness, and general lack of closeness in relationships. Sometimes adults who have been in relationships in which trust has been betrayed develop a shell around themselves, avoiding situations that threaten their independence. They've been hurt before and don't want it to happen again. Yes, trusting may be scary; you have to take that leap. But a lack of trust is not good for either romantic or platonic relationships.

Close relationships seem to integrally involve doing favors, trusting, helping others, being helped and "owing" someone, giving and receiving. If you cannot do this because of a lack of trust or a fear of being taken advantage of, you will tend to keep people at a formal distance and be unlikely to have close, satisfying interpersonal relationships.

Conclusions

Interpersonal needs (inclusion, affection, and control) may be symmetrical or complementary in relationships, and they are so subtle that we often fail to recognize they are influencing us. Nevertheless, they do guide our interpersonal behavior as we seek to meet those needs. Not understanding our own and others' needs may cause difficulties in a relationship. (Think of the potential problems if one roommate has very high inclusion needs and the other has low inclusion needs.) Misbehaviors, broken promises, or even perceived uncaring may all be attempts by someone to get his or her interpersonal needs met.

Part of understanding ourselves in relationships is being aware of our needs. If we don't realize what we must have to be happy, how can we expect someone else to magically meet our needs? We have to develop communication in relationships to help meet them. Building that process will involve creating a relationship, trusting someone, opening up through self-disclosure, and being honest, accepting, and flexible about both our own and our partner's interpersonal needs.

REFERENCES AND RECOMMENDED READINGS

Cotterell, N., Eisenberger, R., & Speicher, H. (1992). Inhibiting effects of reciprocation wariness on interpersonal relationships. *Journal of Personality and Psychology, 62,* 658–668.

Eisenberger, R., Cotterell, N., & Marvel, J. (1987). Reciprocation ideology. *Journal of Personality and Social Psychology, 58,* 743–750.

Fehr, B., Baldwin, M., Collins, L., Patterson, S., & Benditt, R. (1999). Anger in close relationships: An interpersonal script analysis. *Personality and Social Psychology Bulletin, 25,* 299–312.

Furnham, A. (1996). The FIRO-B, the Learning Style Questionnaire, and the five-factor model. *Journal of Social Behavior and Personality, 11,* 285–299.

Gurtman, M. (1992). Trust, distrust, and interpersonal problems: A circumplex analysis. *Journal of Personality and Psychology, 62,* 989–1002.

Schutz, W. (1966). *The interpersonal underworld.* Palo Alto, CA: Science and Behavior Books.

INTERPERSONAL TRUST

Here is a list of interpersonal problems that people who score low on measures of interpersonal trust report that they encounter. Do any of these describe you? How does it make relationships difficult?

1. I am too suspicious of others.

2. I feel competitive even when a situation does not call for it.

3. It is hard for me to trust others in a variety of situations.

4. I often feel attacked by others.

5. I tend to be too envious and jealous of others.

6. I criticize others too much for fear they will criticize me.

7. I have difficulty telling someone personal things.

8. I worry about my family's reaction to me.

9. It is hard for me to put somebody else's needs before mine.

10. It is hard for me to express my admiration for another.

11. I sometimes focus on getting revenge against people too much.

12. It is hard for me to feel close to others.

I N T E R P E R S O N A L   N E E D S

For each of the following statements, respond from 1 to 5 based on how applicable this is to you generally in your life. There are no "correct" answers, just your answers.

Not like me at all	**Very little**	**Sometimes**	**Quite a bit**	**Yes, that's me!**
1	2	3	4	5

____ **1.** I like to make decisions for myself.

____ **2.** I tend to be a very affectionate person.

____ **3.** Being a part of groups is very important to me.

____ **4.** I may not want to boss others around, but I really don't want others to tell me what to do on a regular basis.

____ **5.** I feel upset when other people don't let me know they like or love me.

____ **6.** I often prefer to work alone.*

____ **7.** I often feel that others ought to take the lead rather than me.*

____ **8.** I often show how much I like people in a variety of direct and indirect ways.

____ **9.** I tend to enjoy doing activities, especially social activities in groups.

____ **10.** I tend to believe that my opinions, ideas, and ways of doing things are really the best way to do something.

____ **11.** I have little need to express affection to others even if they're important to me.*

____ **12.** I often find groups to be superficial and a "waste of time."*

____ **13.** I prefer to take the lead and direct actions around me.

____ **14.** When I like someone, I want to express that and I feel frustrated if I can't.

____ **15.** I enjoy the stimulation and activity of communicating with people in group settings.

Scoring:

1. Reverse the score for items with asterisk. (1 = 5; 2 = 4; 4 = 2; 5 = 1)

2. Add up the scores for each segment:

    Items 1, 4, 7, 10, and 13   Total C _____

    Items 2, 5, 8, 11, and 14   Total A _____

    Items 3, 6, 9, 12, and 15   Total I _____

Interpretation: Scores on each segment can range from 5 to 25.

EXPRESSION OF INTERPERSONAL NEEDS

In Groups of 2–5 People:

1. Individually complete the answers to the questions below.

2. When that is done, discuss what you have written and exchange ideas for communicating about your needs.

1. I think my *inclusion* needs are _____ (high/moderate/low). I find myself expressing that need when I . . .

2. I think my *affection* needs are _____ (high/moderate/low). I find myself expressing that need when I . . .

3. I think my *control* needs are _____ (high/moderate/low). I find myself expressing that need when I . . .

5 Personality Traits in Interpersonal Communication

OBJECTIVES

If you want to do well on a test over this information, you need to be able to

1. Define what a trait is and why traits are not entirely bio-genetic.

2. Explain affective orientation and how it relates to communication in an interpersonal relationship.

3. Differentiate between argumentativeness and verbal aggressiveness. Be able to recognize each pattern of communication in a scenario.

4. Define the traits Machiavellianism, humor orientation, and tolerance for ambiguity. Discuss how each might affect a relationship.

5. Describe someone who exhibits the trait of conscientiousness.

6. Distinguish between a person who has an internal versus an external locus of control. Describe how each might affect a relationship.

7. Compare the patterns of behavior and reactions of someone who is an introvert and someone who is an *extravert.*

8. Discuss why an extreme level of any trait is more stable and identifiable than moderate levels of a trait.

CHAPTER OUTLINE

Description of Traits

Link to Communication Process

Traits Operating in Communication Interactions
    Affective Orientation
    Argumentativeness versus Verbal
        Aggression
    Machiavellianism

Tolerance for Ambiguity
Conscientiousness
Humor Orientation
Locus of Control
Androgyny = Versatility
Extroversion versus Introversion

When Personality Traits Will Have the Most Influence

"He's a creep." "She is a such a bitch." "They're low-life losers." "What a conniving liar!" Have you ever heard someone describe acquaintances or even relational partners like this? When we describe people, chances are we are describing their *personalities*. We are describing what we think of them as a person, both positive and negative. Personality is made up of the total configuration of all our traits.

Description of Traits

What *is* a personality trait? *Traits* are relatively enduring characteristics of an individual that predispose us to respond in certain patterns. Personality traits appear to be a combination of *inherited qualities and social reinforcement.*

Many personality traits appear to have their roots in genetics, and the predispositions to behave in a certain way are inborn. No, this doesn't mean that if you are born with high levels of aggressiveness you will always respond with aggressive communication, constantly getting into fights. But it does mean that you will *tend* to respond that way more than others might. Recent research has observed that in extroversion, inhibition, anxiety, aggression, responsibility, sociability, and a wide variety of other characteristics tend to be inborn traits.

Traits also represent predispositions to patterns of response across situations. They won't affect the person only in one context, but will be present in many varied environments and situations. If someone is very intelligent and has a good memory, that will likely carry through in work situations, diverse classes in school, and even on vacations. Similarly, if you tend to be a jealous person, you will feel jealousy around different partners and under varying circumstances, more so than a person who is low on the trait of jealousy.

Although not all personality traits are inherited, they are often formed very early in childhood through reinforcement patterns. You probably don't even remember your parents and other caregivers reinforcing you for being creative, obedient, adventurous, or cautious. But the way families communicate with very young children no doubt has an impact on the personality traits that develop. For example, if a child constantly is rewarded for trying new things, making attempts on her own, and is forgiven for making mistakes, that child is more likely to develop independence and creativity.

Does this mean that "biology is destiny"? No. Personality is consistent, but it is also *dynamic*. That means people can change. Certain characteristics may be punished and therefore be minimized, for example, leadership, sympathy, risk taking. In contrast, other traits that are present very early in life are actually made stronger and enhanced by societal reinforcement. A good example of this is aggressive tendencies in little boys (Maccoby & Jacklin, 1974). Male infants are born with higher levels of testosterone than most baby girls are, so boys begin life with more aggressiveness. Differences are notable even in early infancy. Then parents, siblings, schools, and society in general encourage aggression in various ways, especially in little boys. Young boys are more likely to play fighting and competitive games, to respond to tasks with forceful aggression, and to be discouraged from being timid or weak. Thus, males' initial higher levels of aggression (biological) are emphasized and positively reinforced by others around them (developmental) to result in even larger gender differences as they mature.

By the time people get to be young adults, their personalities are fairly well established. Any significant change will probably be slow and incremental. It won't happen overnight. In addition, personality change in adulthood often necessitates active involvement of the individual in the transformation. In other words, the person typically has to decide to change a particular characteristic (e.g., dominance, self-control, anxieties), and then participate in activities or thought processes to make those changes. (Why do you think self-help books and classes are so popular? People often *want* to modify their traits, but need guidance and support when doing it.)

Link to Communication Process

A question you may be asking at this point is, "Why should we be studying personality traits, seems like a psychological area, in a *communication* class?" The answer of course is that our traits influence how we communicate—both encoding messages and decoding them. Remember from Chapter 1 that "meanings are in people." Well our personality traits are part of what determines our meanings.

To illustrate, our shyness (trait) may influence us to talk less in a group situation even when we know we ought to talk more. It may influence us to communicate nonverbally so that we do not draw attention to ourselves. (Have you ever noticed that some people dress to "blend in," whereas others dress to be unique and memorable?) In contrast, if we are *extravert*ed (trait) we may go out of our way to be where other people are and to meet them.

In decoding messages, traits affect how we *perceive and interpret* the messages coming in to us. Again, if we are shy, it may seem intimidating or overwhelming when someone starts a conversation with us. If we are low on "argumentativeness," we may perceive any challenge to what we have said as an attack; but people high in this trait view challenges as positive and as opportunities to discuss an issue. Thus, our individual traits impact how we put communication messages together and how we understand and respond to messages as they come to us.

Traits Operating in Communication Interactions

Although we don't have the space or time to go through all the personality traits which may influence relationships, here are a few traits that have received attention from communication researchers. See if you recognize them in people around you.

Affective Orientation

Affective orientation is the degree to which we are aware of, value, and really use our emotions as guides in communicating and making decisions (Booth-Butterfield & Booth-Butterfield, 1990). Some people are very aware of their emotions; they think about them and carefully consider them. Others, low affectively oriented folks, tend to be less sensitive to their own emotions and when they do become aware of them, reject their value for making decisions. In other words, some people follow their "gut-level response" and others follow the facts and objective logical analysis.

To compare the two types, the high affectively oriented college student who is homesick may go home on the weekend for company, despite having a major paper due. On the other hand, a homesick low affectively oriented student with a major paper due would be more likely to put feelings aside and work diligently during the weekend.

Affective orientation has been found to be associated with greater conversational and nonverbal sensitivity and better comforting behaviors. Overall, people who are more affectively oriented tend to feel their emotions more strongly and to be aware of even subtle changes in how they view themselves and the interactions around them. Sounds like they'd make desirable relationship partners, doesn't it?

Argumentativeness versus Verbal Aggression

Verbal aggression is a destructive communication act and should not be confused with argumentativeness, which can be constructive. How can we distinguish these forms of communication traits? *Verbally aggressive messages* are those which attack the self-concept of another person with the intent to cause psychological pain. Some types of hurtful messages include attacks on one's character, competence, or physical appearance. Verbal aggression may also include malicious teasing, ridicule, threats, profanity, and nonverbal actions.

In contrast, *argumentativeness* is when people want to discuss and argue about the issues. They can debate without getting personal. They can fight over an issue, such as abortion rights, without trying to hurt the other partner. Argumentativeness has been found to be a desirable trait when used competently in organizations and relationships. But there is no study which has found that verbal aggression is productive for interpersonal interactions.

The psychological pain produced by the verbally aggressive messages includes: embarrassment, feelings of inadequacy, humiliation, hopelessness, or depression (Infante, 1987), and obviously such patterns of interaction don't encourage open communication. In fact, one study showed directly that verbally aggressive people were perceived as less popular and socially attractive (Wanzer, Booth-Butterfield, & Booth-Butterfield, 1996).

Where does the trait of verbal aggression come from? It is probably developed within the family. Infante, Myers, and Buerkel (1994) concluded that the family environment may support verbal aggression because family members have a lower need for social desirability in that setting than in other social settings. Bayer and Cegala (1992) found that parents who are verbally aggressive with their children often use messages that are hostile, sarcastic, and belittling, and suggested that parental verbal aggression and authoritarianism has the potential of damaging the child's self-concept. Individuals who come from a verbally aggressive family environment tend to be more verbally aggressive themselves, and experience less satisfaction in their relationships with others (Beatty & Dobos, 1992). Not surprisingly, verbal aggression in sibling relationships has also been linked with lower relational satisfaction and interpersonal trust (Martin, Anderson, Burant, & Weber, 1997).

One of the main reasons people resort to verbal aggression appears to be deficiencies in communication skills. If people are not competent communicators, especially when it comes to disagreements, they may resort to lashing out and "winning" the fight the only way they know how—by hurting the other person. This is termed an argumentative skill deficiency and has been linked to violence in relationships, as well as to more low-level aggression. For these reasons argumentativeness is viewed as a trait to be encouraged, whereas verbal aggression is seen as an unproductive personality trait.

Machiavellianism

Some people are manipulators. They want to arrange events and strategize about how to get people to achieve some outcome that they see as positive (maybe they want to get you to clean the apartment, but they figure you would be resistant). When people typically use manipulative strategies to accomplish their goals, they are referred to as *Machiavellian.*

Machiavellian personality types tend to believe that people won't do what you want them to, so you have to trick them, or be indirect in order to get them to do what you desire. People high in this trait are unlikely to be totally open and authentic in relationships. They will prefer "games" and manipulations to straightforward conversation. This makes them somewhat more difficult to deal with as intimate relationship partners. For one thing, high Machiavellian partners have more difficulty trusting others. Researchers have also found that high Machiavellian people are better at the art of deception than people low in the trait. Hmmmmm.

Tolerance for Ambiguity

A trait that is frequently difficult to see and understand in others is tolerance for ambiguity. Some people want a great deal of structure and guidance in their lives—whether in task or social arenas. They want certainty and have a *low tolerance for ambiguity.* Other people live quite happily with uncertainty and a general lack of planning; they value spontaneity and discovering things for themselves as they go along. We call this having a *high tolerance for ambiguity.*

How people plan their vacations offers a good illustration of individual differences in tolerance for ambiguity. Folks with higher tolerance for ambiguity just jump in the car and head toward their destination—assuming they have one. They're lucky if they have a map in the car. Others want to plan details and know what to expect every step of the way—from exact routings, to where they'll be staying each night, to what activities they can anticipate each day. And they may expect their interpersonal relationships to be like that too!

In relationships some people "take it a day at a time." They don't necessarily need to know where the relationship is going or what the rules are. In contrast, people with low tolerance for ambiguity want more certainty. They want to understand "where they stand" with their partner and what to expect, so they can cope. Keep in mind that neither high nor low tolerance for ambiguity is necessarily productive or unproductive in every situation. Certainly there are times when we want spontaneity (high ambiguity "surprises"), and times when we do *not* want uncertainty and unexpectedness (how class assignments will be graded or "pop quizzes"). However, things may work more smoothly in relationships if the partners are similar on this trait.

Conscientiousness

The personality trait of *conscientiousness* refers to social dependability and responsibility. (Think of having an active conscience guiding you.) People who are highly conscientious follow through on what they say they will do, they are responsible, and they try to do what is right and good. They also tend to be orderly and relatively free from selfishness and arrogance. Sometimes we think of them as people of high "character."

People who score low on conscientiousness tend to be self-interested and enact behaviors that will benefit themselves regardless of the consequences for others. For example, low conscientious individuals may "cut corners" on an assignment, whether it be a task for class or building a multistory apartment complex.

There have been numerous studies of trait conscientiousness, and some of the findings may be surprising. Children who are conscientious live longer as adults, partly because they are less likely to smoke and drink heavily. They are less likely to get divorced or have what are called "unstable marital histories" (Friedman et al., 1995). Conscientious people are probably good bets for relationship partners. Wouldn't you rather have friends who stand by you and follow through on what they promise, rather than ones who let you down?

Humor Orientation

Have you ever known people who are just plain funny? They can reliably make you laugh in a variety of ways. According to Booth-Butterfield and Booth-Butterfield (1991), persons who enact humor frequently and successfully perceive themselves as effective in communicating humor, and employ diverse humor strategies across a number of situations exhibit a trait known as *humor orientation*. These people are funny. They may encode their humor through joking, acting things out, nonverbal mannerisms, changes in their voice or witty language—but they do keep people entertained.

High humor-oriented people are perceived by observers and independent coders to be funnier than low humor-oriented people when telling jokes, and as communicators in general, are viewed as more humorous. This contributes to making them more socially attractive (Wanzer, Booth-Butterfield, & Booth-Butterfield, 1996). People high in humor orientation seem aware of others' responses to their humor and tend to use it frequently to get others to like them (see *affinity seeking* in upcoming chapters). People who are low in humor orientation tend not to be very effective at telling humorous stories, remembering punch lines, and so forth. They will be the audiences for the high humor-oriented people and will use other methods of communication to attract others.

Although we focus on the positive characteristics of effective use of humor, we should also mention that in relationships being too funny *could* have some drawbacks. High humor-oriented people may have difficulty in serious relational discussions. Sometimes partners need to discuss issues or problems, and it may be hard to get people with high humor orientation to focus on the topic. They may want to joke their way out of straight talking and serious discussion.

Alternately, people who use humor regularly may have problems getting others to view them as responsible partners. They may be viewed as comics, but not as romantic leads. In other words, it seems reasonable that humor should not be overused in interpersonal interactions, and high humor-oriented people need to know when to adapt to another style to be competent.

Locus of Control

Locus of control is a very important personality trait because it relates to how we believe our lives are controlled. If we have an *internal locus of control,* that means we believe we control our lives, we are in charge, and we can make things happen. If we have an *external locus of control,* that means we believe we are controlled from outside, external forces. In other words, we don't make things happen, things happen to us. If we constantly believe that our circumstances are because of other people, situations, luck, or Fate, we are not believing in our own ability to control happenings.

As a simple example, if you want to meet someone you find attractive, you might go over and talk to him or her if you have an internal locus of control. You would take charge of the situation. If you have an external locus of control, however, you would wait for the person to come over to you. People with an external locus of control often feel that their instructors determine their grades rather than their internal mechanisms of motivation, hard work, and ability. If a romantic relationship is floundering, the external-locus-of-control person will tend to "wait it out," waiting for circumstances to change or for the other person to make a decision. In the same situation, the person with an internal locus of control may decide to do something to try to either fix or end the relationship.

It has been found that people who are extremely lonely tend to have an external locus of control. They often wait for someone to call them, or someone to invite them out, rather than taking the initiative themselves. Compare this to the internal-locus-of-control person who happens to be lonely in a certain situation. That person will probably get on the phone, or go to the mall, or do something to communicate with someone so he or she won't feel lonely.

Most people are somewhere in the middle on locus of control, which is probably positive. In life there truly are things that we may not be able to control. Accidents and random events do happen. If we persist with an internal reason for *everything* we might drive ourselves crazy. ("I *should* have . . ." "If only I had . . .") On the other hand, we have to realize that many outcomes are attributable to our own actions. We cannot be external on everything or we will never take responsibility for positive change— whether it be in our school and work life, health, or interpersonal relationships.

Androgyny = Versatility

Androgyny refers to how versatile and adaptable a person is on what have been traditionally masculine or feminine personality characteristics. Some people are strong on the stereotypically masculine characteristics such as self-reliance, being analytical, taking charge, decision making, and independence. Others are strong on classical feminine characteristics including nurturance, emotionality, tenderness, sympathy, and attentiveness. All of these are admirable traits. But a person will be even more competent if he or she can enact all of them, depending on what the situation calls for, rather than be limited to either one set or the other. We term individuals who have high levels of both types of communication traits *androgynous* or *versatile*.

Think about it. If you can act on the masculine traits, but not the feminine traits, there will be large areas of your life, especially relationally, in which you are lacking competence. Yes, you are fiercely independent, but you lack human warmth. If you have the feminine characteristics in your communication, but not the masculine ones, there are also gaps. Yes, you may be good with your family, but you can't make a decision and take a stand. So the most complete communicators can enact messages in both dimensions. That way, they are flexible and adaptable to the varying situations they may encounter.

Extraversion versus Introversion

Do you know people who are very sociable and outgoing while others keep to themselves and seem content to have very little social interaction? These may be examples of extraverts and introverts. Because of a lower need for external stimulation, *introverts* are less motivated to communicate with others. They simply don't need it and are sufficiently stimulated with solitary activities. In fact, one reason introverts draw back from social encounters is that they may become overactivated, a feeling that is negative.

On the other hand, *extraverts* crave stimulation—and one way to get it is through people and lots of social interaction. Extraverts may be highly willing to engage in communication because they want the fun and excitement associated with such interactions. Extraverts may go out of their way to find communicative encounters. Extraverts may want to live in very accessible or high-traffic areas in apartment complexes or residence halls. They may situate themselves in very visible, open-to-communication areas in social gatherings. Extraverts have high needs for stimulation and therefore are very willing to communicate in order to get those needs satisfied.

In contrast, one conversation per day with a friend may be sufficient for introverts. They don't need any more interaction, chit-chat, or new experiences to feel good. But an extravert may desire multiple conversations with numerous different people on a daily basis because of the rich diversity and opportunities such encounters bring. One point to consider here is whether our society is adapted for introverts or extraverts. Which personality do you think fits in with most U.S. college environments, complete with active social programs, residence halls, and sports bars? Many extraverts assume that everyone wants as much social activity as they do—an assumption that is often incorrect.

Introverts and extraverts have also been found to differ in the emotions they experience. Extraverts have been found to have a predisposition to experience and recall positive emotions, and to be happy, upbeat people. Introverts, on the other hand, are more likely to feel and recall negative affect. The introversion/extraversion trait has been found to be one of the most unchanging across the life span, so don't expect your extraverted friends to change their love of socializing very much (Roberts & DelVecchio, 2000).

Introverts are not "shy" individuals, although many people mistakenly think that because they choose to work alone or spend large amounts of time with only one other person. Introverts and extraverts often have difficulty understanding each other and living together. If you are an extravert with an introverted roommate, you may think he or she is lonely or in a rut. In contrast, your introverted roommate may think you are overly driven to be with others and you must be insecure. Your roommate can't imagine why you find social interactions exciting. Because their own traits are so strong (in either direction), including both psychological and physical involvement, introverts and extraverts have significant difficulty in taking the perspective of the other.

When Personality Traits Will Have the Most Influence

We all have some levels of these traits that operate to guide our communication and interactions in relationships. But they will have the most impact when they are at either very high or very low levels. People who are moderates on a trait will be more variable in their behavior. For instance, very high trait aggression is noticeable in almost all interactions with aggressive communicators. They will react aggressively with very little provocation. But if the aggression trait is moderate, then the specific situation will come into play and have more influence. Maybe someone provokes you. Maybe traffic going across town is frustrating.

People who score in the middle ranges of traits, whether it be locus of control, humor orientation, or introversion, will be more variable in their communication. The display of those moderate traits is more dependent on situational causes, such as who you are with, stress level, and environmental features. People who score high or low, at the extremes of the traits, will be more affected by their personality traits regardless of external situation, because the trait is a stronger, more intense drive in them than it is in moderates.

Conclusions

Don't enter a relationship with the objective of making your partner over. If you are aware of personality traits in a potential friend or romantic partner (whether it be sloppy relaxation, extreme sociability, or violence), don't expect this person to change just because you're in a relationship together. Personality change can occur, but it will be slow if at all. In addition, behavior is more likely to change than actual personality. That is, we might be able to avoid yelling at someone, but we might still *feel* like yelling. In order to avoid disappointment, frustration, and ongoing conflict, you had better be ready to accept those traits that are apparent in your relationship partners.

What if the traits I notice in my partner are really irritating or even dysfunctional? Should I dump my partner? Again, if you are not prepared to accept the partner with those characteristics, to notice only small "improvements," or to work around the traits in your relationship, get ready for a bumpy ride. Sometimes people get married thinking, "My partner will change once we're married." That's doubtful. Adults don't change overnight, even with the best motivation and efforts. Yes, you can teach an old dog new tricks, but it's not easy. You may have to decide whether or not you can safely and happily live and have a productive interpersonal relationship with a partner with that personality type.

R E F E R E N C E S   A N D R E C O M M E N D E D   R E A D I N G S

Bayer, C. L., & Cegala, D. J. (1992). Trait verbal aggressiveness and arguementiveness: Relations with parenting style. *Western Journal of Communication, 56*, 301–310.

Beatty, M., & Dobos, J. (1992). Direct and mediated effects of perceived father criticism and sarcasm on females' perceptions of relational partners' disconfirming behavior. *Communication Quarterly, 41*, 187–197.

Booth-Butterfield, M., & Booth-Butterfield, S. (1990). Conceptualizing affect as information in communication production. *Human Communication Research, 16*, 451–476.

Booth-Butterfield, M., & Booth-Butterfield, S. (1997). Emotionality and Affective Orientation. In J. McCroskey, J. Daly, & M. Martin (Eds.), *Communication and personality: Trait perspectives* (pp. 171–189). Cresskill, NJ: Hampton Press.

Booth-Butterfield, S., & Booth-Butterfield, M. (1991). The communication of humor in everyday life. *Southern Communication Journal, 56*, 205–218.

Friedman, H., Tucker, J., Schwartz, J., Martin, L., Tomlinson-Keasy, C., Wingard, D., & Criqui, M. (1995). Childhood conscientiousness and longevity: Health behaviors and cause of death. *Journal of Personality and Social Psychology, 68*, 696–703.

Friedman, H., Tucker, J., Schwartz, J., Tomlinson-Keasy, C., Martin, L., Wingard, D., & Criqui, M. (1995). Psychosocial and behavioral predictors of longevity. *American Psychologist, 50*, 69–78.

Geen, R. (1983). The psychophysiology of extraversion-introversion. In J. Cacioppo & R. Petty (Eds.), *Social psychophysiology: A sourcebook* (pp. 391–416). New York: Guilford Press.

Infante, D. (1997). Aggressiveness. In J. McCroskey and J. Daly (Eds.), *Personality and interpersonal communication* (pp. 157–192). Newbury Park, CA: Sage.

Infante, D. A., Myers, S. A., & Buerkel, R. A. (1994). Argument and verbal aggression in constructive and destructive family and organizational disagreements. *Western Journal of Communication, 58*, 73–84.

McCroskey, J. C., & Beatty, M. (1984). Communication apprehension and accumulated state anxiety experiences: A research note. *Communication Monographs, 51*, 79–84.

Maccoby, E., & Jacklin, C., (1974). *The psychology of sex differences.* Palo Alto, CA: Stanford University Press.

Martin, M., Anderson, C., Burant, P., & Weber, K. (1997). Verbal aggression in sibling relationships. *Communication Quarterly, 45*, 304–317.

Roberts, B., & DelVecchio, W. (2000). The rank-order consistency of personality traits from childhood to old age: A quantitative review of longitudinal studies. *Psychological Bulletin, 126*, 3–25.

Snodgrass, S., Hecht, M., & Ploutz-Snyder, R. (1998). Interpersonal sensitivity: Expressivity or perceptivity. *Journal of Personality and Social Psychology, 74*, 238–249.

Wanzer, M., Booth-Butterfield, M., & Booth-Butterfield, S. (1995). The funny people: A source-orientation to the communication of humor. *Communication Quarterly, 43*, 142–154.

Wanzer, M., Booth-Butterfield, M., & Booth-Butterfield, S. (1996). Are funny people popular? An examination of Humor Orientation, loneliness, and social attraction. *Communication Quarterly, 44*, 42–52.

IMPLICATIONS OF TRAITS IN YOUR RELATIONSHIPS

1. Of the personality traits discussed here, what are ones that *you* find most attractive in a relationship partner? Least attractive?

2. What are some additional trait-like communication characteristics that you have encountered which have an effect in relationships?

3. Give an example of how each of the traits discussed in this chapter might be observed in an interpersonal relationship—whether platonic or romantic.

6 Shyness, Communication Apprehension, and Avoidance

OBJECTIVES

This entire chapter is devoted to exploring the specific traits related to communication anxiety and avoidance because of their impact on life in our communicative country. Whether you engage in communicating whenever possible because it's fun for you, or whether you would just like to be left alone because having to talk makes you tense and nervous, you need to know these things.

1. Define shyness and its link to social encounters.

2. Describe someone who would qualify as love-shy.

3. Explain what communication apprehension is and three of the four ways it affects the communication process. Use examples to support your responses.

4. Differentiate between willingness to communicate and communication apprehension.

5. Explain how self-esteem, alienation, communication apprehension, cultural divergence, introversion, and self-perceived communication competence are related to *low* willingness to communicate.

6. Discuss what tends to happen to shyness, communication apprehension, or low willingness to communicate once someone gets into a relationship.

CHAPTER OUTLINE

Shyness
  Description
  Love-Shyness
Communication Apprehension
  How Communication Apprehension
    May Influence Communication

Willingness to Communicate
  Description
  Predictors of Willingness
    to Communicate

The United States' social and work cultures thrive on communication. We appreciate people who are excellent conversationalists. We reward students who participate actively in class discussion. We pay professionals who are expert communicators. We are suspicious of people who don't talk much. We base our relationships on active interpersonal communication.

But for some people such communication doesn't come easily. Conversations make them tense and nervous. They get clammy hands. They avoid eye contact. They feel out of place. They may not talk to others, even when they realize it would be beneficial to do so. The question is, "Why?" If you know that communication is essential to forming and maintaining relationships, important to gain positive impressions from others, why don't you *do* it?

There is not just one answer to this question. Individuals avoid communication for differing reasons. Sometimes we're nervous and anxious, but other times we may simply make conscious decisions not to interact. In this section, we will discuss several major patterns that motivate interaction avoidance: shyness, willingness to communicate, communication apprehension, and self-perceived communication competence. Although each typically leads to avoidance of social interactions, the patterns are distinguishable and necessitate different ways of handling the communication in order to achieve the most positive outcome.

Shyness

Are you a shy person? Is your roommate quiet because she is "shy"? Does your friend have difficulty meeting people because of his shyness? This is a term that many people toss around without really knowing what it means. Many people are probably labeled "shy" who really are not shy at all. But all you have to do is go to your local bookstore or magazine stand to see that there are numerous books and articles out there discussing "shyness"—so it must be a problem.

The definition of *shyness* used by most researchers centers on two dimensions: (1) fear and (2) inhibition in response to social communication (Leary, 1984). Both of these factors must be present in order for a person to be considered shy. This means that the shy person is nervous, anxious, and fearful of communicating, and because of this anxiety, he or she avoids, minimizes or "inhibits" interaction. (Inhibition refers to restraining or minimizing a behavioral plan of communicating. You want to communicate, but can't bring yourself to do so.) Can people be nervous about communication and still interact? Yes. It may not be easy for them, but they do it. Can people be quiet and have minimal communication for reasons other than fear? Yes, and we will discuss some of these patterns. Shyness involves both. Shy people avoid and minimize (inhibit) communication because of the emotional discomfort brought on by the nervousness.

Shyness appears to be fundamentally a *social* problem. That is, social interactions—making friends, getting to know roommates, beginning potential romantic encounters—are the most difficult for shy people. Many people who are shy and worried about others' evaluations of them in social contexts are quite confident and interact freely in work situations.

You can see how being shy makes it difficult to form relationships. Someone has to make the first move! The two interactants have to converse and talk about things. They need to self-disclose. Shy individuals may communicate actively one-to-one after a relationship gets started, but they have problems getting to that point.

Love-Shyness

An extreme and particularly unproductive form of shyness is love-shyness. The concept of *love-shyness* refers to severe anxiety and fear of communication with the opposite sex. This anxiety is so extreme that it has totally inhibited formation of adult romantic relationships. To date, love-shyness has only been studied among males, and although it's not a common problem, you can probably think of someone in your community who may fit that description. Love-shy males are not homosexuals, but they are adults who are virgins and are not engaging in dating relationships (Gilmartin, 1989). They are probably quite withdrawn from social interaction and often may go unnoticed.

The communicative basis of love-shyness is not a fear of commitment in relationships, nor a negative attitude toward romance and communication, but rather extreme apprehension about communicating in order to form those romantic relationships. Thus, the relationship itself is not anxiety-provoking, but the necessary communication involved appears to be.

This does not mean that love-shy males never tried to have relationships. In fact, when these love-shy boys were quite young, they formed romantic attachments to girls. However, love-shy males don't seem to be able to communicate to sustain romantic relationships, and so these young romances were often only one-way and more in thought than in action. In addition, because of their shyness and their attitudes differentiating them from the all-American boy image, upon reaching adolescence they find it extremely difficult to engage in expected dating patterns. Hence, they miss out on practice at forming important adult relational skills.

For the most part, even hesitant young men overcome their anxiety sufficiently to develop romantic relationships later in life. For example, in Gilmartin's study it was much more difficult to locate love-shy males age 35 or older than it was to locate them in a college-age group. But in the small segment of our society where love-shyness overwhelms other interpersonal drives, you can see that it could be a serious problem for their lives and interpersonal relationships.

Communication Apprehension

One of the primary reasons individuals may not communicate is that they are apprehensive or fearful of communication. *Communication apprehension* (CA) is defined as the fear or anxiety associated with real or anticipated communication with others (McCroskey & Beatty, 1982). Thus, communication apprehension is based in the individual's emotions and feelings, not attitudes or behavior. The person is nervous about interacting, initiating a conversation, or giving a prepared presentation. Communication apprehension is an emotional response.

We need to recognize that people may become anxious because of a perception that they're out of their depth, unprepared, or because they feel estranged from the group they're communicating with. But the foundation of CA is emotional—fear. Other factors create or intensify the fearful response, but emotion is at the core. And typically it is related to a fear of some form of negative evaluation.

Interestingly, just because people are communication apprehensive does not necessarily mean they will avoid communicating, especially when another person initiates the interaction or when they are "forced" to communicate in a social situation. Even the most anxious student will typically have some sort of response when called upon in class. You probably know people who are desperately apprehensive about communicating, but continue to make themselves engage in interactions anyway because they know how important talk is in our society.

In general, however, we avoid what we fear. If we fear snakes, we make sure we don't hike in snake-filled woods. If heights make us nervous, we don't climb to the top of the tower. If we fear communicating, we tend to avoid it as much as possible and, when we can't avoid it entirely, our communication may be minimal. Unfortunately in our society, it is much more of a problem to be anxious and apprehensive about communicating than it is to be anxious about heights.

A key point to remember about communication apprehension is that it may not be easily observable to people around the high CA individual. He or she may seem quiet or tense but still communicate to some extent, and so others may have a tendency to conclude that the anxiety "can't be that bad." Not true. It *is* that bad. But it's difficult for low CA communicators to have empathy for high CA communicators, and to realize how nerve-wracking conversations are for them.

An outgrowth of this lack of observability and lack of understanding is that highly apprehensive people are often misperceived. Numerous studies have found that high CA individuals are perceived to be less motivated, involved, and capable in classes. They are viewed less positively as a social companion or group leader, and even fare poorly in organizational perceptions. There is no indication that CA is related to lower intelligence or motivation, but observers may believe it is. Further, because high CA people experience such extreme anxiety, they may not communicate to clear up the misunderstanding.

How Communication Apprehension May Influence Communication

There are four main ways that high communication apprehension can affect the individual's communication: communication avoidance, minimization/withdrawal, disruption, and cognitive interference (Booth-Butterfield & Booth-Butterfield, 1997). The emotions of fear and anxiety can be manifested in multiple ways; that is, each person may react differently, and you may see more than one category of behavior among your apprehensive friends.

Communication Avoidance. Probably the most common effect of CA is to avoid communication altogether when possible. High CA people may go out of their way to get out of social situations in which they would be expected to converse and meet people. High CA students may simply not take courses that expect participation or performances. Adults may not apply for jobs that require interaction. These are all examples of how CA motivates the escape or avoidance mechanism—we simply do not put ourselves in situations where interaction is expected. But we cannot always avoid communicating entirely. That is where the next category comes in.

Communication Minimization or Withdrawal. Sometimes it is impossible to get out of communicating. A course is required. You are in a social situation. In these cases, high CA people tend to interact as little as possible. They may give short answers, speak only when spoken to, avoid eye contact or other nonverbal involvement. They may try to "hide out" and stay in the background so no one will notice them. In addition, high CA communicators often remove themselves from the situation as early as possible. They want to terminate the interaction. For example, it has been found that people with high CA end their interactions with physicians as quickly as possible. Such brief interactions could have implications for health care. If you are constantly trying to talk as little as possible, to withdraw from interaction, it will be difficult to begin and deepen interpersonal relationships. There will be a lot of "quiet time."

Communication Disruption.   A third way communication apprehension affects interaction is that it can cause physical disruptions. The tension leads to nervous mannerisms, such as finger drumming, fidgeting, or playing with glasses. It may be difficult to get words out, so the high CA person fumbles over words, misspeaks, and has numerous awkward pauses. Any of these outcomes has the potential to disrupt communication because they draw attention to themselves, rather than to what the person is saying. We may remember how nervous the person acted rather than the similarity of his or her ideas.

Cognitive Interference.   Finally, CA may affect our internal ability to put ideas together to express ourselves or our ability to recall information (encoding and recall). This is termed cognitive interference. Apprehensive individuals are so focused on the fear and anxiety that other thoughts are pushed out. They find they have difficulty formulating thoughts or holding thoughts in memory. Why? It isn't because they don't have the ideas or cognitions, but because the anxiety interferes with processing the information.

Some people have had a similar experience with test anxiety. You study for the exam. You know the material. But then when you get into the test situation, anxiety takes over. You can't remember what you read. You can't find the correct answers even though you knew them just a few minutes before. What happened? Did you just get struck stupid? No. The anxiety floods your thought capacity, leaving little room for effective recall of information. The anxiety effectively acts as a block. To solve this, you need to get rid of the anxiety.

As you can see, high communication apprehension can lead to other difficulties with communication. Although CA is an emotion-based problem, the emotion motivates and creates other kinds of communication problems—from complete avoidance to disruption to jumbled thoughts.

Willingness to Communicate

A concept that encompasses several types of communication avoidance is willingness to communicate. *Willingness to communicate* very simply is an individual's desire for talk. For a variety of reasons, some people want to communicate more than others do. Some enjoy talk and will converse easily with almost everyone in almost any situation—waiting to use a phone, in the line at the cafeteria, or when sitting next to any other student in class. In contrast, some people believe communication is not a particularly important or worthwhile activity. Or they may be low in willingness because communication interactions are not rewarding to them for some reason.

People who are low in willingness will avoid communicating whenever possible and communicate freely only when the circumstances are exactly right for them. This might be when the receiver is someone they really like or feel attracted to, or when the topic is one they find very interesting or in which they have expertise. The concept of willingness to communicate suggests a motivational perspective, one in which the individuals make a conscious decision about their interaction.

All of us can think of times when we were *situationally* unwilling to communicate. We were just not in the mood, hung over, disinterested, or we disliked the person we were with. But several different factors may cause someone to be consistently low in willingness to communicate. We refer to these communication concepts as *predictors* of willingness to communicate.

Predictors of Willingness to Communicate

Self-Esteem. Wilma has low self-esteem. She doesn't think she's very intelligent, attractive, or fun to be with. Marianne, in comparison, has high self-esteem. She feels confident of her abilities to get along with others and perceives herself to be a reasonably attractive student who can also get good grades if she works at it. It's probably no mystery which of these two students would be higher in the trait termed willingness to communicate. Marianne probably feels that she has something to offer others when she interacts and that communication can be rewarding, whereas Wilma does not perceive communication as positive due to her poor self-image.

People who have low self-esteem, or a negative self-concept, are less willing to communicate in most cases because they can't foresee positive outcomes for it. "Why would anyone want to get to know me (I'm such a loser)." "Why should anyone want to listen to my presentation (when it's so stupid)." If individuals have low self-esteem, the only feedback they can envision for themselves is negative. They believe receivers will ridicule them, ignore them, think they're incompetent—and they believe the receivers would be justified in those responses.

However, if communicators have high self-esteem they no doubt find communication more potentially rewarding and exhibit higher willingness to communicate. They have probably had positive experiences communicating and can predict positive outcomes from their interactions. High-willing communicators foresee that receivers will respond with laughter to their jokes, will listen attentively to what they say, and will conclude that their message is worthwhile. High self-esteem communicators tend to perceive communication as a way to gain rewards or admiration, or to enhance their position and influence in some way. Hence, they will tend to approach rather than avoid communication encounters.

As we discussed in Chapter 2, a positive self-concept is one of those personal dimensions that influences many aspects of our lives and relationships. Certainly one of the reasons for this is that high self-esteem makes us more willing to attempt communication, regardless of the context. We aren't as afraid of failure or negative evaluation and so people with high self-esteem tend to say, "What the heck, I'll give it a try."

Alienation.   Sometimes people feel very alienated, estranged, or isolated from the people around them. They don't think they fit in or "belong." They feel as though the values and attitudes they hold are not similar to the ones held by people around them: "These people are fools, why waste my time." When a person feels this alienation, he or she is likely to exhibit less willingness to communicate.

We've probably all had periods in our lives when we felt alienated or estranged from our society (e.g., we move to a new and different culture, we're experiencing some form of life transition that we think no one understands). But for some people, alienation appears to become a way of life. We might surmise that hermits, or people who choose to physically separate themselves from human contact, do this because the values and norms of mainstream society don't fit them.

It is not at all uncommon for adolescents to feel extremely alienated and withdrawn from communication with most people—particularly with adults. Why does this occur? Teen-agers are challenging the norms and values of the adult world. Values and beliefs that were not questioned when they were younger now become perceived as barriers to their independence, happiness, and who they want to be as a person. For example, a 13-year-old may want to get a tattoo as a demonstration of her adult persona. A college student may believe he shouldn't have to check in with parents about his schedule or activities when he's home on breaks. Parents may see both of these attitudes as dangerous and inconsistent with the norms of their society.

When you feel this alienation, and do communicate about it, conflict often arises—quarrels and disagreements with teachers, parents, coaches, or almost any adult. Such conflict is a negative communication outcome. Subsequently, any alienated individual will tend to exhibit lower willingness to communicate ("when I *do* communicate it leads to a hassle"). Thus, initially alienation may tend to increase overt conflict, and continuation of this pattern will probably result in lower willingness to communicate.

Communication Apprehension.   It may seem obvious that we are less willing to confront situations we fear than those that do not evoke fear. Thus, if communication-apprehensive people (discussed earlier) are anxious, tense, and fearful of communicating, it makes sense that most of them will also avoid interactions and hence exhibit less willingness to communicate.

This anxiety is an aversive emotional condition that people wish to avoid. Some highly apprehensive people report sleeplessness, disorientation, and even vomiting when threatened with a public presentation or social engagement. It's little wonder they seek to avoid such circumstances.

Cultural Divergence

Robert enrolls in a family communication class where he finds himself to be the only male student in a classroom with twenty-six females. He is reluctant to speak up in this class.

Kimberly is an African American accountant in an organization with predominately white male coworkers. Although she is highly competent, she rarely interacts with others.

You are an older, nontraditional student returning to the college classroom after working for twenty-five years in sales. You don't seem to have anything to discuss with other students in your classes.

Each of these examples illustrates how cultural divergence could lead to lowered willingness to communicate. Cultural divergence occurs when your background, upbringing, economic group, or some other aspect is quite different from most of the people around you. People may also be culturally divergent because of any number of differences: gender orientation, disability status, ethnic background, age, and so on. Any of these differences can cause many barriers to open communication.

For example, cultural divergence may cause language problems. International students in American schools simply may not have fluent English skills, and it's unlikely that most American students are fluent in Japanese, Swedish, or other foreign languages. Because the students have great difficulty making themselves understood and understanding others' language, they may be less willing to engage in interaction.

Even if the language itself is not a problem, accents can emphasize cultural divergence. If people consistently remark on your Midwestern twang or Southern drawl you might find yourself pulling back from communicating, because your vocal patterns draw attention and emphasize differences.

It is also important to note that not all cultures place the importance on talking that the United States does. People from some cultures (notably the Japanese and Native Americans) are much quieter and more selective about communicating than most Americans are.

Sometimes there are nonverbal difficulties between culturally divergent communicators. These may include differences in proxemic expectations, interpretation of facial expressions and gestures, coordination of talk, use of scent, and even perceptions of attractiveness. After you have had a few perplexing or upsetting nonverbal encounters you might decide to minimize communication. Remember that no one culture is "right," but the culture represented by most of the people will be the one that dominates.

In general, just feeling different or as though they don't fit in will tend to make people uncomfortable. If you think that people won't understand your perspectives, your customs, or your way of thought, then you may find yourself less willing to speak out because you constantly need to explain, clarify, or defend those ideas. Low willingness to communicate is a result.

Introversion–Extraversion.   As we discussed earlier, introverts are less motivated to communicate with others than are extraverts because of differences in their need for stimulation. Introverts, then, are less willing to communicate than extraverts.

Extraverts may be highly willing to engage in communication because they want the fun and excitement associated with such interactions. Extraverts may go out of their way to find communicative encounters. They may want to live in very accessible or high-traffic areas in apartment complexes or residence halls. They may situate themselves in very visible, open-to-communication areas in social gatherings or in the classroom. Extraverts have high needs for stimulation and therefore are very willing to communicate in order to satisfy those needs.

Introverts, in contrast, are lower in their willingness to communicate with most other people because they don't want or need such social stimulation. One conversation per day with a friend may be sufficient for an introvert. But an extravert may desire multiple conversations with numerous people on a daily basis because of the rich diversity and opportunities such encounters bring. Hence, the differences in willingness to communicate between introverts and extraverts are understandable.

Self-Perceived Communication Competence.   *Self-perceived communication competence* refers to how we evaluate our own communication skill. If we perceive ourselves to be communicatively incompetent, we will probably be less willing to communicate than if we judge ourselves to be competent. We like to do what we are "good" at. The better we are at something, the more we tend to be willing to demonstrate that skill. Thus, if people believe they have something worthwhile to say, and can be fluent about saying it, they may more readily volunteer to share that message. Or said another way, they'll exhibit higher willingness to communicate. People with low self-perceived competence want to hide what they view as their flawed performance, so they are less willing to communicate in more situations.

With many physical skills, avoidance of the activity doesn't present a significant problem. I may not consider myself mechanically competent with autos or a particularly good roller skater, but my avoidance of working on my car or of roller-skating rinks does not pose a significant obstacle in my life. The same is not true of communication. If I don't feel communicatively competent and because of that perception I avoid situations where I would have to communicate, I will be greatly disadvantaged in our society.

If someone believes he is a poor communicator, he may not introduce himself to another student he'd like to get to know better. The sophomore who thinks her speech ability is low may take a failing grade on a presentation rather than get up in front of class and, in her mind, "make a fool of herself." Clearly low self-perceived communication competence creates obstacles for achievement.

Notice that this concept is called "self-perceived" communication competence. That means the evaluation is within the source rather than an objective evaluation of communication skills. People who are low in self-perceived communication competence may or may not actually be skilled communicators. I'm sure you've known some individuals who are extremely poor communicators, but had no idea they were perceived that way. As a result, they made no attempt to avoid communication (even though at times you might have wished they *would* avoid communicating). Therefore, it is our own perception that we're unskilled communicators that leads to avoidance.

Sometimes low perceptions of communication ability are well-founded. If we are not fluent in a language, we may be less participative than usual. If we have a physical speech disorder and have difficulty making ourselves understood, we may avoid communicating unless absolutely necessary. If we aren't competent in a particular topic, we may do more listening than talking. Such cases create situational self-perceived communication incompetence.

Notice that if people feel inadequate and unskilled about communicating, they may become anxious about communication. They reason, "I know I'm not a good speaker and I'll look stupid, so I become very nervous about the prospect of showing everyone how clumsy and unskilled I really am." Thus, sometimes low self-perceived communication competence leads to heightened anxiety.

Overall, people may be unwilling to communicate for a variety of reasons, one of which may be a perception of low competence. But not all unwilling people see themselves as poor communicators. Some people may be unwilling because of anxiety, lack of motivation, or other reasons that cause them to avoid communication encounters.

Conclusions

A final note is in order regarding these causes of communication-related anxiety and avoidance. We sometimes confuse, and lump together, various types of communicative anxieties and avoidance. But it is important to be able to distinguish shy behaviors from the fearful feelings of communication apprehension, and from the attitudes and other components creating unwillingness to communicate. They originate differently and their interpersonal outcomes will be different. Clearly, however, they are linked—for example the ways in which high communication apprehension, cultural divergence, and low perceived competence may create lowered willingness to communicate.

These traits, whether shyness, low perceived competence, or high anxiety, will cause the most difficulty in early stages of interpersonal relationships. After you get acquainted and start a relationship with your shy friend, it is very likely that he or she won't act shy with you. Relationships have a way of overcoming the communication avoidance problem. The person may still become nervous talking with strangers or other people not well known, but feel at ease with friends and family. The fear of negative evaluation for disrupted communication or for long silences recedes. Your friend learns that you understand and accept him or her, and so feels safer in communicating with you. However, the difficulty is in getting to that relational point.

In order to solve the problems caused by communication avoidance in our society, you must understand the basis of the problem. Is the avoidance caused by fear? By negative attitudes toward the act of communicating? Low skill levels? Each reason for avoidance requires a different response in helping friends to communicate more effectively. What works to assist shy friends may have little effect on the avoidance of friends with low communication skill levels or others who feel culturally divergent. Therefore, understanding these different sources for communication anxiety and avoidance is essential to adapting to communication in relationships.

REFERENCES AND RECOMMENDED READINGS

Ayres, J., & Hopf, T. (1993). *Coping with speech anxiety.* Norwood, NJ: Ablex.

Booth-Butterfield, M., & Booth-Butterfield, S. (1997). *Communication apprehension and avoidance in the classroom.* Acton, MA: Tapestry Press.

Booth-Butterfield, M., & Booth-Butterfield, S. (1997). Communication anxiety and people with disabilities. In J. Daly, J. McCroskey, J. Ayres, T. Hopf, & D. Ayres (Eds.), *Avoiding communication* (2nd ed., pp. 285–302). Cresskill, NJ: Hampton Press.

Cheek, J., Cheek, B., & Rothstein, L. (1989). *Conquering shyness: The battle anyone can win.* New York: Bantam Doubleday Dell.

Geen, R. (1983). The psychophysiology of extraversion-introversion. In J. Cacioppo & R. Petty (Eds.), *Social psychophysiology: A sourcebook* (pp. 391–416). New York: Guilford Press.

Gilmartin, B. (1989). *The shy-man syndrome: Why men become love-shy and how they can overcome it.* New York: Madison Books.

Leary, M. (1984). Affective and behavioral components of shyness: Implications for theory, measurement, and research. In W. Jones, J. Cheek, & S. Briggs (Eds.), *Shyness: Perspectives on research and treatment* (pp. 26–38). New York: Plenum Press.

McCroskey, J. C. (1984). The communication apprehension perspective. In Daly, J. A., & McCroskey, J. C. (Eds.), *Avoiding communication: Shyness, reticence, and communication apprehension* (pp. 13–33). Beverly Hills, CA: Sage.

McCroskey, J. C., & Beatty, M. (1984). Communication apprehension and accumulated state anxiety experiences: A research note. *Communication Monographs, 51,* 79–84.

APPLICATIONS TO YOUR LIFE AND RELATIONSHIPS

1. List television personalities (either real people or animations) who are definitely shy. Also make a list of television personalities who are *not* shy.

2. Describe two situations in which you would no doubt feel communication apprehension and two in which you would not. What are the differences in these communication situations in terms of context, expectations, and so on?

3. Think of someone you know who is quite unwilling to communicate most of the time (high trait). Apply the predictors of low willingness to them to attempt to explain why they don't want to interact.

7 Pattern of Relational Stages

Coming Together and Falling Apart

OBJECTIVES

Though short, this is one of the most important chapters in this book. You need to be able to analyze and understand the following terms and concepts in order to understand the processes and transitions of interpersonal relationships.

1. Explain the differences between coming together and coming apart stages as two major processes in relationships.

2. List and describe each of the 10 stages, using an example of communication to illustrate that you understand the function of each stage and what is occurring in it.

3. Be able to recognize the pattern (or examples) of communication that occurs in each stage, as well as communication that would *not* be typical in each.

4. Describe a situation in which differentiation is unproductive and leads to termination and one in which differentiation is productive and leads to a stronger relationship. What is the major difference?

CHAPTER OUTLINE

Stages of Coming Together
  Initiating
  Experimenting
  Intensifying
  Integrating
  Bonding

Stages of Falling Apart
  Differentiating
  Circumscribing
  Stagnating
  Avoiding
  Terminating

Think back to when you first met the person who is now your best friend. Maybe it was in elementary school, maybe it was when your family moved to a new location, or perhaps it was more recently at a summer job. Consider how you met and got to know each other. Try to picture what you thought of the person then or how you talked with him or her. Or, think about someone you used to care deeply for, but now don't even want to spend time with. Remember how it felt to be with that person in the good days of your relationship—how you interacted then, how exciting, funny, entertaining, smart, or attractive you found the person to be. These changes in perceptions and interactions illustrate how interpersonal relationships are ongoing processes. They don't just happen all at once. Instead, they exhibit *stages of coming together and falling apart.*

All interpersonal relationships go through recognizable stages as the participants interact, discover things about each other, adapt, and either grow closer or put distance between themselves. Stages in relationships are sequential. We go from strangers, to acquaintances, to friends to close friends and intimates. We also may travel in the opposite direction—being close but then as situations change or information is revealed, the relationship transforms into complete noncaring or even warfare.

At the most general level there are two major directions for a relationship to move. It can come together, or toward greater intimacy, or shift apart, toward less intimacy. When a relationship is coming together it is characterized by increasing psychological, emotional, and usually physical *closeness.* When a relationship is deteriorating or falling apart, it is characterized by increasing psychological, emotional, and usually physical *distance.* But relationships don't constantly fluctuate. People don't typically keep on bouncing around. They may also reach a plateau within a stage as the partners maintain a certain level of intimacy.

Knapp noted ten separate stages that are recognizable within the two overarching stages (1978). Interactants can identify these stages from the styles of communication apparent in each and from the function each stage serves in the progress of the relationship. (Keep in mind here that "progress" means not only moving forward, but any movement.)

Stages of Coming Together

Initiating

The first stage of any relationship is its *initiating.* This is typically a very brief interaction in which people decide the extent to which each interactant is interested in forming a relationship. In other words, the major question at this point is, "Do you have any interest in getting to know me?" We rely on both visual and auditory cues here. In social settings this may include a greeting that is warmly reciprocated, positive nonverbal cues such as smiling, extended eye contact, and a direct body orientation, and verbal extensions when you answer questions. (For example, if someone asks, "How do you like Brown's class?" or "Is this the first time you've shopped here?" an extended answer is a more positive cue toward initiation than a brief "yes" or "no.") In the initiating stage if the answer to the major question, "Do you want to get to know me?" is "No," then the relationship goes nowhere. (This would be true unless the initiator was very highly motivated to begin a relationship with the other.) If on the other hand, the answer is at least somewhat positive, then the interactants will move on to the next stage and begin experimenting.

Experimenting

The second stage of coming together is *experimenting* and follows after a positive initiating stage. In a sense, the experimenting stage is a screening process because during this phase people share more information to ascertain whether they are compatible, interesting, or have similar values. Thus, entry-level self-disclosure is very important here ("You're a Laker fan? No kidding, I am too!). In our culture, "dating" is a good example of an experimenting pattern in romantic relationships. But other relationships experiment too as we test the waters of a potential friendship—we may play ball and then order pizza at a friend's, spend the afternoon going to a museum, or just hang out together and go out for cheeseburgers.

It is important to note that most relationships never progress beyond experimenting. We may enjoy many people on a fairly superficial basis, but not find sufficient overlap to want to pursue a deeper relationship. Students in classes may have many acquaintance-type friends, lots of people they know to "chat" with, but they have far fewer close friends. A significant amount of experimenting occurs in Internet chat rooms in the twenty-first century.

In addition, this stage varies greatly in length. Some people experiment for a long time or with several different people prior to moving to a closer stage. Either they are quite cautious or they just want to keep a relationship simple. Other people move quickly to a closer, more committed relational level—from experimenting to intensifying.

Intensifying

In the *intensifying* stage, you can recognize a decided shift in the communicators' focus as they change from interacting regularly with a variety of others to focusing resources and time on one partner. Having numerous friends changes to having a "best friend." Dating around changes to "going steady." You may decide that this person would make a good roommate. In this phase, communication partners are clearly choosing one partner over other potential partners.

You can observe distinct communicative changes in this stage as partners self-disclose more deeply and become more emotionally close. The use of "we" or "us" rather than "you" and "I" becomes more prevalent. Partners often begin to reference future interactions ("We ought to work together on the next class project" or "Maybe we'll go rafting this summer"). Statements like these signal something very important—the partner's assumption that the relationship will still be together in the future.

Typically, physical interaction and nonverbal intimacy will also increase during the intensifying stage. As people spend more time together, touch becomes much more accepted and casual. The hand-holding that was previously a noticeable gesture, becomes almost automatic. Leaning together, putting arms around each other, and so on, become commonplace. Increased touch occurs in platonic relationships as well as romantic. If your friend needs assistance with getting dressed, with a smudge on her face, or with something caught in her hair, you may feel no discomfort at all with touching her or helping her. In contrast, if an acquaintance asked you to help in this way, you might not want to.

Other verbal changes occur. Based on additional disclosures verbal shortcuts begin to appear in conversations. For example, there is no longer any need for Jen to explain her strained relationship with her mother and how it came about. Instead you'll hear Jen say, "You know how it is with my mother," or maybe she'll just roll her eyes at the mention of her mother's actions, and the message will be clearly communicated. Similarly, you don't have to explain repeatedly who Newton is, because your relationship partner already knows it's your cat.

Integrating

If all goes well in the intensifying phase of coming together, the relationship will often move into the *integrating* stage. There are some important changes that occur between partners in this stage. Here the individuals attempt to share "self symbols"; that is, they want to take on characteristics of their partner's self or aspects that are important to him or her. The goal is to merge or integrate with each other as much as possible, so you may observe people becoming more alike in their actions, nonverbal cues, and clothing. They may begin to sound similar as they integrate laughter patterns or verbal phrases. (It is logical that we pick up similarities with people we spend a great deal of time with; however, we do not adopt sayings or non-verbal cues of people we do not like or admire.)

Partners in the integrating stage may also begin to merge their social circles as one is "adopted" into the other's family, and friends are no longer yours or mine, but ours. Property such as apartments, audio equipment, or even pets may be possessed together as a symbol of integration.

Self symbols can also involve activities we care about. We may join the church or a photography club as a pair, or learn to windsurf, line dance, or develop Web pages together. The importance here is the symbolism of taking on aspects of the other person's identity for your own.

As it becomes clear that values are shared, then hobbies, friends, possessions, and the like are used to reinforce to each other, and to others outside the twosome, the strength and closeness of this relationship. Although individuals may go on to bond without a thorough integration stage, significant areas that remain dissimilar create more potential areas of future conflict. For example, if you still feel like "company" rather than "family" with the in-laws, this could be a point of contention at holidays or other get-togethers. If all of your activities center on outdoor sports activities and your friend is totally involved with computer interactions but you aren't, it may be difficult to maintain closeness.

Bonding

The *bonding* stage is the final stage in the coming together process. This follows when there is a ceremony of some sort that publicly communicates the commitments the partners have made to each other. Up to this point, individuals make most of their own personal rules for each relationship. But when partners bond, then legally recognized, or at least normative, rules from external agencies also apply. You're no longer making it up as you go along.

In our society the most common form of bonding is marriage, but other types are prevalent as well. Adoption is formal bonding between parents and a child. When people become godparents, they generally take on recognized obligations to a friend's children. Even a formal ceremony in which friends become "blood brothers" signifies commitment. Although perceptions of expectations of the relationship may shift after bonding, in many cases communication will not significantly change. If people are already well integrated, they may simply continue this process with minimal internal communication change.

A bonded relationship often continues for many years, maintaining the same level. But other times relationships may begin to disintegrate or enter the process of "falling apart."

Stages of Falling Apart

Differentiating

A relationship may terminate at any time or skip to the termination stage rather than going through each stage of disintegration. This is particularly true in early stages of coming together. But relationships often begin "falling apart" with signs of *differentiating*. The differentiating stage is the opposite of integration. During integration when our goal was to become as similar as possible to our partner, with differentiating we attempt to reassert our own individual identity. One of the key symptoms of differentiating is an increase in the amount of dissension and disagreement experienced as we recognize the ways we are different from our partner. We cannot assume we are alike anymore. Such an increase in disagreement may be voiced if we argue openly about it, or it could just as easily be recognized but not communicated by the members of the relationship. Thus, just because you don't *see* fighting or overt disagreements, that doesn't mean that differentiating is not occurring.

Differentiating is not necessarily bad for a relationship, nor is it necessarily a signal of the relationship's deterioration. Some relationships become so thoroughly meshed that one partner loses his or her sense of self or independence entirely. This is particularly true when one partner is clearly dominant over the other. In such cases, differentiating can be positive. It can lead people to "blossom" as they discover ways they are unique and have special talents.

In classrooms, this can sometimes be seen when close twins are separated for some activities. Such a move can give the less dominant twin an opportunity to achieve on her or his own. In marriages, such differentiating may be observed when a "traditional wife" returns to college to finish her degree. Or, among close friends differentiating may take the form of joining different social groups. Again, this does not mean the relationship will disintegrate because of recognized differences. Relationships that are extremely differentiated may still be very stable and happy.

Whether a relationship will disintegrate during differentiation seems to depend strongly on what is *done* with those different patterns. How are the differences treated in the relationship? If partners accept and enjoy their differences and each brings her or his newfound skills, interests, and information back into the relationship to enrich and revive it, then differentiation will be positive for the relationship. People don't have to do everything together, think alike, and act identically to have a strong relationship. On the other hand, if differentiating is viewed as negative and threatening, it may lead to quarrels or to unspoken avoidance of topics—both unproductive directions. If the changes are not discussed but still cause discomfort, then this pattern tends to lead to greater and greater psychological distance.

Circumscribing

Assuming that differentiating does drive a wedge into the relationship, the next stage of falling apart is circumscribing. *Circumscribing* means carefully keeping communication to "safe" or nondisputed areas. The communication pattern is selective and careful rather than open and spontaneous. When partners are in the circumscribing stage, they are more cautious and self-protective about their communication. They realize that if certain sensitive topics are brought up communication will become difficult or unpleasant. In some friendships you might avoid discussing political issues such as abortion, private versus public schooling, or interracial marriage. You might skirt around personal issues such as your new job or the partner's recent behavior because you're afraid the other may disagree—or even become angry. When people are circumscribing in communication, interactions are more careful and polite, less spontaneous, and generally less personal. On the surface, a circumscribing relationship may appear to be quite trouble-free. But it is difficult to be relaxed and free with someone when you have to constantly monitor what you say or anticipate problems with the interaction.

Stagnating

If circumscribing continues, however, it eventually becomes *stagnating.* When relational partners continue to be cautious in their communicative patterns with each other, more and more topics emerge that cannot be discussed. Soon nothing new is brought up. The only "safe" areas are old business, past experiences, or routine daily events. "How was class?" "Let's rent a video." "How's your mother?" "Pass the salt."

Partners almost unanimously describe this phase of a relationship as "boring." You wonder what you ever found interesting or rewarding about the other because everything is so dull now. Partners won't try new activities or attempt new communication patterns because of relational inertia or a fear of negative outcomes. Sometimes people avoid asking important questions for fear of the answers they may receive. It is often easier to just go along in the deadly routine of a stagnant relationship than to do the work or take the risk to get beyond this stage. Roommates may feel stagnant in their relationships, but not do anything but "stick it out." We may find ourselves putting up with a stagnant relationship with a neighbor because, although it doesn't meet our interpersonal needs, at least it doesn't cause trouble. At times, people even put up with a stagnant relationship because they know it has a distinct termination point—graduation, the family is moving away, a job transfer is upcoming—so they don't have to put forth the effort to try to repair it. One of the real dangers of stagnant relationships is the difficulty of motivating partners to do anything about it. Stagnation takes very little effort.

Avoiding

Nevertheless, stagnation is generally not a pleasant experience and so we often find ourselves moving into the *avoiding* stage. Here the emotional reaction tends to be more negative and the person actively avoids being in contact with the partner—both physically and psychologically. Whereas in the intensifying stage we might have made excuses and strategized ways to see our partner more frequently, in the avoiding stage we do the opposite. We find that we "can't" arrange our schedule in order to have lunch with our friend. "Working late" isn't an excuse to cover infidelity, but rather an indication of what we currently find rewarding in our life. When we are with the relationship partner, things are uncomfortable, boring, and not enjoyable, so why be there? Why not be at work where you can get something accomplished? In the avoidance stage we can observe drastically reduced amounts of talk and time spent together.

Terminating

A logical outgrowth of avoidance is movement into the *terminating* stage. Most people think of termination as the actual ending of a relationship, but it is also a stage and can happen very suddenly (as in an unexpected death or a goodbye note left on the kitchen counter). Or the terminating process can be more long-term. In general, the more thoroughly integrated a relationship is, the longer it will take to terminate. The more you and your partner share friends, family, activities, and possessions, the longer it will be before the relationship can be entirely ended. It is possible that in a divorce when there are children, termination may never be completed. Compare this with the relative ease of terminating a relationship that is only in the experimenting stage. All you have to do is not call again, or decline an invitation in order to quit the relationship. When you become more highly involved and integrated, however, voluntary termination does not occur without some communicative ending point.

The process of terminating may also differ depending on how you feel about the other person. If you care about the person's feelings and well-being, you may try to "let them down easy," to communicate positively about the end of the relationship. ("It's really better this way." "We've had a lot of good times together.") This involves using more other-oriented strategies of communication. By contrast, if the progress throughout the deteriorating stages has been rocky, resulting in coldness, neutrality, or hostility toward the partner, the parting may be abrupt and angry. ("I'm out of here, you no-good so-and-so) Understandably, the manner in which you communicate at the end has an impact on potential for remaining friends or having any kind of positive attitude about the relationship experience.

Of course, voluntary termination is not the necessary destination of all relationships. One of the goals of understanding these stages is to help people recognize where their relationship is and where it is going. The relationship process is not irreversible. Partners *can* save their relationship if they really want to. But to do so, early awareness of danger signals is important. With interpersonal relationships, just as with cancer, if early warning signs are noted the chances of recovery are much greater.

If people are not cognizant of circumscribed communication, differentiation, and what those patterns indicate, the deterioration of a relationship is likely to continue. By the time you reach the stagnating or avoiding stages there is much less hope of reviving the relationship without outside intervention. One reason for this is that by the later stages of coming apart, the partners are not communicating openly and honestly. They may not even be talking to each other. When they do talk it's likely to be mundane topics rather than open discussion of the relationship issues, or the interaction is likely to be characterized by negative affect and antagonism. The philosophy may be, you don't even *like* this person anymore, why should you put forth effort to continue the relationship?

In addition, when a person is in the unpleasant, ending stages of one relationship he or she may be in the pleasant, beginning stages of another. This complicates matters because one relationship is boring, unrewarding, and going downhill, while the new relationship is exciting, interesting, and rewarding. It is not surprising, then, that many people decide the old relationship isn't worth the work necessary to rejuvenate it and opt to terminate it. In marriage, this may translate into divorce; in romances, this probably means breaking up; in platonic relationships, it means finding a new "best friend"; in relationships at work, it may mean changing jobs.

So you see, it is important to understand and recognize these stages and the communication that accompanies them in order to help participants have the happiest, most productive relationships possible. It can also be helpful for us as concerned friends when we have others who are experiencing interpersonal relationship development and disintegration.

Conclusions

We can describe ten different stages in the development and deterioration of interpersonal relationships. They may at times seem to merge together, but they can be identified by the communication and behavior that takes place. As we become aware of the communicative patterns, we can make decisions about the relationship itself—where we want to go with it, do we want to maintain, deepen, or what? Not all relationships can last forever. We simply don't have the time and energy to maintain every relationship. Sometimes the most productive thing that could happen to some unhealthy relationships is termination.

But many interpersonal relationships are important to us, and we want to assure that they remain vital. The goals and motivations of both partners will influence the eventual outcome. In many cases, if trouble arises, knowing what communication patterns lead to increased closeness and positive emotions and comparing them to the communication patterns associated with negative emotions and disassociation can help get a relationship back on track. Having the knowledge is a first step. The more you know, the better informed your decisions and communicative behavior can be.

Stages Relationship Partners Experience When "Coming Together and Falling Apart"

PARTNER 1	PARTNER 2
Initiating	Initiating
Experimenting	Experimenting
Intensifying	Intensifying
Integrating Integrating	
Bonding	
Differentiating	Differentiating
Circumscribing	Circumscribing
Stagnating	Stagnating
Avoiding	Avoiding
Terminating	Terminating

REFERENCES AND RECOMMENDED READINGS

Clark, M., & Reis, H. (1988). Interpersonal processes in close relationships. *Annual Review of Psychology, 39,* 609–672.

Coupland, N., Giles, H., & Wiemann, J. (1991). *"Miscommunication" and problematic talk.* Newbury Park, CA: Sage.

Knapp, M. (1978). *Social intercourse: From greeting to good-bye.* Boston: Allyn & Bacon.

Knapp, M., & Miller, G. (1985). *Handbook of interpersonal communication.* Beverly Hills, CA: Sage.

Montgomery, B. (1993). Relationship maintenance versus relationship change. *Journal of Social and Personal Relationships, 10,* 205–223.

Murray, S., & Holmes, J. (1997). A leap of faith? Positive illusions in romantic relationships. *Personality and Social Psychology Bulletin, 23,* 586–604.

COMMUNICATION IN STAGES OF RELATIONSHIPS

Communication messages and strategies differ depending on what stage of the relationship the people are in. Working with a partner, give examples of communication (words or behaviors) you have noticed in each of the ten stages.

Coming Together

1. Initiating

2. Experimenting

3. Intensifying

4. Integrating

5. Bonding

Falling Apart

6. Differentiating

7. Circumscribing

8. Stagnating

9. Avoiding

10. Terminating

IN-DEPTH COMPARISON OF INTEGRATION WITH DIFFERENTIATION

The two stages of *integrations* and *differentiation* are opposite in their intent. Examine and analyze types of communication in the integrating stage. Then compare those with what happens in the differentiating stage. What would you observe in the relationship? These descriptions should be detailed and specific.

How might this differentiation be positive or negative?

8 Expectations, Affinity Seeking, and Immediacy

OBJECTIVES

As we begin interpersonal relationships, these concepts are particularly important. If you have successfully synthesized the information in this chapter you should be able to

1. Explain what short-term expectancies are.

2. Give at least three examples of short-term expectancies and describe what happens when a person doesn't adhere to them.

3. Provide a definition of affinity seeking and three examples of how we communicate when we are affinity seeking.

4. Explain why affinity seeking is a skill and how it can go "wrong" so that you end up looking like a desperate loser.

5. Differentiate between affinity seeking and affinity maintaining.

6. Give the definition of immediacy in communication and examples of verbal immediacy and nonverbal immediacy in an interaction.

7. List three advantages and three disadvantages of immediate communication.

8. Describe how these advantages and disadvantages may depend on the situation and the person.

CHAPTER OUTLINE

Making Contact

Short-Term Relational Expectations

Affinity Seeking
Affinity Seeking as a Skill
Affinity Seeking Compared to
    Affinity Maintaining

Immediacy
Verbal and Nonverbal Immediacy
Immediacy Behavior on a
    Continuum
Disadvantages of Immediacy

Excitement. Fun! New information. Nerve-wracking. Stops and starts. Uncertainty!

When we begin to form new relationships, we notice different communication patterns occurring compared to when a relationship is well established. We don't expect the same communication later in a relationship that we do early on in a relationship. Priorities shift. Whether positive or negative, let's face it, we act differently early in a relationship (before we have the person "hooked") than we do when a relationship is years old. So in this chapter we're going to examine several communication components and strategies that are particularly important in determining whether a "new" relationship continues—answering that all-important question, "How do I move from being just an acquaintance to really having a close relationship?"

Making Contact

We begin with how we get together. Two primary predictors of whether we will initiate contact on our way to forming a relationship are proximity and physical attractiveness. *Proximity* is how close we are physically to the other person. We're much more likely to begin an interaction with someone near us. If you are instructed to "team up" with someone in a class, you probably look around for someone sitting close to you. Few people will go all the way across a crowded room to start conversation with a stranger. It's just logical. The people nearest you are the most accessible for communicating—even if the interaction is very short or superficial. There may be a perfect "soulmate" for you, but he or she is living in New Zealand. If you don't get into physical proximity at some time, there is little chance of your finding each other. The people who live next door to you, people who share your classes, people you work with, and those who ride on the same mass transit you do are your most likely initial communication contacts. So the person you end up standing next to in line will probably be someone you begin a communication interaction with.

The *physical attractiveness* variable (also discussed in Chapter 3) is another predictor of initial communication contact. We are more likely to strike up a conversation with people we perceive as attractive. This does not necessarily mean we will make a beeline for the most glamorous, fantastic-looking person in the room. Often people we view as attractive are those who seem friendly, open, somewhat similar to us, and not *un*attractive.

Notice that these first two predictors in taking steps to initiate a conversation are visual cues, without the necessity of interaction with the other person. We decide who to interact with initially based on who is close and reasonably good-looking.

Short-Term Relational Expectations

Once we make contact with a stranger and we find out that he or she is open to conversation (and a possible relationship) with us, short-term expectancies come into play. That is, we expect people to follow certain communication "rules" of interaction when we are in early stages of relationship development. These rules may not persist long into the relationship, but they exist in the beginning acquaintance stages. Also note, these expectations may affect our judgment of the other person even if we are unaware that we hold such expectations. If these short-term expectancies are violated, it is less likely that we will continue interaction and form a relationship. Thus, if someone is unaware of, or uncaring about these short-term expectations, they may have difficulty establishing productive relationships.

If you look at the list on the following page, you'll notice some themes. These expectations center on putting your best foot forward and being generally polite or following certain courtesy rules with your new potential relationship partner.

If these expectations are *violated* in the early stages (e.g., you have conflict, the person is always depressed, the other pushes you in affection so you feel crowded), you probably will not go on to later stages. You may ask yourself, "If they're acting like this now, what will it be like later?"

You could probably add many expectations that you and your peers hold. Norms of behavior vary from social group to social group. This list is to get you started thinking about your own expectations of what communication should happen early in a relationship.

Affinity Seeking

Given the importance of interpersonal relationships to the happiness and well-being of human beings, it is not surprising that we develop communication skills to enhance the likelihood of attaining friendships. We use *affinity-seeking* communication to get people to like us (Bell & Daly, 1984).

Naive or inexperienced communicators may believe that people with whom they interact will just naturally like them. However, as we gain experience we realize that the manner in which we communicate and interact with others will determine whether they like us and want to become our friends. Affinity-seeking skills are communicative strategies we enact to encourage people to be socially attracted to us.

Affinity seeking is often conducted on a strictly social basis, but we also can observe it at work, toward parents, and with instructors.

Just think of all the ways you might try to get on the "good side" of or simply attempt to "be nice" to your professor. Students become very complimentary when they are engaged in affinity-seeking. They may notice

Short-Term Expectations

Expectations we have when we first meet people, during the initial stages of coming together.

INTERESTS: You expect the two of you will be interested in one another, will pay attention and be responsive to each other. You won't ignore each other.

PEACE: You expect peaceful interactions. You won't fight or argue with one another. You will both work hard at being agreeable.

RULE FOLLOWING: Both of you should closely follow rules of appropriate conduct, common courtesy, and manners. (That is, you won't do bizarre things.)

AMUSEMENT: You expect both of you to try to be entertaining, engaging, and fun to be with.

APPEARANCE: You expect both of you to be physically attractive, to appear neat, with good grooming and appropriate dress for your reference group.

PRESENCE: You expect that when you are with that other person somewhere, you'll stay together. Neither of you will wander off leaving the other alone.

PURPOSE: When either of you wants to see the other, you will have an activity to justify your interaction together. That is, you'll plan to go biking, to a movie, and so on, rather than just getting together with nothing planned.

TIMING: Neither of you will move faster, emotionally or physically, than the other one. Your levels of intimacy will be similar.

AFFECTION: You will each demonstrate appropriate affection cues to the other. Again, this will be reflected by your own social or cultural group.

IMAGE: You expect each of you will attempt to create an impression of being competent and trustworthy toward the other.

RESPECT: You expect that neither of you will treat the other as an inferior. You won't "talk down" to your partner.

PRIVACY: Neither of you will ask questions or make statements that are too intimate or personal for the level of relationship you have.

POSITIVITY: Both of you will be positive, optimistic, and "up" when around the other. Neither will be negative, moody, grumpy, or unhappy all the time.

UNIQUENESS: When together you will treat this person differently than you treat everyone else. There will be some special communication pattern.

what the instructor is wearing and comment positively on it ("That's a hot tie Mr. B."). Students may try to include professors in their activities such as playing basketball, inviting them to fraternity or sorority gatherings, or even buying them drinks at a local establishment—all in an effort to enhance liking.

Nonverbal indicators of affinity seeking are also noticeable. When someone is trying to get you to like him or her, that person will probably smile more, interact at closer distances, make eye contact, and touch you. This is an attempt to become more psychologically and physically close with you and to show their liking.

Communicators may also try to become your friend by disclosing about themselves or by questioning you. Many times this takes the form of telling you about their life at home, or even television shows they have watched. They are trying to maximize perceptions of similarity or homophily with you. When people are engaged in affinity seeking, they may also try to help you by carrying objects, helping with school work, setting up your computer, or even offering physical protection. On the next page is a list of some typical affinity-seeking strategies. Individual communicators may use some or all of these strategies.

Affinity Seeking as a Skill

Even though many of these actions may seem like naturally emerging communication, affinity seeking is a communicative skill that must be acquired. The process necessitates being able to accurately predict what will be pleasing to the target and then having the ability to enact that behavior. Some individuals learn how to gain affinity effectively, but others somehow miss the lesson.

In general, as with most other communication skills, people often become more adept at affinity seeking as they get older. Their communicative skills broaden and their perspective-taking abilities heighten, so they become more complex about the communication. Young children are quite direct and straightforward in their attempts to get you to like them, whereas as people move into adolescence and beyond their affinity seeking becomes more sophisticated, subtle, and indirect. Sometimes college students who work with young children are surprised and gratified when the kids blurt out, "I love you," or tell them directly how great they are. We often become more "sophisticated" and less open about our affinity seeking as we reach adulthood.

The second point to keep in mind about affinity-seeking communication is that, although they *attempt* to seek affinity, some people may not do it *well*. Some people are just not very adept at enacting those behaviors. They may try to do things you like, but inadvertently irritate you in the

Affinity-Seeking Strategies

ASSUME FAMILIARITY: The person engages in behaviors that suggest that her or his accomplishments and abilities are obvious to the liked other. "Remember I told you about breaking that track record. . . ."

COMPETENCE DISPLAYS: The person makes her or his accomplishments known. For example, the individual demonstrates how good he or she is at gymnastics, music, or fighting.

DEPENDENCE: The person acts dependent or reliant on the other in an effort to flatter or engage her or him in more communication. For example, a student who likes you may ask you a number of questions about an in-class assignment. This person is communicating that he or she thinks you are competent.

DISCLOSURE: The other person communicates personal information. This may include details about vacations or home life, feelings, or reasons why the person acted a certain way. The goal is to have you know him or her better.

DYNAMISM: The person behaves in an active, enthusiastic way when around you. And seems animated toward you.

ELICIT SELF-DISCLOSURES: The person encourages you to disclose by asking questions and responding positively to disclosive messages. Then when you do share information, this person often remembers even small details.

FACILITATE ENJOYMENT: The person tries to maximize the enjoyment you experience by being playful, humorous, or generally "entertaining," so that you have a good time with him or her. The person may plan activities or events specifically for your pleasure.

GIVING GOODS: The person brings gifts and objects of small or large value to you. These may be anything from roadside flowers to Christmas gifts to buying drinks.

HELPFULNESS: The individual tries to provide services. He or she may offer to assist with moving furniture, doing laundry, helping you pick out a CD player, or may directly ask what he or she can do to help. This person is trying to become indispensable to you.

INCLUSION: The person invites you to participate in her or his social activities. The person may ask if you are going to go to the football game, or invite you to a party. It may be something as simple as asking if you want to come along with a group going to the mall or church.

INCLUSION OF THE SELF: The person tries to be included in your activities. He or she may visit you, want to go with you to the mall, or attend parties you do.

NONVERBAL IMMEDIACY: The person signals interest through various nonverbal cues such as smiling, closer interaction distances, direct eye contact, and touching.

(continued)

Affinity-Seeking Strategies   continued

PHYSICAL AFFECTION: The person attempts physical affection with you. He or she may move closer, give you a hug, a slap on the shoulder.

PHYSICAL ATTRACTIVENESS: The person tries to look and dress as attractively as possible when in your presence, even pointing out his or her new look, haircut, or clothes.

PRAISE: The person compliments or praises your appearance, skills, possessions, or personality. He or she may mention how good you look, what a nice person you are, that you're a great history scholar.

SIMILARITY: The person expresses tastes and attitudes similar to what he or she perceives yours to be. If you have liberal attitudes, you may hear them espoused by the affinity seeker. The person may claim to like the same cars, music, and movies that you do. (Time will tell if these similarities are real or manufactured.)

SMALL TALK: The person chats with you at length about topics of little consequence—public events around campus, sports, the weather. Such small talk is one of the ways the person tries to spend more time in your presence.

SUPPORTIVE: The person supports you in interactions with other people. For instance, a person might stand up for you if someone criticizes you. Support is shown when he or she defends your perspectives or motives in discussions with others. At the extreme, it could be physical support.

VERBAL AFFECTION: The person says affectionate things to you and may directly tell you that he or she likes or loves you.

---

process. This is the case with the coworker who doesn't know when to *stop* giving compliments, or makes compliments so extreme that they become ridiculous.

Affinity seeking also may not work when it is poorly timed. For instance, there are appropriate times for people to self-disclose to you and times when it's better to be quiet. Trying to use humor or to be entertaining has its place, but jokes are not always appropriate or wanted. Therefore, the timing of specific affinity-seeking communication is important.

Sometimes the entire behavior enacted in trying to get someone to like you may be inappropriate. A young male teacher related an incident in which one of his female ninth-grade students tossed her panties on his desk as she was leaving the classroom. Although this might have been at attempt to seek his affinity or attention, it clearly worked in the opposite direction with the flustered young teacher.

The third fact to be aware of with affinity-seeking messages is that they may seem inappropriate or "wrong," but it may be because they are seeking the affinity of *someone else, not you.* Affinity-seeking communication is tailored for the specific person we wish to impress. Therefore, you might observe a guy in McDonald's acting "silly and stupid" by putting french fries up his nose, but the person the message is aimed at thinks the behavior is "cute," "daring," and "hilarious." In order to understand affinity-seeking communication in general, you need to understand where the message is directed.

Affinity Seeking Compared to Affinity Maintaining

Unfortunately, we often slack off in our affinity seeking once our interpersonal relationship is well established. We may do little *affinity maintaining.* Sometimes that is because it is simply not possible to always be at your best, looking good, and communicating entertainingly with people you live with every day. But many times we just get lazy. We may actually communicate our worst selves to the people we love the most. We may be far more polite and attentive with acquaintances and coworkers than with lovers. We may put our cologne on only when we go out to be with others. Or we might extend ourselves to do extra tasks for acquaintances, when it might be nice to do these affinity-maintaining behaviors with people we care about the most.

Another way to think of ongoing affinity behaviors is as *relational-maintenance strategies* (Canary & Stafford, 1992). These are the communication approaches people use to sustain their relationship. Relational-maintenance communication can be organized into five distinct categories regularly enacted by partners: positivity, openness, assurances, networks, and sharing tasks. The first three involve very direct communicative interaction. When we exhibit positivity, we are communicating with our friend in an upbeat, optimistic, and noncritical manner. We're trying to be nice and entertaining, refraining from saying anything negative about his or her ideas, tastes in music, and so on. Openness involves disclosures about the relationship and one's feelings about it. "I'm wondering where our relationship is going." Assurances have been found to be particularly important because they emphasize the value of the relationship and commitment to the partner. "This relationship is the best thing that ever happened to me. I'll always be there for you." Use of social networks as maintenance means that we involve our friends, coworkers, relatives, and others in the relationship too. Perhaps you all enjoy going out for barbequed ribs together. Sharing tasks seems obvious to linked partnerships. In this category, partners solidify relationships by performing the tasks that are their agreed-upon responsibility; you take care of the car and I handle the taxes. But it could also include the coordination of smaller tasks—one person orders the burgers, while the other gets the ketchup and finds a table. These final two categories still involve communication but may be less direct, and indeed these have been found to have somewhat less impact on the satisfaction in the ongoing relationship.

If you could only enact *one* of these maintenance behaviors, the best one for the relationship would probably be to give assurances. This form of communication signals ongoing liking and dedication, and has been found to have the largest impact on the widest variety of relationships.

Many people gripe and sigh that relationships get "old" and "boring." Perhaps if we did more affinity seeking later in relationships rather than just at the beginning, we could keep those relationships lively and fun. For example, at least one recent study showed that when married people were perceived to exhibit more nonverbal immediacy with their partners, there was more liking and affection. This relationship held no matter how long they had been married (Hinkle, 1999).

Out-of-Class Assignment.   Try some affinity seeking with someone you used to do it with, even though you've declined in such behaviors recently. You already have that relationship, so try some affinity maintaining. Be specific and selective, and see how the person responds.

Immediacy

One specific category of affinity seeking seems to carry a great deal of weight in interpersonal interactions: immediacy. *Immediate communication* is a cluster of communication behaviors that enhances the psychological or physical closeness between people.

Immediacy is a valued aspect of communication in our society, one that has been found to improve teacher evaluations and interview outcomes, as well as to increase perceptions of attraction, likability, and warmth in interpersonal interactions. So, immediacy is an especially positive communication skill to develop and use. It works in personal relationships, at work, in health care situations, and even in public presentations.

Verbal and Nonverbal Immediacy

Immediate communication can be verbal and/or nonverbal. *Verbal immediacy* is when we use words to try to communicate closeness. Compare "Did you see how he looked at us?" with "Did you see how he looked at me?" Or, "We're almost out of milk" versus "I'm out of milk." The verbally immediate communication brings people closer. It gives a sense of inclusion, that you and your partner are more of a team and linked, rather than separate individuals.

Nonverbal immediacy is more subtle than verbal immediacy. Nonverbal immediacy includes actions such as maintaining eye contact, moving closer to the other person, smiling, nodding, leaning toward the other, and even appropriate touching. Such behaviors also signal that you are approachable and open to interaction. Notice that when you are attracted to someone, or you want to influence someone positively, you focus more on them, turn toward them, and have good eye contact. These are examples of immediacy behavior that tend to make people feel close to you.

Immediacy Behaviors on a Continuum

Since immediacy is a communication skill, does this mean people can mess it up? Yes. Some communicators are overly immediate. They touch when they shouldn't. They move in too close when conversing. They smile, laugh, or nod too much in an attempt to get you to like them. Being overly immediate often ends up in having the reverse effect from what was intended. We want to distance these people and keep them at arm's length.

At the other end of the immediacy continuum is nonimmediate communication. When we cannot or do not look our interaction partner in the eyes, that is nonimmediate. When we have a closed or stiff posture, that is nonimmediate. If we maintain a large conversational distance and don't move closer, or if we put physical barriers, such as bookshelves, pillows, or chairs between us, that is nonimmediate communication.

Nonimmediate cues communicate distance, coolness, reserve, and less caring or involvement. Such a pattern of communication tends to formalize interactions and may communicate authority or control in official situations, but it doesn't build positive affect or liking in any situation.

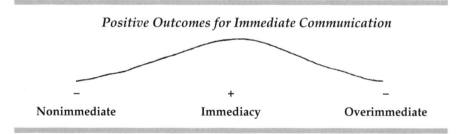

Positive Outcomes for Immediate Communication

−	+	−
Nonimmediate	Immediacy	Overimmediate

Disadvantages of Immediacy

We have indicated here that appropriate immediacy is a positive communication pattern that will tend to enhance others' liking of us if well done. Be we also have to be aware that there may be some drawbacks even to appropriate, well-communicated immediacy in interpersonal interactions.

1. *Immediacy opens up channels of communication that may increase interaction.* What's the drawback? People may want to talk to you more and take more of your time. Being immediate encourages communication from receivers, so the interaction expands.
2. *Sometimes immediacy may be misunderstood as intimacy moves.* People may think you are trying to be more than friendly if you are immediate, especially if they are not used to immediate communication. It is important to be aware that there are differences across cultures in immediacy expectations. So if you are communicating across cultural backgrounds, the norms may be different. Be warned about misinterpretations.
3. *Sometimes immediacy may be mistaken for a lack of control or authority.* In a new job, immediacy may be misperceived as weakness. Some professors report that students interpret their immediacy as being an "easy teacher." Again, especially if communication receivers are not accustomed to seeing immediate cues, they may think that the source lacks authority or credibility. In truth, often the people who are the most secure and sure of their control are ones who can communicate in an immediate manner without loss of authority.

Conclusions

If we look at the big picture, communicating in an immediate manner is overwhelmingly positive in our culture. There is a strong expectation of immediate communication, particularly in relationships that are important to us. The benefits to communication and relationships far outweigh the drawbacks if the immediacy and the affinity seeking in general are skillfully done. However, both can backfire, resulting in negative reactions, if we communicate them poorly, time the actions badly, or simply overdo the communication pattern. For the health of the relationship, it is also important to remember to do relational maintenance. Once we have the interpersonal relationship (whether friend, colleague, or lover) going, we cannot just drop all those positive behaviors and hope that our partners will stay satisfied.

REFERENCES AND RECOMMENDED READINGS

Andersen, J. (1979). Teacher immediacy as a predictor of teaching effectiveness. In D. Nimmo (Ed.), *Communication yearbook, 3,* (pp. 543–559). New Brunswick, NJ: Transaction Press.
Bell, R., & Daly, J. (1984). The affinity-seeking function of communication. *Communication Monographs, 51,* 91–115.

Bell, R., Daly, J., & Gonzalez, C. (1987). Affinity-maintenance in marriage and its relationship to women's marital satisfaction. *Journal of Marriage and the Family, 49,* 445–454.

Canary, D., & Stafford, L. (1992). Relational maintenance strategies and equity in marriage. *Communication Monographs, 59,* 243–267.

Canary, D., & Stafford, L. (1994). *Communication and relational maintenance.* New York: Academic Press.

Hinkle, L. (1999). Nonverbal immediacy communication behaviors and liking in marital relationships. *Communication Research Reports, 16,* 81–90.

Messman, S., Canary, D., & Hause, K. (2000). Motives to remain platonic, equity, and the use of maintenance strategies in opposite-sex friendships. *Journal of Social and Personal Relationships, 17,* 83–101.

Ragsdale, J. (1996). Gender, satisfaction level, and use of relational maintenance strategies in marriage. *Communication Monographs, 63,* 354–369.

Stafford, L., & Canary, D. (1991). Maintenance strategies and romantic relationship type, gender, and relational characteristics. *Journal of Social and Personal Relationships, 8,* 217–242.

Wanzer, M., & McCroskey, J. (1998). Teacher socio-communicative style as a correlate of student affect toward teacher and course material. *Communication Education, 47,* 43–52.

AFFINITY-SEEKING
COMMUNICATION SKILLS

1. What types of things do people do that lead you to like them *more?*

2. What things do people do that make you like them *less*—even though you know they may be trying to get you to like them? What's going wrong?

WHEN IMMEDIACY MAKES A DIFFERENCE

Team up with a partner. Together come up with descriptions of at least five interactions in which someone acted in an "immediate" manner with you. How did they communicate? What did they do? And how did it make a *difference* in your response to them (either positively or negatively)?

Situation 1:

Situation 2:

Situation 3:

Situation 4:

Situation 5:

9 Nonverbal Messages in Interpersonal Relationships

OBJECTIVES

This chapter explores nonverbal communication in relationships. If you can do the following at the conclusion of the unit, that means you understand the main points. If you cannot perform these actions, you need to go back and read it again.

1. Define nonverbal communication.

2. Explain the difference in weighting of nonverbal cues early in the relationship, compared to later in the relationship.

3. Differentiate between how we view nonverbal messages when we are the source versus when we are the receiver. Use an example to complete your answer.

4. List three potential advantages and three disadvantages of being physically attractive.

5. Discuss the evidence that physically attractive people are better as relationship partners.

6. Give two examples of kinesic communicative behavior used in relationships.

7. Explain what the four facial-management techniques (intensifying, deintensifying, masking, neutralizing) are and why they are used in interpersonal communication, and give an example of the circumstances when they might be used in relationships.

8. Touch can communicate a variety of meanings in relationships. Explain the four different categories and create a scenario using each type of touch.

9. Explain four criteria for interpreting touch in our society.

10. Describe how circadian rhythms may help or hinder interaction in a relationship.

11. Define nonverbal sensitivity and list four ways someone could increase his or her nonverbal sensitivity.

CHAPTER OUTLINE

Nonverbal Cues Early versus Later in a Relationship

Interpretation of *My* Nonverbal Messages versus *Your* Nonverbal Messages

Forms of Nonverbal Messages in Relationships
    Physical Appearance
    Kinesics: The Study of Body
        Movement and Gestures
    Facial Expression and Eye Behavior
    Paralanguage

Use of Space and Touch to
    Communicate
Meanings of Touch in Relationships
Interpreting Interpersonal Messages
    of Touch
How the Use of Time
    Communicates in Relationships

Nonverbal Sensitivity
Definitions
Increasing Your Nonverbal
    Sensitivity

We are often more aware of what we *say* in interactions than of how we *act* in those interactions. Our words are closer to consciousness and we can remember them more easily. And yet, nonverbal communication is a primary means of communicating in relationships (Burgoon, Buller, Hale, & deTurck, 1984). Understanding how we encode and decode nonverbal messages can help us develop and keep interpersonal relationships.

By definition, *nonverbal communication is all the ways we communicate other than through words in relationships.* Nonverbal communication is nonlinguistic. The specific words, whether spoken or written, constitute the verbal means of sending messages. So nonverbal messages include our physical appearance, our facial expressions and eye behavior, gestures and posture, voice variables, touch, and even how we communicate with time.

Nonverbal Cues Early versus Later in a Relationship

It's important to understand that these nonverbal variables will not hold equal weight throughout a relationship. Some are more influential in early stages, but diminish as time passes. For example, when you first meet someone, physical appearance—how you look and what you're wearing—carries a lot of weight. People start forming impressions based on these visual cues (whether accurate or not!) before they even interact with you. The fact that you're wearing a certain ball cap, type of shoes, or even how you wear your hair communicates. But how people dress, how fat or thin they are, and other appearance aspects tend to be noticed less as the relationship gets going.

In early stages of relationships, any nonverbal message will carry a disproportionate weight because our potential friends have so little other information to go on. They have nothing to balance off the initial impressions. So, if you are late for the meeting when you first interact with someone, that communicates more than you probably think. Similarly, if you speak with someone on the phone prior to meeting him or her, impressions are formed based on the sound of your voice. Is it strong or weak? Soft or loud? Accented? Hesitant or confidant?

Later on, after you get acquainted, individual nonverbal messages may have less impact. (This is not to say they have zero impact, but each cue will carry less individual weight.) As partners have more information about you, they will interpret any one nonverbal message in the context of the whole event. That is where *patterns* of nonverbal communication are recognized and noticed. For example, maybe you tend to be a very "touchy" person. Initially that may stand out to your co-communicators, but as they get to know you, your touching will just become a part of the pattern expected from you when conversing. People who know you will gauge your nonverbal messages compared to your regular pattern of behavior rather than isolated cues.

1. Nonverbal cues are heavily weighted in first impressions.
2. Later in relationships, nonverbal cues are viewed as part of an overall pattern of communicating.

Interpretation of *My* Nonverbal Messages versus *Your* Nonverbal Messages

We tend to be much more aware of our verbal messages and how we put the words together than we are of our nonverbal communication. We may not even be aware of when and how we encode and display nonverbal messages. They often seem to flow naturally, without any conscious thought. Unfortunately, this is one of the reasons so many misunderstandings are generated by nonverbal actions.

Although we are often unaware of our own nonverbal messages, or think of them as unintentional and "natural," we are very aware of others' nonverbal messages. If someone frowns in our direction, we think they're irritated with us or don't like something we've done. But they may not even realize they are frowning. This can be dangerous because we *attribute intent* much more to someone else's facial expression, bodily movements, and tone of voice than we do to our own. (Have you ever "smiled back" and waved at someone who you later realized was just smiling to himself?)

Our nonverbal messages are relatively out-of-consciousness in that we don't notice them as much. But because other people attribute meaning to them, it would be productive to become aware of our own nonverbal cues, and at the same time, recognize that nonverbal cues we receive from others may not be intentional.

This is not a "cookbook." Notice that you will not find phrases such as "Hands on your hips indicate aggression" or "Folded arms mean you are defensive"—phrases sometimes seen in magazine articles or books that are used like recipes in a cookbook. Nonverbal communication is far more complex than that. Each nonverbal behavior may be motivated by a variety of reasons. To give a straightforward "recipe" for effective nonverbal communication or interpretation would be misleading. Instead, the intent here is to describe what research has found nonverbal cues to indicate, and how they tend to be interpreted in order to bring those nonverbal actions into your awareness. Then you make the decisions about use.

Forms of Nonverbal Messages in Relationships

Several different categories or forms of nonverbal messages can have impact in interpersonal relationships. We start with physical appearance.

Physical Appearance

How you look to others may not be relevant to who you are, but the fact is that your appearance sends messages. In our culture, physical attractiveness tends to elicit positive responses and makes people want to communicate with you. Keep in mind that what is physically attractive to one person may not be as attractive to another. But, overall, there are some benefits, especially in initial interactions, of being perceived as physically attractive.

Having physically attractive partners appears to be more important in males' judgments than in females'. That also holds true for platonic friendships, where males have been shown to be more similar in physical attractiveness to their friends than are females. In addition, being physically attractive appears to garner more benefits for females than for males in a variety of contexts. Perceivers may gauge males more on their competence and less on their physical appearance.

Being perceived as beautiful or handsome has benefits in the educational, organizational, and legal settings. Especially in public schools it has been found that attractive students receive more "teacher attention." Teachers spend more time with them and less with the unattractive students. This may in part explain why physically attractive students tend to score higher on achievement in school.

In organizations, physical attractiveness seems to be a benefit in getting interviews, doing well in interviews, and getting your foot in the door of the organization. Of course, it could be in part that attractiveness helps the communicator to feel and interact in a more confident, poised manner. (Word of warning here: There is some indication that being extremely physically attractive can work against females in the interview process.)

Even in legal settings, there is some evidence that good-looking people have an advantage. It may be harder to convict a physically attractive defendant. And if convicted, attractive people tend to serve less time. Of course, in such studies there are many factors going on, but the fact is that being good-looking gives one an advantage. The exception to this case appears to be if the accused seems to be *using* his or her attractiveness to commit the crime or to "get over," as in fraud or selling worthless stock. In that instance, their punishment ends up being even more strict than that of their less attractive counterpart.

Good-looking people are perceived by others to be better communicators, more socially skilled, and so on. But are physically attractive people really better at social interaction? Some studies suggest that they are. Studies of interactions by phone when the people couldn't see each other find that attractive people were rated as more desirable partners and more socially skilled. And this occurred when participants could not see the person to gauge attractiveness. It makes sense, doesn't it? Good-looking people probably receive more positive feedback when communicating throughout their lives, starting with positive reactions when they are toddlers. They learn very young that interaction is fun, that people say nice things and react positively. So the attractive child practices communicating frequently and does indeed become better at it.

Are there any disadvantages to being physically attractive? Yes. Physically attractive people often have a difficult time convincing others that they really are competent and are not just getting by on their looks. In other words, people may not take them as seriously. Further, because others view them so positively, when attractive people do have problems, others may not be as sympathetic. "Yeah, I should have your problems." Finally, extreme attractiveness can be intimidating. Some people may be intimidated or jealous and avoid contact.

So where does this leave all the rest of us average-looking people? First of all, there is no evidence to suggest that beautiful people are better relationship partners. Some good-looking people are probably great in relationships, but others may not be at all. After you get to know someone, you tend to forget about how attractive or unattractive they are. Beauty *is* only skin deep. And physical attractiveness is only one type of attractiveness, probably not the most important for interpersonal relationships.

For initiating relationships or interactions when you don't know the people involved, good advice would be to try to look your best. Many first impressions and judgments are based on physical attractiveness. Obviously, after people get to know you, they will realize that physical attractiveness is only one part of who you are.

Kinesics: The Study of Body Movement and Gestures

The main categories of body movements that are studied for interpersonal communication are *emblems, illustrators, regulators, adaptors, and affect displays*. Although these are discussed in detail in entire courses on nonverbal communication, they should be mentioned here with a relational application. You can no doubt supply your own examples in each category.

Emblems are nonverbal symbols that have specific translations. They are always intentional communication and may serve as a substitute for saying the words. Basic examples are the hitchhiker's thumb and the OK sign. But there are others in relationships. When you see an acquaintance at the student union and she waves you over to the table, that emblem means "come here." Sometimes within relationships partners may develop their own emblems, which have specific translations for them but which others may not recognize. These private symbols serve to demonstrate closeness in the relationship and the exclusion of others who are not in the relationship.

Illustrators involve using gestures and your body to help describe something. The nonverbal messages assist in making the verbal description clearer or more vivid. You may gesture as you tell someone how tall a person was or how hard you hit the wall, or when you point to give directions. Illustrators may occur more often when you are excited about an issue, or when words are difficult to select in explaining the idea you want to get across.

Regulators help control conversational flow so that you have smooth interactions. This may be by communicating to others that you want to take a turn speaking by leaning forward, gesturing with your hand, and so on. Nodding at your partner when you want him or her to take a turn or respond is another nonverbal message that aids conversational flow.

Keeping eye contact or avoiding eye contact is also important in regulating interactions, because we look directly at people when we want to contribute or want them to contribute, but we look away when we don't want to talk to them. Shy people tend to send contradictory regulating messages. They may *want* to talk with someone but feel nervous about it, so they look down. Avoiding eye contact is a signal of not wanting to interact.

Interestingly, we typically are only aware of these regulators when people don't enact them effectively. When regulating is not well done, it tends to increase awkward pauses and talk-overs, and contribute to a general clumsiness in the interaction.

Affect displays are very prevalent in relationships. Affect displays entail how we communicate the emotions we are feeling, and they can be focused in either body movements or facial expressions. For example, giving someone a spontaneous hug is an affect display. Or when you are out shopping or are at a boring fishing boat show with your friend and you tap your foot and shift back and forth as a signal of impatience, those are also affect displays.

Adaptors tend to be signs of either tension or boredom, and are generally not positive. Adaptors are excess unmotivated movement, usually in the extremities such as hands or feet. The presence of adaptors suggests energy or tension that we cannot let out. When people are tense you see them playing with things (object adaptors)—for example, ripping up or folding a paper napkin. Or tense or bored people may enact body adaptors such as playing with their own hair, cracking their knuckles, drumming their fingers, or scratching themselves. Whenever you notice adaptors in your relational partners, you can be assured that there is more going on with them than they are directly telling you.

Facial Expressions and Eye Behavior

Eye behavior and facial expression are two relatively controllable channels of nonverbal communication. That means both can be fairly conscious and under our control once we become aware of the implications. To illustrate, compare how easy it is to focus your eyes or manage your face to look "honest" with how difficult it often is to control the quaver in your voice or to remember *not* to bob your knees when you are nervous.

Eye behavior may be quite diverse, including eye contact, gaze avoidance, and shifting eyes. Think of eye contact as directly looking at a person, an act that opens communication channels with another and invites interaction. When we avoid eye contact it closes channels, suggesting that we do not want to interact.

In our society eye contact between communicators is viewed positively, whether in social, instructional, or work settings. Don't you expect your partner to look at you when you are conversing? Whether accurate or not, we perceive that partners are more truthful, confident, concerned, and trustworthy when they maintain eye contact with us. Eye contact is especially expected when we are in the listening role. Interestingly, there are some gender differences in eye contact patterns. Females tend to maintain eye contact more than males do, especially when they are listening.

Gaze avoidance, or a lack of eye contact, carries multiple potential meanings. It may communicate that you are shy, ill at ease, deceptive, respectful, uninterested, angry, or involved in something else. The important thing with gaze avoidance is to understand what message it may send, and make sure that is the message you want to communicate.

Shifting eye movement tends to be a negative nonverbal behavior. Although everyone moves their eyes, rapid shifting back and forth carries meanings similar to gaze avoidance—deception, anxiety, lack of confidence—and tends to make people suspicious.

We all want to think that our *facial expressions* are the true communication of what we feel. But this is not always productive. *Facial management techniques* are used extensively in interpersonal interactions, and their objective is to make whatever emotion you are feeling more acceptable to the receiver. They control expressions so that they are appropriate for the circumstances. Sometimes we may feel that we cannot be totally genuine, natural, and authentic when interacting, even with a good friend. So we use facial management techniques to restructure the message.

Intensifying occurs when you want the emotion you are communicating to be more extreme than the emotion you actually feel. This may happen when your roommate is telling you something that is really exciting for him or her, but is only marginally interesting to you (e.g., a play-by-play account of her golf game). You want to be a supportive friend, so you intensify the interest shown in your face. Intensifying in relationships may also occur when receiving gifts or expressing affection.

Deintensifying is just the opposite. This is when you don't want others to know how strongly you feel about something. You may deintensify how touched you are by a card, the sadness you feel watching a movie, or how angry you are with your partner. In this case, you judge that the full strength of your emotion would not be received well by the person you're with, and so you need to downplay the intensity.

We *neutralize* our facial expressions when we don't want another person to know how we are feeling at all. This entails keeping your face carefully blank, as in the "poker face." Neutralizing is a cautious management technique, often used to keep the partner guessing about what is going on with you.

Masking is substituting one emotional expression for another. Typically, masking is used when we think our emotion is not socially desirable in the situation. If we are actually happy when someone we're with receives a bad grade, but we communicate concern for them, that is masking. If we feel frustrated with a task, but we communicate as if we are calm, or if we want someone to think we are in love with him or her, when we actually want the person for an ulterior purpose, we may use masking. Of all the facial-management techniques, masking is the least authentic and the most deceptive. But if you think about it, all of these techniques are deceptive to some extent. We are not being nonverbally honest with our interaction partner, either because we think it is not productive to do so, or because it's inappropriate for the situation, or because we believe that the person could not handle the truth.

Paralanguage

When we communicate specific messages through the use of our voice, this is called *paralanguage*. If you have ever said to someone, "Don't use that tone of voice with me," you are aware of the impact of paralanguage. We can convey hostility, warmth, or a businesslike tone. We can speak confidently or anxiously. Paralanguage includes everything we do with our voice and voice characteristics outside of the specific words we use.

Paralanguage is often used unconsciously in relationships. It may be out of our awareness, sometimes leading to conclusions we did not anticipate. We may not realize that we sound bored when talking with a friend. We may not be aware of how loud or harsh-sounding our voice becomes during a disagreement. Because we cannot hear ourselves effectively, it would be beneficial to have a close friend give us feedback about these vocal characteristics.

Paralanguage also influences interpretations of our responses in other situations. The intensity and vocal variety you inject into responses to a partner can be encouraging. If someone declares his or her love for you, this person probably expects an impassioned response. Flatly spoken, even saying "I love you" may be disappointing. In contrast, if your friends disclose a problem to you and you can't keep the shock or disgust out of your voice, they may close you off.

Thus, vocal tones, volume, variety, and so forth, which are appropriate to the situation and consistent with the actual words you say are very important parts of nonverbal relational communication.

Use of Space and Touch to Communicate

We also communicate interpersonally through the use of space. Our society has norms for typical conversations, but expectations of comfortable and appropriate interaction distance differ by person and by situation. Touch and spatial "norms" are communication rules (either spoken or unspoken) that guide the use of space and touch in interactions. In individual relationships, these norms are developed by the participants; they create their own "rules." But in any society there are certain norms that are expected in general as well.

Some people feel more comfortable interacting at closer distances than do others. We say they have need for a smaller personal space. *Personal space* is the area around you that you consider an extension of yourself; therefore, you feel uncomfortable if someone violates that space in some way. People with smaller interpersonal space needs may seem to move "too close" to you if you have larger space needs.

In addition, your needs for space may vary depending on who your interaction partner is. With family you may sit close together and hug, enjoying the touch. But with colleagues at work you may keep a greater distance. In the United States, female-to-female interaction distance is typically closer than male-to-male interaction distance. Male–female interaction distances will often depend on the relationship and liking levels. In general, we keep smaller distances with people we like and know well.

To some extent, personal space is a sign of status too. We allow higher-status people larger and more private spaces (e.g., parents), whereas we quite freely invade the space of low-status others (e.g., children).

Interaction distance needs may also differ depending on what you are discussing. Public information and general social conversation may occur at a greater interaction distance, in part because you don't care who joins in the conversation. But if your topic is more private or important, the distance tends to close up. This serves to both exclude others and focus more fully on the partner. The marriage proposal that is written across the sky, cut into a field, or publicly videotaped for all to see is indeed a rarity.

Meanings of Touch in Relationships

An extension of the "personal space" concept is touch. Many have asserted that touch is the most intimate form of nonverbal communication in relationships. No other channel is so direct. But touch is also one of the most complex forms of nonverbal interaction, and misunderstanding often occurs. Our interpretation of messages based on touch is a function of several factors, including status, type and location of touch, our gender, and the context of the touch.

Touching someone has the ability to communicate at least four different categories of messages. First, touch can communicate *status,* or your relative rank in a social hierarchy. People with more status tend to be the ones with the prerogative of initiating touch, at least in organizational or acquaintance-type interactions. Typically, the boss or supervisor touches first. It is less clear whether status has much of an impact in interpersonal relationships. It is presumed that both friends are equal partners, so either of them may initiate the hug or other form of touch.

A second category of touch meanings is *liking* or *affection.* We use touch to communicate our affinity or liking for another person. Notice that you do not tend to touch people you don't like, but you may find yourself patting or leaning against people you do like. This form of touch is also used to communicate that you want a closer relationship with the other person, such as when you touch someone's arm as you converse with him or her. An important aspect to remember here is that people with high affection needs may touch quite a bit more than those with low needs. Thus, the absolute amount of touch may not be telling, but the amount you touch one person relative to another is likely to be a sign of liking and warmth.

The third category of touch meanings is *instrumental*, or touch used to help accomplish some goal other than relational. You might touch an opponent when playing racquetball or when helping him or her to climb over a fence. This form of touch happens often in relationships, but it is not due exclusively to liking. It's a function of needing to get something done.

It is probably also true, however, that we may mask affectionate touch by calling it instrumental if we are unsure of the other's reaction. For example, as you are working in the kitchen you may find yourself putting your hands on your partner to move him or her out of your way. That could be strictly instrumental, or it could also be more frequent because you are attracted to your partner.

Obviously, if we need to accomplish a goal *and* we like someone, touching will increase. Your roommate just found out that her fiancé cheated on her. She is in need of some comforting. You will probably comfort differently if you have a positive relationship (hug and staying close) than if you have a negative relationship (brief pat on the shoulder.)

Finally, touch is often very *role-oriented*, although this form of touch may be less important in interpersonal interactions that go beyond roles. Role-oriented touch is when you initiate touch solely because it is your job. It doesn't communicate anything relationally. This might occur if you work at a shoe store and have to help people try on shoes. You don't touch them because you like them; you do it to sell the shoes. Similarly, a physician or a nurse touches a patient and a football player touches an opponent because of their roles, not because of the relationship.

Interpreting Interpersonal Messages of Touch

How can we tell how to interpret touch behavior? What does it mean? Is this touch appropriate to the relationship? When we are the receivers of touch communication, we need to be able to interpret what that touch symbolizes and where it might be leading in order to avoid difficult situations. Here are a few pointers. Ask yourself these questions.

1. *What* type *of touch is it?* Perhaps the most obvious influence on how we decode touch in interpersonal communication is through the type of touch. Is this a slap? A pinch? A caress? A pat? Generally speaking, nonsustained touch, such as patting, is less intimate and used with more different people, regardless of relationship. We pat someone's back in congratulations. We pat children on the head. In comparison, sustained touch tends to communicate more intimacy and hence we tend to use it with fewer people. If you leave your hand on someone's arm rather than just patting them, or if you stroke someone's knee instead of just tapping it to say "good job," the message is very different. It tends to communicate more closeness and intimacy.

Akin to the type of touch is the *force* of the touch, how much pressure is behind it. Gentle touch seems nice and friendly, unless it is perceived as sexual. You might playfully hit someone's shoulder, but if too much force is used that can be perceived as a challenge or aggression. Therefore, we also interpret touching by how much force is behind the touch.

2. *What is the* location *of the touch? And what is your* relationship *with the person touching?* Although it may seem simplistic, where on your body the other person touches you has influence on your interpretation. Think of it this way. We are selective about who has the option to touch us in various areas. The pat on the shoulder for congratulations has a different interpretation than the pat on the fanny. In general, "safe" areas of the body to touch include the head and shoulders, the upper back, and the forearms. Few friends will perceive a casual touch in these areas negatively. And indeed, touch in those areas has been found to have very positive interpretations resulting in favorable responses—even from strangers. Research has verified this benefit of casual touch in restaurants, stores, libraries, and to obtain help on the street. So touch in the United States is fairly safe if limited to those specific areas.

We are more selective about who we allow to touch other areas of our body (legs, lower back, and face). For example, if you notice someone has a smudge on his face, or dust on his lower back from leaning against a chalkboard, you probably hesitate to brush it off for him. We will tend to touch people in these areas of their body only if we know them fairly well, or if touch is instrumental in nature.

Finally, there are areas of our bodies that we reserve for our intimates because they tend to be sexual in nature. Most people are not allowed to caress our genitals, breasts, or butt. So touch in those locations is highly restricted, and if we *do* receive touch there from a nonintimate, it should set off warning bells in our response system.

As you can see, where you are touched is tied up with the relationship you have with the toucher. If you have an intimate friendship, you will no doubt allow touch to many areas of the body and perceive it positively. But if the relationship is more of an acquaintance type or even unfriendly, you will allow fewer areas of touch and interpret it negatively if this is violated.

3. *What is the* physical context *in which the touching occurs?* The physical context or environment where touching happens strongly influences how we will interpret that message. In a crowded mall while shopping, or at a packed rock concert, being shoved close together and touching will not seem out of place (and may even add to the overall experience!). But in those same areas, if it were not crowded and people were very close and touching you, you might feel strange.

In general, public touch is less intimidating, intimate, or threatening than touch when you are alone with a person. An arm placed across your shoulder out in public with dozens of people around may be interpreted as friendship or congratulatory, and therefore it is inoffensive. But if that same person put an arm around your shoulders when you were alone on an elevator, you probably would react quite differently. The reasoning here is that when out in public the touch is unlikely to escalate to anything more intimate. There are too many people around. But in private that same touch behavior has more potential to lead to further touching, and for that reason is highly limited.

Greetings and good-byes are times of heightened touching—at airports, ends of conferences, beginnings of a stay at home. In the process of saying hello or terminating a conversation, people may touch even when they don't do so throughout the interaction. If you doubt this, the next time you greet someone with a hug or even a handshake, don't let go. Continue that touch. You will quickly see that this is a violation of expectations for the situation.

Other specialized contexts in the United States have norms for increased touching as well. Think of the amount and type of touch that occurs on the dance floor, the basketball court, when cheerleading or during other athletic events, and even on New Year's eve. These are examples of contexts that have developed special allowances for touch that go beyond the regular relational expectations. But those touch norms change back when you leave that particular context.

4. *Is the touch coming from a* male *or a* female? We have to admit that, as with many other areas of interpersonal communication, there are gender differences in the interpretation of touch. Although there is considerable variability within this category, much of our interpretation of touch depends on whether we are a male or female and being touched by a male or female. There are a few generally accepted differences to be addressed here.

First, in our culture it is more acceptable for females to touch other females than for males to touch each other, except in highly normative ways. That means that male-to-male touching will follow clear rules (e.g., hand-shaking, clapping someone on the back, or instrumental touch in athletic endeavors). Male–male touch that is outside of those norms tends to be looked at closely to determine whether it has a romantic motivation. Females in our culture are not bound quite so closely to normative touching patterns. Females use touch with other females to show support, comfort, happiness, solidarity, and affection—typically without people wondering whether they are romantically inclined. The sources for these differences are not well understood and require longer discussion than is appropriate here. But there are several books that deal extensively with male and female differences in nonverbal communication and how they developed (e.g., Canary & Emmers-Sommer, 1997; Hall, 1985).

In our culture, females develop more detailed schemas for touch, probably because they tend to be the recipients of more touch throughout their lives. Females receive touch from both women and men, but adult men receive touch primarily from women. In addition, females initiate touch to both women and men, but men initiate touch primarily toward women. So women grow up with more differing sources and types of touch communication and hence develop more elaborate category systems for interpreting and judging touch.

For example, many males differentiate "good" from "bad" touch primarily depending on who initiates the touching. In many cases, if a female initiates touch to this guy then it is interpreted as "good." Most males tend not to interpret touch coming from a female as "intimidating," and in fact, may make the mistake of thinking too many types of touch are sexual. This can lead to some very serious mistakes if this is in a dating-type encounter.

In comparison, females have more different categories. They may gauge touch according to whether it is playful versus serious, sexual versus comforting, from a male or a female, intentional or unintentional, and so on. Their labeling process is much more detailed, specific, and rapid because females tend to have more experience with touching and being touched. They have grown up with it. Females appear to be less likely to think a touch from a male is sexual when he really intended it to be friendly (Abbey, 1982).

Advice: Women, don't assume that because *you* think a touch from your male friend is just casual that *he* thinks that too. Be careful how you touch your college male friends, if you don't want to be misinterpreted. Men, don't assume that the touch you label as a sexual come-on from your female colleague is indeed sexual. She may believe she is communicating friendliness or trying to be comforting. Don't jump the gun.

How the Use of Time Communicates in Relationships

Chronemics is how time communicates, and is often discussed in organizational or intercultural contexts. We will focus on our use of time in interpersonal relationships, particularly circadian rhythms, punctuality, and timing.

Body time or body cycles are termed *circadian rhythms*. Simply put, some people are morning people. That is when they are most alert, do their best work, prefer to take classes, and so on. (We sometimes refer to these people as "sparrows" because of their early morning activity.) Other people are on a different circadian rhythm. They are night people (owls) who prefer to work and play at night, and often don't function very well in the mornings. If you are someone who *begins* writing papers for class at 10 P.M., and find it easy to stay up for the late, late show, you are probably an owl.

Interestingly, circadian rhythms, because they are biologically based, seem to be in place at birth. Parents can often tell whether their young child is going to be a "morning person" or a "nightowl" from very early behavior patterns. (Yes, even before they get to be teenagers and stay up late, some people have great difficulty waking up in the morning.)

Now, what do circadian rhythms have to do with relationships? Researchers have found that people are more satisfied and successful in relationships with a partner who is on a circadian rhythm similar to theirs. It makes sense, doesn't it? If you are living with someone who wants to go to bed by 11 P.M., which is when you are just getting started for the evening, this may cause difficulty. When they get up all cheery and fresh at 7 A.M. and you are groggy and grumpy until noon, that doesn't help either! Partners with similar circadian rhythms have less conflict because they tend to want to do things on similar time schedules—everything from scheduling classes, to arranging travel plans, to having sex. Time is at least one thing they don't have to argue over.

Conflict in relationships often occurs over punctuality as well. *Punctuality* is being "on time" and what constitutes on time may differ by situation. For instance, being punctual for a job interview may mean arriving 5–10 minutes early, whereas punctuality for a campus party may be one-half to one hour (or more) after the designated starting time.

But what about relationships? What is "punctual" there and what does it mean when people violate punctuality expectations? Think of it this way: Making someone wait for you is a power strategy. It communicates that you have control over that person's time and hence what he or she does during that time. If you agree to meet a friend at 8:00, but you don't show till 8:30, your friend has been "on hold" for a half hour.

Think of how you feel when a professor is consistently late for class but expects you to be on time. Use of time in this way communicates that you perceive that you hold higher status and that your time is more valuable than the person who is waiting. Typically, the individual with lower status (e.g., patient) has to wait for the individual with higher status (physician). Therefore, punctuality communicates equality and respect.

Time can, in a similar way, communicate relative importance or liking. When you receive a phone message from someone, how quickly do you respond? Do you get back to that person immediately, or sometime later when you get around to it? There is generally a relationship between how rapidly you respond to a message and how high the esteem or value you place on that relationship.

There is at least one more important way time can have an impact in relational communication, and that is in timing. The *timing* of communication messages refers to how we sequence information, or how rapidly we move from one message to another. We may want to bring up an issue about keeping the apartment clean, but realize that the "timing" is poor to do this; perhaps your partner just got back from a rough shift at work. Understanding timing is important in avoiding needless conflicts or irritations. Timing can also be crucial in the pacing of a relationship. How fast or slow should you move in the relationship? Is your friend ready to move into more intimacy with you? Sexual timing is an aspect that has been implicated in acquaintance rape discussions. Sometimes one partner feels ready to move into a sexual relationship and pushes the issue before the other partner is ready for that type of commitment.

Overall, you can see that how we structure and use time with our partners may communicate important relational messages. They may be intentional or unintentional, but communication via time has a significant impact on the success of our relationships.

Nonverbal Sensitivity

Some people are better at "reading" nonverbal cues than others are. They can tell what the meaning of the message is by how the sender acts, sounds, moves, or even uses time. They are nonverbally sensitive. *Nonverbal sensitivity* is when a person is adept and skilled at decoding nonverbal messages. Clearly, this is a valuable talent. You might be aware of what is going on in a relationship before it is put into words. You might be able to tell if your partner is becoming bored in the relationship before that feeling is voiced, or when someone is beginning to get angry with you prior to a blowup. Sometimes people communicate nonverbal cues they are not even aware of, so you can head off problems in a relationship before they become larger issues.

Several studies have found that women tend to be more nonverbally sensitive than men (Hall, 1985; McClure, 2000). Women tend to pay close attention to speakers, watching what is being communicated and listening for small cues. Women also tend to think about and process relational information, so they devote resources to "figuring out" what the source really means. Men are more likely to disregard such nonverbal cues, thinking that people will come right out and say what they mean if it's important to them. Unfortunately, people are usually not that direct. Although men may not get as much practice at decoding nonverbal messages, this does not suggest that men *cannot*, because studies have found that men who are in careers like counseling or nursing are just as nonverbally sensitive as women. They focus on different aspects. This means that many men need attentional training to improve their skill at reading nonverbal cues accurately.

Increasing Your Nonverbal Sensitivity

If being nonverbally sensitive in a relationship is positive, what can someone do to be more nonverbally sensitive? A key point here is that nonverbal sensitivity is a skill; it's not inborn. Nonverbal sensitivity is learned, and you can practice to improve. Here are a few tips:

1. *One of the first steps is to really focus on the other person's communication.* Look at that person, not at other things occurring around you. Turn off the TV. Don't have serious discussions when driving in traffic. Pay attention to your relational partner.
2. *Watch for eye contact or the lack of it.* Eye behavior says a great deal. When people are not looking at you, they are closing off the communication channel for some reason. Disinterest? Guilt? Embarrassment? Check it out.
3. *Listen closely for changes in vocal quality.* Are they talking loudly as if they're excited, or in a monotone as if they are depressed? Are there long silences when no one is talking? Does the person seem nervous and agitated, talking rapidly? These are often good indicators because the sender may be unaware of the vocal changes.
4. *Notice even small things about your partner's general behavior, such as alterations in muscle tension, attention span, emotionality, patterns of dress, or social activities.*
5. *Observe your partner over time so that you can notice even minor differences in the way he or she behaves.* When a pattern is changed, there is typically a good reason for it.

What each of these tips have in common is the need to pay attention to the partner and be less involved with what is going on inside ourselves. We often get so caught up in our own lives that we neglect to notice what our relationship partners may be trying to tell us through nonverbal channels. Because nonverbal cues are often less obvious, we have to observe and interpret carefully to pick up what is really being "communicated." However, the payoff for this attention and sensitivity is improved understanding of your partner, which inevitably affects the relationship.

Conclusions

Nonverbal communication is so fundamental in interpersonal relationships that to fully explore all the aspects of it would take much more than the one chapter devoted here. *Much more.* So we can say that this represents an introduction to some of the basics by looking at various forms of nonverbal messages—for example, kinesic emblems, facial affect displays, the impact of our voice in paralanguage—and how they impact interpersonal communication.

Touch sends particularly strong messages in interpersonal interaction. Hence, how we interpret various kinds of touch from differing people in different contexts has significant implications for relational outcomes. Nonverbal sensitivity, the skilled decoding of nonverbal messages, is a skill that can be enhanced to improve our overall ability to understand others in interpersonal situations.

But verbal communication cannot be overlooked in relationships either. In the following chapter, we'll take a look at how the verbal cues may coincide with, contradict, or enhance the nonverbal messages.

REFERENCES AND RECOMMENDED READINGS

Abbey, A. (1982). Sex differences in attributions for friendly behavior: Do males misperceive females' friendliness. *Journal of Personality and Social Psychology, 42,* 830–838.

Burgoon, J., Buller, D., Hale, J., & deTurck, M. (1984). Relational messages associated with nonverbal behaviors. *Human Communication Research, 10,* 351–378.

Burgoon, J., Walther, J., & Baesler, E. (1992). Interpretations, evaluations, and consequences of interpersonal touch. *Human Communication Research, 16,* 237–263.

Canary, D., & Emmers-Sommer, T. (1997). *Sex and gender differences in personal relationships.* New York: Guilford Press.

Hall, J. (1985). Male and female nonverbal behavior. In A. W. Siegman & S. Feldstein (Eds.), *Multichannel integrations of nonverbal behavior* (pp. 195–225). Hillsdale, NJ: Erlbaum.

Langlois, J., Kalakanis, L., Rubenstein, A., Larson, A., Hallam, M., & Smoot, M. (2000). Maxims or myths of beauty? A meta-analytic and theoretical review. *Psychological Bulletin, 126,* 390–423.

Leathers, D. (1997). *Successful nonverbal communication: Principles and applications.* (3rd ed.) Boston: Allyn & Bacon.

McClure, E. (2000). A meta-analytic review of sex differences in facial expression processing and their development in infants, children, and adolescents. *Psychological Bulletin, 126,* 424–453.

Motley, M., & Reeder. H. (1995) Unwanted escalation of sexual intimacy: Male and female perceptions of connotations and relational consequences of resistance messages. *Communication Monographs, 62,* 255–382.

Muehlenhard, C. (1988). Misinterpreted dating behaviors and the risk of date rape. *Journal of Social and Clinical Psychology, 6,* 20–37.

Mynatt, C., & Allgeier, E. (1990). Risk factors, self-attributions, and adjustment problems among victims of sexual coercion. *Journal of Applied Social Psychology, 20,* 130–153.

Parrot, A. (1989). Acquaintance rape among adolescents: Identifying risk groups and intervention strategies. In P. Allen-Meares & C. H. Shapiro (Eds.), *Adolescent sexuality: New challenges for social work* (pp. 47–61). Haworth Press.

Shotland, H. L., & Hunter, B. (1995). Women's "Token Resistant" and compliant sexual behaviors are related to uncertain sexual intentions and rape. *Personality and Social Psychology Bulletin, 21,* 226–236.

Snodgrass, S., Hecht, M., & Ploutz-Snyder, R. (1998). Interpersonal sensitivity: Expressivity or perceptivity. *Journal of Personality and Social Psychology, 74,* 238–249.

Snider, M. (1991). Circadian rhythms and marital bliss. *USA Today,* January 22, 2D.

Stets, J., & Pirog-Good, M. (1989). Sexual aggression and control in dating relationships. *Journal of Applied Social Psychology, 19,* 1392–1412.

10 Saying It Right
The Impact of Words

OBJECTIVES

Although we humans react individually with regard to meanings in interactions, the specific *words* chosen have an impact all their own. Here you'll be studying (a) connotative versus denotative meanings, (b) the impact of who says what and where it was said, and (c) how intense language affects us. You know you understand this chapter if after studying it you can

1. Describe the difference between denotative and connotative meanings, giving an illustration of each.

2. Give examples of how language use often differs as we proceed through stages of relationship development and decline.

3. Explain how "hate speech" is not just "free speech."

4. Describe the effects of intensifying your language, and what happens with repetition of intense language.

5. Define and give an example of euphemisms in interpersonal communication.

6. Give at least three examples of how language is expected to differ from work to social contexts.

7. Explain what verbal assurances are and how they are used to maintain life in a relationship.

8. Describe two types of language that typically are viewed as "powerless" and explain why.

9. Give an example of "accusatory language" and a counterexample that would be preferable in a relationship.

CHAPTER OUTLINE

Words Have Intentional and Not-So-Intentional Meanings
  Connotative versus Denotative
    Meanings
  Words as Intentional
    Communication
Word Selection
  Words Used to Wound
  Accusatory Language
  Language Intensity
  Powerful and Powerless Language
  Personality Effects on Word Choice
Situations Affecting Verbal Communication

  Context: The Workplace versus
    Your Place
  Source Effects
Verbal Communication: A Requirement for Interpersonal Relationships
  Necessity of Verbal Interaction
  Vocabulary Development
Verbal Communication Reflects Relationship Processes
  Link to Stages of Relationships
  Conclusions about Verbal
    Interaction

> *A word is not a crystal, transparent and unchanged; it is the skin of a living thought and may vary greatly in color and content according to the circumstances and time in which it is used.*
>
> —Oliver Wendell Holmes, Jr.

How many times have you ever rewritten a letter or note to get the wording *exactly* the way you want it? Or, have you ever rehearsed an important message (whether to your boss or to your mother) to make sure the words come out right? We have already established that "meanings are in people," but the words have impact too—sometimes too much impact. John Locke wrote, "We should have a great many fewer disputes in the world if words were taken for what they are, the signs of our ideas only, and not for things themselves."

Words are not the "things," but we cannot ignore the fact that words trigger meanings. And, as we will see, words vary in their impact. Certain types of words trigger certain meanings. Skilled communicators use words to try to create very specific meanings and images in the minds of their receivers. First we'll look at the different types of meanings words may have.

Words Have Intentional and Not-So-Intentional Meanings

Connotative versus Denotative Meanings

A *denotative meaning* is the official meaning of a word, the explicit definition of a term. It is what you would find if you looked a word up in the dictionary. For example, in the *New Oxford Dictionary*, anger is defined as "extreme or passionate displeasure; wrath." A quarrel is "a complaint against or disagreement with another or his/her action or opinion; cause of unfriendly feeling." Yes, these denotative meanings are straightforward and clear. Often in interpersonal communication, though, we are affected as much by the meanings we put on the words as the words themselves, that is, their connotative meanings.

A *connotative meaning* is a suggested meaning, the implied meaning of the word, or the definition that exists in addition to the denotative meaning. This is where the "meanings are in people" principle is most noticeable. Connotative meanings are a function of our past experiences, our culture, and immediate contexts. Often connotative meanings are very difficult to predict, because they are not straightforward and out in the open. To illustrate, the denotative meaning of "dog" is a four-legged canine that barks, pants, and sheds a lot. However, there may be many more connotative meanings of "dog" (both four-legged and two-legged) depending on the context in which it is used.

Differences in connotations have also been studied in words we use to describe females versus males. Positive gender descriptors for females include elegant, graceful, tender, peaceful. Positive descriptors for males include debonair and valiant. Notice that these words tend to connote the sex of the person being described. It may sound odd to hear "he certainly looked elegant tonight" or "she was debonair in that dress." More negative descriptors also carry gendered connotations. Personality trait terms that tend to be used to describe only women are nagging, sassy, gossipy, mushy, and clingy. Negative trait terms that tend to be used primarily to describe males include bigheaded, cocky, rowdy, rough, and messy (Sankis, Corbitt, & Widiger, 1999). This does not mean that the words change their exact meaning, but rather that when we use them, the connotation is that we are describing either a male or female, but probably not both.

Another example of connotative meanings can be seen in verbal descriptors. When grading student papers, in addition to the numerical score, I often put words as encouragement at the top of the paper. "Terrific" "Excellent" "Good Job!" Many students don't just accept the actual numeric grade; they compare papers to check what *words* others received and to see how they measured up. Is "terrific" a better score than "outstanding"? Does "good job" suggest a weaker rating than "fantastic"? The language used has connotative meanings. Think how much more prevalent connotative meanings are in interpersonal communication where exact meanings of words are often uncertain. What does a "committed" relationship connote? What is "cheating"?

Words as Intentional Communication

Verbal interactions overwhelmingly tend to be *intentional communication*. Although we can all think of examples of when we accidentally misspoke, a certain word just "slipped out," or we even "talked in our sleep," most words are consciously selected and incorporated into an interaction. By comparison, we may be much less aware of our nonverbal behaviors such as our facial expressions or posture. Verbal communication tends to be one of the purest illustrations of motivated and intentional communication.

It is not uncommon for communicators to rehearse what they plan to say or talk about before an important event—and not only in public speaking contexts. Partners often carefully consider and select the best wording when preparing to confront the other about an issue—whether picking up the apartment or larger issues such as fidelity. People who are unfamiliar with "dating" (adolescents or previously married adults who may be rusty) regularly plan out how to ask someone to go to a movie or dinner with them. Verbal messages can be crafted and practiced, especially when they deal with important areas of relationship such as escalation, de-escalation, interactions with others in their network, relatives, or any other topic that has the potential to turn into a quarrel.

Another area where we focus on interaction almost exclusively through words in is computer-mediated communication (CMC). More and more, computer interactions are used not only in the workplace but also socially. In addition, CMC is used not only to maintain existing relationships but to *begin* relationships. Look at the number of computer users who "meet" people in chatrooms. Internet dating services have sprung up that try to match people on their interests and goals. These Internet exchanges are primarily verbal. People can carefully select the words and phrases they want to use. They can even practice and rewrite the exchange before sending it without worrying about how they look and sound. Some sources have said the verbal exchanges over the Internet are ideal for individuals who are extremely shy or have disabilities. The focus is on the verbal interaction.

Word Selection

Words Used to Wound

Unfortunately, in relationships people sometimes select words specifically to wound their partners—intentional and deliberate cuts. The people we are closest to are usually the ones who know how to hurt us the most with their communication. Previously we discussed communication in general that was intended to damage the self-concept of another person (termed "verbal aggression," although actually these strategies use both verbal and non-verbal tactics). Part of this negative behavior is choosing words that will hurt, embarrass, shame, humiliate, or cause some other kind of pain to the other person.

A type of verbal communication that is clearly employed to harm others is *hate speech* (Leets & Giles, 1997). Although hate speech is typically conceptualized in more public contexts, the premise also holds for interpersonal communication. Yes, we have free speech in America, but there are some things you cannot say due to the direct harm they cause. You cannot legally spread lies about people that defame their character. You cannot scream "fire" in a crowd, which may lead to mayhem and injury. You cannot incite someone else to assault an individual or to do violence. Many legal and communication scholars are now viewing hate speech, acts that are intended to denigrate people based on a group to which they belong, as illegal because of the harm it causes. Hate speech (everything from racial slurs to insults on your gender or physical abilities) is thought to lead to depression and paranoia, stress, loss of self-esteem, and harm to one's human dignity. The effects can result in both short-term pain and long-term pain. Hate speech involves selecting phrases and words with the goal of harming the receivers with the acid, disparaging words.

Intentionally using words against a partner is part of the definition of emotional abuse. Communication such as ridiculing or insulting the other person's feelings, race, or values, humiliating the person in public or private, threatening to do harm to the person or someone the person loves would all qualify as emotional or psychological abuse (Chez, 1997; Gazmararian et al., 1996). Both emotional abuse and hate speech have been made illegal and are not just a matter of personal choice about your verbal communication.

Accusatory Language

Have you ever noticed that sometimes what comes out of our mouths sounds much worse than we meant it to sound. We may blurt out words that lead our roommate to feel blamed, hurt, or accused. Then our roommate becomes all huffy and defensive and shoots back at us. At this point, we have a negative downward cycle going.

Accusatory language is any wording that implies the other is at fault, responsible, or to blame for a negative occurrence. Two major forms of accusatory language are "you" messages and unqualified statements.

First, let's look at "you" versus "I" statements. If you say, "You are driving me crazy channel surfing with that remote," it sounds worse than saying, "I would like to leave the TV on one channel for a while." You might be communicating pretty much the same thing, but by framing the message with an "I" it sounds less antagonistic. Or consider this: "I waited and waited for you after work today," as opposed to, "You were late to pick me up after work today." The focus of the issue is your response rather than "accusing" the other of neglect, carelessness, or inconsideration.

A second way verbal messages may be perceived as accusatory is if they are totally unqualified. To qualify a statement you insert words or phrases that lessen the directness and suggest less certainty. There may be other explanations, it may not happen all the time, you might be misunderstanding, and so forth. For example, telling your friend that he or she "drinks too much" is likely to start a fight. However, if you say, "I think you drink too much" or "sometimes you drink too much" or "it seems like you drink till you get falling-down drunk really regularly," these frame the message in a more qualified way and sound less accusatory. You might even rephrase a statement as a question in order to avoid sounding accusatory. "Do you ever notice how often you get drunk?"

Now I have to note here that such qualifiers should be selected intentionally with knowledge of the possible outcomes, because they tend to weaken your message. If you are at a political rally and want to appear decisive and forthright, qualifications may not be the best tool. Notice the difference in a message worded "we can do this" versus a message worded "I think it's highly likely that we can do this." Qualifications may weaken your advocacy. However, in interpersonal relationships there may be times when adding qualifiers to your statements is highly productive with your partner.

Language Intensity

We sometimes use words intentionally to shock, revolt, move, or otherwise engage our receiver's emotions. In general, language that is vivid, intense, and unique is more likely to get someone's attention and rile them up than will milder language. Intense language also tends to be more memorable than everyday language. Saying "I despise your liver-sucking face" is no doubt more memorable than "I dislike you."

Sometimes extreme profanity is used in this way for emphasis or its shock value. Note, however, that extreme language loses its shock effect when it is frequently and continually used, an effect called *desensitization*. If you incorporate the same words over and over again in your interactions, whether they are profanity or love words, receivers habituate to them and the intensity of the words loses its impact.

Words are not objects or actions, but words trigger other meanings in our minds. Clothing with certain words or phrases is banned in schools or blocked out, either by bleeping or blurred images, in the media. Sometimes people will talk around the actual words. Notice how people will explain, "He used the N-word," or "And then she said the F-word," rather than using a specific word that could receive a very negative reaction.

At the opposite end of the intensity continuum are euphemisms. *Euphemisms* are terms used to soften the impact of a word, when we want to say something a "nicer" way. For example, we might say that someone's employment was terminated, rather than that they were fired. Or we explain that our significant other changed his or her mind about the relationship, rather than admitting we got "dumped." Euphemisms also illustrate the impact words can have. Why would anyone bother to try to tone down, or soften, the word if words didn't have impact?

Powerful and Powerless Speech

Certain forms of verbal expression tend to be perceived as ineffectual, uncertain, or wishy-washy. The speaker comes across as being "low in the hierarchy." Although studied mainly in public contexts, rather than interpersonal ones, these forms of communication have been termed *powerless* language because the source is viewed as weak and incompetent. In comparison, other direct forms of language are interpreted as forceful or strong and hence viewed as *powerful* speech. Some types of language use that lead to evaluations of powerlessness are hesitations, hedges, tag questions, polite forms, intensifiers, and disclaimers.

Hesitations in speaking signal uncertainty, nervousness, or being unsure of yourself. "Well I, um, saw that, er, car coming around the, um, corner." If you heard this from a witness on the stand, how believable would the statement be?

Hedges are words used to qualify your statements, making them less absolute: Saying "I guess that would be a good movie" rather than directly stating your opinion, "that's a good movie."

Tag questions are phrases tacked on to the end of a declaration that weaken it. "I was good last night, wasn't I?" Tag questions seem to beg your listener to agree with you, instead of directly asserting your claim. "Hey, I was good last night!"

Polite forms of speech indicate respect for, deference, or submission to the other person, as in when you say, "I would appreciate it if you would take a look at my paper, sir." Note that in the military no "polite" forms of speech soften orders. This is not to be rude, but it serves to make clear who has the authority, rank, and power to issue the order, rather than ask a favor.

Intensifiers are words that fortify or make another word stronger. "I like you very, very much." "This is a really lousy idea."

Disclaimers are phrases we put before our statements to show that this might not be absolutely true or may not be our fault, or in some other way divert the responsibility from the source. "Now I may not be an expert in this, but. . . ." "I know this may sound outrageous, but. . . ."

I think we all can recognize that these verbal patterns are not perceived identically in all situations. Hesitations, hedges, and tag questions have been found to be particularly weak-sounding. Disclaimers may somewhat weaken your arguments, but don't necessarily undermine them.

Some researchers, however, have noted that intensifiers and polite forms of communicating are not always perceived as weak. These forms tend to be interpreted as "powerless" only if combined with other powerless styles, such as hesitations (Bradac & Mulac, 1984). So the message here is definitely not to avoid being polite. It may be the combinations of styles rather than the specific styles that undermine your points.

In addition, we have to remember that these effects have been studied primarily in presentational contexts rather than in interpersonal interactions. It is quite a different context if you are in a debate, or making a public statement to a committee. In such cases, your goal will be to create the image of strength and assuredness. However, there are numerous times in interpersonal situations when you want to *avoid* coming across too powerfully. You don't want to intimidate your interaction partner. You may want to get your partner to open up with you, to share his or her opinions, and so on. In these cases, you need to use language that won't seem so assured and will not be perceived as overwhelming or domineering.

Personality Effects on Word Choice

Finally, different people talk differently. Yeah, no kidding. But those differences in word choice are consistent across situations and time, and they form recognizable patterns. There seem to be personality types that are recognizable from the language people select to use. For example, it was found that negative emotions in language—that is, relatively harsh talk whether talking about past experience or the weather—were associated with more alcohol and tobacco use. People who score higher on the trait of dominance also tend to use more intense language to get their ideas across (Pennebaker & King, 1999).

Therefore, your personality to some extent drives your patterns of word selection, and in contrast, your pattern of verbal interaction reflects a great deal about your personality.

Situations Affecting Verbal Communication

Context Effects: The Workplace versus Your Place

Simply put, we tend to use different language and words at our place of employment than we do at home. The context or physical surrounding affects what words we select to encode our messages. Think about how you talk when hanging around your apartment watching TV with friends compared to how you talk on a job interview, or even after you enter your chosen organization. Some job sites include rougher talk than others (compare a construction site with a law office), but most work contexts are at least different from social contexts. One area in which we can see word selection is in our use of people's titles.

The titles we use with people denote status. How you refer to coworkers or friends, the specific term or title you use, communicates how much respect you have for them or their status in the organization. In general, the more informal the language, the more interpersonal the relationship. Some professors prefer to be called "Doctor," whereas others are comfortable with a first-name exchange. But informality isn't the only consideration. We also have to look at the differential levels of formality in the respective titles. When we call someone by his or her title (e.g., Reverend) and that person calls us by our first name (James), this communicates the differential status of the individual. When we move to calling our supervisor by her first name (Michelle rather than Ms. Wyer), that signals a change in the relationship. This change suggests more interpersonal communication and getting beyond the societal roles of supervisor and subordinate.

Source Effects

Sometimes how you interpret specific words depends on who says the words. If you and a close friend call each other "bitch," neither will probably take offense. Why? Because you know you both mean it affectionately or humorously. But imagine someone you don't know well using the same terminology, the same words. Imagine an authority figure calling you "bitch." At that point you might react angrily because of the "insulting" language. Actually the words stay the same thing, but the source, and therefore the meaning, changes.

We attribute consciousness and intent to the source. (Remember that verbal communication is perceived to be intentional and conscious, even if we think something just "slips out.") If we have a negative past history with a person, we will tend to read that person's words more negatively. Teasing takes on a different meaning. However, if we have a positive relationship with someone, we tend to interpret his or her words in a more positive light.

Same words, different sources of the words. This can also be an example of selective perception.

Verbal Communication: A Requirement for Interpersonal Relationships

Necessity of Verbal Interaction

Interpersonal relationships need verbal exchanges to progress. Although we recognize the importance of nonverbal communication, relationships usually don't progress and grow deeper without effective use of verbal communication. For most relationships, nonverbal exchanges are necessary, but not sufficient. We disclose about ourselves verbally; we use language to express our emotions and to explain our opinions, our relational expectations, or our commitment level to partners. Typically, all of these processes necessitate words. We get into trouble relationally if we assume our partners "understand" what we mean, even if we don't say it out loud.

One area in which specific words have a great impact in romantic relationships is the first time someone says, "I love you." If you think about it, that's a big step. After the initial declaration of love, such expressions may come fast and furious. But until one person breaks through the psychological barrier and actually says the words "I love you," both may hold back. These words are "risky" and weighed very heavily in the progression of a relationship. I mean, what if our partner doesn't reciprocate? What if she laughs? What if he says, "uh . . ."? Relationships typically change significantly—either for better or worse—following the first statement of "I love you."

However, it's not just the initial expression of love that is important. One of the ways we *maintain* relationships is through what are called "assurances" (Canary & Stafford, 1992). *Assurances* are verbal expressions that directly tell the partner of your commitment to the relationship, or that you're happy, that you love him or her, that you'll be there, and so on.

Sometimes after we develop an ongoing relationship, we believe there is no need for continued verbal expressions of affection and commitment; "You know that you're the best roommate I've ever had" or "Well of course I love you. I married you, didn't I?" But our partners may not see it quite that way. Without reassurances many partners begin to wonder whether the relationship is going well. They may doubt the depth of feeling, question whether the other person is satisfied and still cares for them. Although this uncertainty may decrease over time, even after several years together people may question the continued vitality of the relationship. Some people (whether due to their self-concept, past experiences in relationships, or other difficulties) may need more verbal reassurance than others to maintain relationships.

Verbal (and nonverbal) expressions of caring and affection are positive tools no matter how well established and long-term the relationship may be.

Vocabulary Development

The greeting card industry has made a fortune from people who do not have the verbal skills necessary to communicate what they would *like* to express to a relationship partner, acquaintance, or colleague. Go into any greeting card department and you will find far more than the traditional birthday, anniversary, and get-well cards. Cards today express verbal messages that may be too subtle or difficult for us to communicate—everything from "words of encouragement" to coping with the death of a pet, to apologizing for being a jerk. Hallmark knows the value of well-constructed verbal messages.

As with any other communication skill, we need to work on our relationship vocabulary in order to be able to communicate competently. Without the words, our meanings and our interpretations of others' meanings may be either unclear, severely limited, or even mistaken.

So how do you build your relationship vocabulary? You have to think about concepts, talk about them, and practice using the terms. Consider the various connotations of the terms *trust, security, fun, sexy, commitment, cheating, acceptance, independence,* and *fighting fair.* Each partner may have a slightly different definition or explanation of such concepts, which can lead to major misunderstandings.

This is why the use or development of verbal communication is discussed in multiple chapters in this book. Note that the chapter on expressing emotions contains guides for verbal communication, as does the chapter on assertive communication. Specific language choice strengthens various communication skills, so applications and examples of verbal communication are interwoven throughout the text.

Verbal Communication Reflects Relationship Processes

Link to Stages of Relationships

As interpersonal relationships develop and grow closer, the language used in them also tends to change. Often the words we use become more casual and informal, or tailored to our individual relationship. Verbal shortcuts may be created as we have more shared experiences. Close friends and relational partners may even develop words with special meaning only for them (Bell & Healey, 1992). This has sometimes been termed *idiosyncratic language.*

Such individualized, made-up verbal codes are not uncommon between identical twins, lovers, even teenage friends. The codes serve to cement the private, special relationship between the partners, and accentuate in-group/out-group lines, excluding any other people who do not understand the language.

We also see language effects that may reflect stages when peoples' names are altered. The shortening of names or use of nicknames can suggest increased closeness in the relationship. Or, such alterations could suggest that the sender wants others to *think* that the relationship is more friendly and intimate than it may actually be. Do you know people who consistently try to abbreviate or somehow alter their co-communicators' names? George becomes "Georgie," Melissa becomes "Missy," John Reed changes to "J. R.," Doctor to "Doc." Take note of the fact that sometimes name alterations can backfire relationally if both people don't appreciate the name shortening, so you might want to check it out when you call someone by a nickname.

The specific words we use when we introduce our relationship partners carry a world of meaning. Consider this: You are meeting your significant other's parents for the first time. Imagine your surprise when he introduces you as "Alexa, a friend from school." You probably thought you would at least be introduced as a "girlfriend," or even "fiancée," perhaps. Did the relationship change, or did just the words change? Verbal language provides us with labels for our relationships so that we can categorize them as important/not important, platonic/romantic, short-term/long-term, and so on. In part, when we hear others describe our relationship with words, it tells us how they envision it.

But what if the relationship is turning bad? Falling apart? Do we see changes in verbal messages? We can witness the opposite effects with language when the relationship becomes less psychologically close. As individuals feel more estranged in a relationship (whether a friend or romantic partner) they are less comfortable with interactions, and words reflect that discomfort and unease. Suddenly they're talking in generalities, or in highly scripted ways. They may include more negative language and more "I/me" references instead of "we/us." Such language reflects the fact that the person is thinking more of a single unit rather than two people in a solid relationship.

Verbal interactions when a relationship is in decline tend to become more formalized, less spontaneous, more stilted and careful. The language tends to be less playful or creative. People may fall into verbal routines in which they say the same things over and over—or don't speak to each other much at all. Such patterns are very evident in stagnating stages of relationships. All of these verbal indicators reflect a lack of psychological closeness with the other person. Often the language changes are very subtle, but they should be recognized as a sign that the relationship is changing—probably for the worse.

Conclusions

Remember, even though we may believe that "sticks and stones may break our bones, but words can never hurt us," words *are* an important part of the communicative process in relationships. They are symbols we select to express our feelings, thoughts, and ideas. And if we don't have use of those words (whether due to language barriers or simple lack of an adequate vocabulary), we will be frustrated and perhaps unsuccessful in our interpersonal relationships. Our relationships don't develop and grow exclusively through nonverbal communication. We have to select and incorporate words, language, that is, verbal communication. You will be more effective with your relationships if you can use words to interpret what others are saying precisely and to express yourself accurately when you interact.

REFERENCES AND RECOMMENDED READINGS

Bell, R., & Healey, J. (1992). Idiomatic communication and interpersonal solidarity in friends' relational cultures. *Human Communication Research, 18*, 307–335.

Bell, R., Berkel-Rothfuss, N., & Gore, K. (1987). "Did you bring the yarmulke for the cabbage patch kid?" The idiomatic communication of young lovers. *Human Communication Research, 14*, 47–67.

Booth-Butterfield, M., & Trotta, M. (1994). Attributional patterns for expressions of Love. *Communication Reports, 7*, 119–129.

Bradac, J., Bowers, J., & Courtright, J. (1979). Three language variables in communication research: Intensity, immediacy, and diversity. *Human Communication Research, 5*, 257–269.

Bradac, J., & Mulac, A. (1984). A molecular view of powerful and powerless speech styles: Attributional consequences of specific language features and communicator intentions. *Communication Monographs, 51*, 307–319.

Canary, D., & Stafford, L. (1992). Relational maintenance strategies and equity in marriage. *Communication Monographs, 59*, 243–267.

Chez, R. (1997). Women battering: It can happen anywhere. *Contemporary OB/GYN*. May 1997, 78–87. Medical Economics Company.

Forgas, J. (1999). On feeling good and being rude: Affective influences on language use and request formulations. *Journal of Personality and Social Psychology, 76*, 928–939.

Gazmararian, J., Lazorick, S., Spitz, A., Ballard, T., Saltzman, L., & Marks, J. (1996). Prevalence of violence against pregnant women. *Journal of the American Medical Association, 275*, 1915–1920.

Kirn, W. (2000). The love machines. *Time*, February 14, 73–74.

Leets, L., & Giles, H. (1997). Words as weapons—When do they wound? Investigations of harmful speech. *Human Communication Research, 24*, 260–301.

Motley, M. (1992). Mindfulness in solving communicators' dilemmas. *Communication Monographs, 59*, 306–314.

Pennebaker, J., & King, L. (1999). Linguistic styles: Language use as an individual difference. *Journal of Personality and Social Psychology, 77*, 1296–1312.

Sankis, L., Corbitt, E., & Widiger, T. (1999). Gender bias in the English language? *Journal of Personality and Social Psychology, 77*, 1289–1295.

SAY IT ANOTHER WAY

We often alter our words to communicate something another way. We may change the words so the meaning will be harsher or more intense, or we may try to soften the message and make it less extreme. In the following phrases or statements, choose other words to intensify or deintensify the meaning. The boldface words are the ones you change.

1. **Vomit**

   More Boldly:

   More Mildly:

2. You're **taking advantage of me**.

   More Boldly:

   More Mildly:

3. My father is **an authoritarian person.**

   More Boldly:

   More Mildly:

4. That song is **really awful**.

   More Boldly:

   More Mildly:

5. I'm **doing badly** in class.

   More Boldly:

   More Mildly:

6. The person **died**.

   More Boldly:

   More Mildly:

7. I have to **go to the bathroom.**

   More Boldly:

   More Mildly:

8. **I love you.**

   More Boldly:

   More Mildly:

C O N S I D E R   Y O U R
R E L A T I O N A L   V O C A B U L A R Y

Step 1: Individually write out your definition or understanding of the following concepts as you think they apply to interpersonal relationships.

1. What is *stimulating* in a relationship?

2. What does *acceptance* mean in a relationship?

3. Define a *long-term relationship.*

4. What is interpersonal *trust?*

5. What do you mean by *independence* in a relationship?

6. What is *security* in a relationship?

7. How would you describe *a fair relationship?*

8. Explain what you mean by *conflict?*

9. What do you think is *sexy?*

10. What do you define as *cheating?*

Step 2: Now in pairs or in groups go over the lists. Does everyone agree on the meanings? Who is "right"?

CHAPTER

11   Self-Disclosure

OBJECTIVES

Self-disclosure is a complex process—certainly difficult to do well, and more complicated than just "talking about yourself." To be more effective you should be able to complete this information about self-disclosing.

1. Define self-disclosure, explaining the importance of intentionality.

2. Describe four of the five functions of self-disclosure and use a relationship example to illustrate each.

3. Explain and give an example of the three levels of self-disclosure.

4. Be able to recognize and label disclosive statements at their appropriate level.

5. Give an example of self-disclosure with negative valence, one with positive valence, one of high risk, and one of low risk.

6. Analyze at least four factors you would take into consideration prior to self-disclosing.

7. Discuss the finding that females receive more self-disclosure than do males. Why do you think this occurs?

8. Explain why perceived self-disclosure may be more important to a relationship than the actual, objective amount of disclosure that occurs.

CHAPTER OUTLINE

What Is Self-Disclosure?

Functions of Self-Disclosure

Levels of Self-Disclosure

Valence

Risk

When Is Self-Disclosing Appropriate?

Male and Female Differences in Disclosure Patterns

What Happens When You Don't Disclose in Relationships?

Relational Implications

One of the communication skills most crucial for both individual and relational well-being is self-disclosure. People need to talk appropriately about themselves in order to stay healthy and to be effective in social, work, and more intimate roles. You do some self-disclosing every day, but do you do it *well?* In this section we will discuss what self-disclosive communication is, how it may function, and how to deal most effectively with disclosure.

What Is Self-Disclosure?

Self-disclosure is defined as intentionally revealing personal information about yourself that other people probably wouldn't know if you didn't disclose it to them. This doesn't necessarily include extremely intimate, sensitive, or secret details. But it does entail information that not everyone knows, and thus is not public knowledge. (If I tell you, "My hair is blonde," that probably isn't self-disclosure because you can see that for yourself. However, if I tell you, "My hair hasn't *always* been blonde," then that would qualify as self-disclosure.)

Notice that this definition also includes the concept of *intentionality*. You make a decision to self-disclose. It's not accidental or coerced. If you happen to overhear two people talking in a restaurant, they have exchanged messages with each other, but they have not self-disclosed to you. Self-disclosive messages have a clearly designated target.

You will see many qualifications about the information in this chapter. That is because the effectiveness and interpretation of self-disclosure depends on many variables. Who does it, when, to whom, about what, in what context? We simply do not completely understand the complexity of disclosing. The patterns presented, however, give a start to the study of this rich area of interpersonal communication interaction.

Functions of Self-Disclosure

Although we most often think of disclosure as a way to build and maintain relationships, and that is the central focus of this book, self-disclosure can serve diverse functions: (1) expressive, (2) clarification, (3) information giving, (4) impression management, and (5) relationship building. We can observe the *expressive* function when someone decides to communicate in order to relieve pent-up feelings or emotions. Your roommate may come rushing back from a weekend to tell you he got engaged over the weekend. He obviously can hardly wait to share the excitement with you. Sometimes the expressive function is seen when people are very upset and just have to tell *someone* what's occurring in their lives. Maybe you've disclosed in this way when you received some excellent news and were about to burst before you told someone. It seems natural for human beings to want to share their intense emotions with someone.

The *clarification* function occurs when self-disclosure is used to help people understand themselves better. Clarifying disclosures may be similar to "thinking out loud." Sometimes we may be mulling over decisions or ideas in our heads, but it is not until we discuss them with someone that the idea becomes clear and understandable. Many professionals report such clarification with research ideas prior to undertaking a project. Friends may use you as a "sounding board"—hearing how the thoughts or ideas sound. ("I've been thinking about transferring to the community college.") Often clarification disclosure occurs as you are considering a big step and you may be looking for feedback from others.

Much professionally related disclosure is for the purpose of *information giving*. The message is straightforward and intended to give the recipient certain information the sender thinks is important to know. For example, students may disclose to professors that they are on medication, have financial aid problems, or have to be absent from class because they play in the university band. Information-giving disclosure gives the recipient background on others and thus facilitates interactions. If someone mentions to you that she has lived in Australia for five years, or grew up in the projects in Chicago, that information may help you to understand her better. But we use self-disclosure as information giving in day-to-day interaction as well, such as when we tell our partner that we dented the car. We need him or her to have the information.

A function we may not be immediately aware of is self-disclosure as *impression management* communication. That is, disclosure can be used to create or maintain a specific image the sender wants others to have. This is not lying or making things up, but rather selectively sharing information with others. For instance, if you want others to have an impression of you as a well-traveled individual, then you mention the travel you've done. On the other hand, if you don't want to seem intimidating and you want a more down-to-earth image, you would probably not disclose all your traveling but focus instead on how much you enjoy watching TV and spending time with your family.

Impression-management disclosure depends on our perceptions of what the audience wants to hear or what they can cope with. We all do this at times. Of course, this function *could* be overdone, becoming extreme and creating significant gaps in knowledge about the other person. This leads to obstacles to greater closeness in the relationship. Your friends may one day find out that they don't know the "real you."

For the purposes of this class on interpersonal communication, one of the most common, and yet complex, functions of self-disclosure is *relationship building*. We often disclose with people when we want to become closer to them, to deepen or strengthen the relationship. We want our partner to know the person we truly are. (Recall that self-disclosure is one form of affinity seeking.) If you are in a relationship that has been stuck at the same stage, try self-disclosing to move it to a different level. Reciprocated disclosure is a reasonable sign that the other person also desires a closer relationship.

Levels of Self-Disclosure

Not all disclosure occurs at the same level of intimacy. Sometimes we are merely "pastiming," having social conversation about well-known happenings with little of ourselves involved. But more personal levels of self-disclosure include opinions, expressed feelings, and shared feelings.

Opinions are disclosures in which we express our thoughts and views on a subject. "I think that senior comprehensives are a good idea." Obviously opinions may be popular or unpopular, but they are yours. Opinions involve thinking and attitudes and cognition.

Expressed feelings contain feeling statements. This level of intimacy includes emotions that you have felt in the past, or that you are currently feeling about something or someone who is not present. In other words, expressed feelings are "there and then" feelings. If you say, "I used to feel intimidated by my boss," this is an example of expressed feelings, as is "I feel nervous in heavy traffic." Expressed feelings are a step removed from the intimacy of shared feelings.

Shared feelings are disclosures of the emotions you are feeling right now about the situation you are in, or person you are with. These are the most immediate. Shared feelings are sometimes called "here & now" feelings. For example, "I feel very uncomfortable right now" is a disclosure at the level of shared feelings.

Note that we are not necessarily sharing feelings just because we begin a sentence with "I feel. . . ." We often verbally substitute "I feel . . ." for "I think . . ." and this is actually an opinion rather than the expression of an emotion. You can check by determining whether there is an affect statement, an emotion term in the phrase. For example, "I feel concerned about our constant fighting" is different from "I feel that we fight too much." The first disclosure is one that expresses the emotion of "concern," whereas the second disclosure states the opinion that you are doing too much fighting. You could substitute the word "think" for "feel" in the second statement (making it an opinion), but not in the first.

Valence

Just as all disclosures are not the same intimacy level, they are not equally positive. The *valence* of a disclosure refers to its positivity or negativity. In general, we tend to disclose positively valenced information earlier in a relationship, and we save more negatively valenced information for later. It's like putting your best foot forward. We want to create a positive impression.

Although we can't determine what disclosures will be positively or negatively valenced 100 percent of the time, there are some messages that most people would agree are either one or the other. If we give someone negative criticism, that is probably negatively valenced. If we spent time in jail, that would probably be a negative disclosure to most people.

On the other hand, when we tell people how much we respect or like them, or when we express positive emotions, most people would rate these disclosures as positive. When we appropriately disclose about an award we won, or our 3.0 GPA, those are probably positively valenced. Of course, an exception would occur if the listener thought we were bragging about the event.

Risk

The risk level of self-disclosures is a complex aspect of the process. *Risk* refers to how much perceived negative outcome could occur as a result of the disclosure. Some statements are much more risky than others, and we tend to be very selective about the recipients of high-risk disclosures. We're careful about these because they could hurt us.

For example, there is very little risk in disclosing to your teacher that you like his class. There would be minimal risk in disclosing to a friend that you feel "comfortable" with her. I mean, who could argue with that! Probably everyone would like to hear those disclosures, and little harm could be imagined from them.

But what about the risk of disclosing to a friend that you cheated on an assignment, "borrowed" money from the till at work, or that you think you are in love with a friend of hers? Think about the interpersonal risk you are taking if you are the first person in a relationship to tell the other "I love you." What if she looks shocked? What if he seems uncomfortable or doesn't reciprocate? What if she laughs? So the risk involved may include both real, concrete negative outcomes (e.g., you could get kicked out of school) and perceived, emotional negative outcomes (e.g., feeling embarrassment if someone laughs or tells others).

Assessing the risk value involves carefully understanding and predicting the reactions of your audience. Sometimes we believe that there is no risk if we know the person well enough and know that we can reveal anything to him or her—even if the content has potentially negative consequences.

The risk may be higher if we know that our receiver disagrees with us on a topic. If we are the only one in the room to believe in creationism, vampires, or conspiracy theories, disclosing on those topics may be viewed as risky.

When Is Self-Disclosing Appropriate?

If self-disclosure is supposedly good, how can you tell whether you should disclose or not? The appropriateness of self-disclosure depends on many aspects of the situation, the relationship level, and the receiver. Consider the following a sort of checklist of questions to ask yourself before you engage in an important disclosing message.

1. *Trust:* Do you trust this person? Has this person proven to you that he or she can "keep a secret"? Can you depend on this person not to betray you if this disclosure is a big one with potentially serious consequences, either emotionally or socially?

2. *Setting and timing:* Is it appropriate to reveal this information about yourself here and now? If you are in the middle of Wal-Mart, it may not be the best time to bring up the topic of dissatisfaction in the relationship. Even if the setting is appropriate, you need to consider the timing of the disclosure. Has your partner had a rough day? Is your receiver in the middle of finishing a major project? The timing of self-disclosure may affect how it is received. We don't want to overload the receiver. We want our disclosure to be carefully considered. If the information is important, make sure you wait until the receiver has the time to listen more fully.

3. *Level of the disclosure appropriate to relationship development:* Some people have a tendency to rush things. Ask yourself, "Is this too much too soon?" Might you scare the person away if he or she knows this about you right now? Disclosing at too intimate a level could include both positively and negatively valenced information. For example, it might be too early in the relationship to tell your friend that you love him (positive valence), just as it might be too soon to tell him that you just got out of a mental hospital (negative valence) (unless he was just released too!).

4. *Reciprocation:* Does your partner self-disclose too? If you are doing all the disclosing, and your partner doesn't reciprocate, something might be wrong. Perhaps she is trying to give you a message that she doesn't want to be closer in the relationship. Maybe he doesn't care. Perhaps she doesn't know that you expect her to take her turn and self-disclose to you. In either event, if the disclosure pattern is one-sided, it is not a good sign for the relationship and should cue you to check out their perceptions.

5. *Constructive outcome:* This is an important consideration. Will the outcome of the disclosure be productive or destructive for the relationship? There may be long-term and short-term constructive outcomes. That is, sometimes we have to get through the short-term discomfort with a self-disclosure in order to make the relationship better. For example, if someone is gay, that may be a fact of life that would cause initial discomfort to a roommate, but it is important to understand for the ongoing relationship.

In contrast, are you just disclosing out of guilt, or to get something off your chest when there is no relational reason to do so? If we have been hurt by our partner, we may want to strike out and disclose something just to hurt the person back. No productive outcome here! Ask yourself, "Why am I telling this person this?" Remember, communication is irreversible; you can't take it back. Will the outcome eventually be positive for the relationship itself?

If you consider these factors—*can I trust this person, is the time and setting right, does the person reciprocate, is the level of intimacy consistent with the development of the relationship, and will the outcome of the disclosure ultimately be productive for the relationship*—you can make good decisions about when to self-disclose and when it might be better to say nothing.

Male and Female Differences in Disclosure Patterns

A great deal of study has been directed at the potential differences in self-disclosure patterns based on whether one is male or female. Many of the studies contradict each other. Some are flawed by small samples. Some are driven by the content of the disclosure. However, there are a few general findings about male–female disclosure patterns that are applicable to interpersonal relationships.

In general, *females receive more* disclosure than males do. More people talk about themselves with women. This is in part because both other women and men disclose to women, but men tend not to disclose to other men in our culture. But females may also be primary targets of disclosure because they are seen as more receptive, nonintimidating, and sympathetic recipients of the information.

An extension of this finding is that mothers tend to receive more disclosure from children than fathers do, and parents who are perceived as "supportive" receive more than nonsupportive parents. Some studies have also found that parent–child disclosure is linked to having fewer social and behavioral problems. That may mean that problems are headed off as they are discussed, before they become large issues. However, keep in mind that parents tend to believe that their family climate is more open and disclosive than their children do.

It has often been thought that females disclose more than males do, but a better interpretation is that males and females disclose about different topics. Women are more likely to talk about their feelings, their emotional state, and the relationship, whereas men are more likely to discuss topics such as politics and business. Men may be less reluctant to talk about money issues with their friends than are women.

What Happens When You Don't Disclose in Relationships?

We can observe several patterns in relationships where the participants are not disclosing to each other. None of them are positive.

First, relationships without self-disclosure don't deepen. The interaction remains on superficial levels, and though it may be pleasant and easy, there is little chance for intimacy and closeness to develop. The relationship will remain at an acquaintance level and be bound by societal roles.

Second, people who are in relationships and then stop disclosing tend to grow apart. They aren't keeping up on what is really going on with their partners. What used to be rewarding may be less so today; people alter their life goals. When people change, that change is not communicated. So partners may perceive stability in the relationship until the relationship is in deep trouble.

Third, when people are not disclosing in a relationship, they will notice numerous misunderstandings. Perhaps they think their partner *should* have known they were upset, or that a letter was important to them, or that they were particularly stressed. But due to nondisclosure the partner wasn't made aware of these occurrences. When partners feel misunderstood in a relationship, satisfaction decreases, leading to the feeling of being lonely even when with that person. They may believe their partner is "clueless," even though they haven't given him or her the clues.

Fourth, in relationships without disclosure, partners often feel very uncertain and may resort to other means to find out information. We don't like uncertainty in relationships. It makes us nervous. So if our partner is not talking to us, discussing feelings or goals about the relationship, we may go to indirect methods of acquiring relational information. One form that this has been found to take is "secret testing." Secret tests occur when one partner wants to assess the relational commitment without discussion and disclosure (Baxter & Wilmot, 1984). Tests may involve showing ones' worst self to see how much your friend will take, setting your partner up for infidelity or trying to make him or her jealous, or forcing your partner to make choices ("It's either me or your Rottweiller"). The bottom line here is that partners in relationships need to disclose to prevent indirect "games" and "tests" being played out to see if they are committed to the other.

Finally, people who fail to self-disclose in relationships end up following routines. Because disclosure allows each partner to adapt to specific needs, timing, and so forth, such spontaneity and flexibility is lost when disclosure declines. Partners find themselves following scripted routine behaviors, whether about daily schedules or sexual interactions, because those are what have been established.

Relational Implications

So is self-disclosure good for your interpersonal relationships? Absolutely. In relationships, it has been found that satisfied couples have a tendency to engage in more self-disclosure. It probably comes as no surprise that dissatisfied couples disclose less to each other, and when they do disclose to their partner, the content is more negative. ("I always thought you looked terrible in that outfit.")

But just because you may not be disclosing as intimately with your partner as you used to doesn't mean your relationship is failing. Self-disclosure tends to decrease in amount as the relationship extends over time. There is simply less *new* information to disclose if you are talking regularly and keeping up with life and changes that may be occurring with your partner.

Finally, some studies have indicated that the actual amount of disclosure may be less important than the *perceived* amount of disclosure in relationships. If partners believe their partners are disclosing to them and that they are learning to know and understand them, they are more happy. There are no absolute amounts of self-disclosure that every friendship must have. Much depends on the expectations of the individuals involved. Of course, the opposite of this is that people may not be satisfied in the relationship even if the disclosure rate is high—if they don't perceive that such disclosure is helping them understand and become closer to their partners.

Conclusions

In summary, self-disclosure is good for relationships and it is good for your own health. But we have to learn to communicate it effectively and appropriately if we really want the outcomes to be constructive for our interpersonal relationships.

Communicators need to understand why they are disclosing (what the function of this particular act is), and the conditions under which the self-disclosure will be most appropriate (right time? right place? right relationship?). Effective communicators will also consider the valence of the self-disclosure (positivity–negativity), the level (information, opinion, feelings, etc.), and the risk of the content before creating the disclosing message. Sometimes people do more harm than good with disclosive messages when they ignore these important indicators. Overwhelmingly, it is positive for interpersonal communication and others' perceptions of us to include disclosures, but you need to develop the skill in order to enhance the potential for positive outcomes. Finally, self-disclosure takes many forms. If all your disclosures are on a superficial level, it won't stimulate much growth in the relationship. You need to get to the feeling levels and allow the other to understand you.

REFERENCES AND RECOMMENDED READINGS

Baxter, L., & Wilmot, W. (1984). Secret tests: Social strategies for acquiring information about the state of the relationship. *Human Communication Research, 11*, 171–201.

Berger, C., & Calabrese, R. (1975). Some explorations in initial interaction and beyond: Toward a developmental theory of interpersonal communication. *Human Communication Research, 1*, 99–112.

Collins, N., & Miller, L. (1994). Self-disclosure and liking: A meta-analysis. *Psychological Bulletin, 116*, 457–475.

Derlega, V., & Berg, J. (1987). *Self-disclosure: Research, theory, and therapy.* New York: Plenum.

Derlega, V., & Grzrelak, J. (1979). Appropriateness of self-disclosure. In G. J. Chelune (Ed.) *Origins, patterns and implications of openness in interpersonal relationships* (pp. 151–176). San Francisco: Jossey-Bass.

Dindia, K., & Allen, M. (1992). Sex differences in self-disclosure: A meta-analysis. *Psychological Bulletin, 112*, 106–124.

Jourard, S. (1971). *The transparent self.* New York: Van Nostrand.

Omarzu, J. (2000). A Disclosure Decision Model: Determining how and when individuals will self-disclose. *Personality and Social Psychology Review, 4*, 174–185.

CASE STUDIES: DECISION TO DISCLOSE

1. You have found out from your physician that you have a serious illness, one that is progressive and will affect your career plans. How long would you keep this information to yourself? Who would you discuss this with first? How would you decide when to disclose?

2. You realize that you have fallen in love with your best friend. This relationship has always been just platonic, but you feel very differently now. There is no indication that he or she feels the same way. You feel that you need to tell the friend about this, but how?

   What would you look for in terms of your friend's readiness to receive the disclosure? How would you prepare him or her for this? Using the information from this chapter, what would you do and say?

3. You have some bad news for your parents. You wrecked your car—again. How do you decide when to tell them? How would you go about actually disclosing this information?

4. You have some great news! You've just found out that you've been accepted for graduate school at Yale. But it means some big changes in your life. It also means that you won't be rooming with your current roommate next year as you had planned. Who do you tell first? How do you set this up?

5. An acquaintance asks you questions about your background and personal life that you really don't feel like talking about. This is not a person you dislike, and you don't want to offend the person or cause hurt feelings, but you just don't know the person all that well. How do you handle this request for self-disclosure?

P R A C T I C I N G   S E L F - D I S C L O S U R E

Directions:

1. Choose a partner from class.

2. Sit together so that you can easily make eye contact and talk.

3. Below is a list of topics to self-disclose about. Look them over and choose several to talk about with your partner.

Describe your tastes in music.

What kinds of vacations you prefer and why?

What important characteristics are you looking for in a romantic partner?

Describe an incident in your life when you were very successful and how you felt.

What do you fear or what makes you nervous about interpersonal relationships?

Describe a very embarrassing moment for you.

How do you feel right now, in this moment?

Describe a time when you felt very hopeless or depressed.

What really ticks you off about roommates?

How do you feel when someone doubts your reliability or integrity?

12 Listening and Understanding in Interpersonal Communication

OBJECTIVES

As competent receivers we need to listen effectively. If you comprehend this chapter you should be able to do all of these.

1. Develop a scenario in which a receiver is listening for information, for the job, and for the relationship.

2. Explain the formula Listening = Attention + Reception + Perception, describing the role of each component.

3. Selective perception may occur for various reasons. Describe three, using examples to illustrate your response.

4. Apply at least four of the potential barriers to listening to your own listening pattern. What barriers do you find yourself dealing with?

5. Provide the definition of receiver apprehension.

6. Describe what each part of the SOLER model means.

7. List at least four strategies for verbal backchanneling.

8. Be able to paraphrase (i.e., perception check) the meaning of a given statement.

9. Explain what "nonverbal perception checking" is and give an illustration.

CHAPTER OUTLINE

Functions of Listening
Listening for Information
Listening for the Job
Listening for the Relationship

Listening = Attention + Reception + Perception
Attention in Listening
Reception in Listening
Perception in Listening

Problems with Listening: Barriers We Construct
Pseudolistening
Information Load

Other Orientation
Time-Consuming
Anxiety about Listening

Behaviors Associated with Listening Competence
Getting Ready to Listen: SOLER
Verbal Backchanneling

Perception Checking

Why Paraphrasing Works

Nonverbal Sensitivity as a Form of Listening
"Listening" for Nonverbal Cues
Nonverbal Perception Checking

If you go back to the beginning of the book and think about the basic principles of interpersonal communication, you will notice that a central component is consistently the *receiver* of the message. Often what the receiver actually does is *listen*. If we want to become better communicators overall, we have to also address how people receive oral messages from others. Many times, unfortunately, we aren't very good listeners.

Why do you think people don't listen very effectively? Is it because they don't care about the information or about the other person? Is it because they don't have the time? Or do they not know what it takes to listen effectively? In this chapter we'll examine why we listen (or don't listen) effectively, what skills are involved in the process of listening, and some specific advice on how to improve your own listening. First, we'll discuss how listening may serve different functions with different goals.

Functions of Listening

Listening for Information

Imagine yourself in an airport waiting for your flight to Tahiti to be called. When the announcement to board the plane comes over the public address system, you listen very carefully (after all, you don't want to get on the flight to Bosnia by mistake). In this situation you are listening for *information*.

We listen to pick up information in classes, in hallways, and even at home when we overhear our parents talking about the possibility of splitting up. We want to receive, understand, and retain the content of such communication events in order to have knowledge that will help us in some way. We want to be prepared. We may especially listen for information when someone is giving us directions about how to get to a specific building on campus, or where a particular restaurant is located, or even where we might find a well-placed parking space around campus. In each circumstance, we are listening for information that will help us to best achieve our goals, whatever they may be in the situation.

Listening for the Job

Sometimes it is our job to listen. We are *assigned a primary responsibility to listen* to others, and we get paid to do it. Don't those phone representatives at L.L. Bean or Victoria's Secret or J. Crew get paid to listen to your order?

Listening as a form of professional occupation may often occur in a counseling or therapeutic setting where one person has a problem and the other listens and counsels. But we may also need to listen as a central feature of other types of jobs in corporate positions such as interviewing or personnel management. One of the primary tasks of personnel managers is to listen to employees—that is, to both receive and interpret what they say. Organizations such as retail stores, banks, and health care facilities have noticed benefits (which may turn into profits) when they listen to people.

In addition, having a person whose job it is to listen to complaints can avoid costly mistakes or lawsuits. Thus some people who have very competent, active listening skills can actually gain employment by emphasizing them.

Listening for the Relationship

It is imperative that we listen to our partners in all types of interpersonal relationships. Unfortunately, we are often the most "rude and inconsiderate" to our significant others. We do other activities when they want to talk, we put them off until a more convenient time for us, or we even watch TV while they are trying to disclose to us. But the support we show them by actively listening and absorbing what they tell us reinforces the *strength of the relationship.*

People form relationships to get their interpersonal needs met. Some of those needs are to feel close and to feel understood by your relationship partner. In this relational function of listening, the surface information may be less important than the underlying feelings or attitudes of the source. That is, it may be less important to know *exactly* what happened at work that afternoon and more important to listen to the fact that your partner is worried or upset. If you care about your friend, you care about how he or she is feeling. And, you uncover those feelings by listening carefully.

Even in relationships that are not particularly close, relational listening is important. Poor listeners are typically poor conversationalists. They aren't good at turn-taking. They may interrupt or break into your thought. They may become distracted and then not respond when you are ready to turn the floor over to them. They seem to "wake up" saying, "huh? Oh. . . ." They may look inattentive, causing us to wonder how boring our thoughts must be to them. In short, we don't like to have conversations with people who are poor listeners.

Can listening in relationships be abused? Yes! Sometimes one partner can take advantage of the other's effective, sympathetic listening and talk him or her to death. Relational listening is a *reciprocal activity*. Like so many other aspects of a relationship, it works best if both parties are equally involved. In other words, if you are doing all the talking because your partner is such a great listener, you might want to step back and see whether you are overtalking. Having a friend who really listens to you is a valuable and scarce commodity. Don't overdo it.

So far we have discussed the functions of listening as a whole concept. Let's break down the process of listening into its component parts.

Listening = Attention + Reception + Perception

The process of listening can be broken down into three major components: attention, reception, and perception. To really understand how listening can be improved (or where potential problems are) we have to examine each component.

Attention in Listening

Much of listening is paying attention; it's *motivational*. We just need to decide to do it and then get rid of some bad habits.

Our motivation to listen tends to increase under certain circumstances. First, we are more highly motivated to pay attention when we believe the information will be useful to us. That is, our partner is telling us something important to the relationship, our boss is giving us instructions on how to do a task, or our instructor is telling us whether this is material will be on the test.

We may also pay more attention, or concentrate harder when the information is specific, not ambiguous. In a relationship with your romantic partner, hinting around is not a great idea. If you talk in broad generalities, people will tend to turn you off and not pay as much attention. So be specific if you want people to listen to you.

When we have a *schema,* a pattern for organizing information, we pay closer attention because the information can readily be categorized and used. For example, if we have previous experience with NASCAR racing or a particular dance club in town, and someone begins talking about it, we are more likely to orient to that information because we can place it. We can make judgments about it.

Several studies have also shown that women pay more attention in conversations than men do (Cross & Madsen, 1997). Women tend to look directly at their partners more often, and recall more features of the interaction (e.g., Buczek 1981). Some of the attentional differences in male and female listening can be observed in children as young as four years old. So this socialized gender difference is in place at a young age.

Finally, it probably comes as no surprise that we attend more closely to receivers when there are fewer distractions. In other words, we will be better listeners if we can focus our attention without many interfering factors (e.g., other people in the room, a rush for time, or watching Brady Bunch reruns on TV).

Reception in Listening

Reception is the *hearing* aspect of listening. People may have problems with the physiological part of their listening, such as when you lose hearing capacity. You can hear something (or someone) without really listening. That means you are just receiving, without really paying any attention or interpreting what you hear. You may have heard people talk about information "going in one ear and out the other." What they mean is receiving without perceiving, or hearing sounds without attaching any significant meaning to them.

Is hearing important? Absolutely! We won't be able to get to the perception and interpretation phase if we don't first receive the information. And yet, many people cannot control this component of the listening process. The largest single type of disability experienced by Americans is hearing loss. It is estimated that over 22 million people experience hearing loss to such an extent that it interferes with their daily lives.

Hearing is so important in interactions that it has been found that when people begin to gradually lose their hearing capacity, they tend to get into bad moods. They become more grumpy and somewhat paranoid. They often believe people are deliberately cutting them out of conversations, talking around them, or talking and laughing *about them* as if they are keeping secrets. When we don't hear what our partners or colleagues are saying, and we would like to, it can be problematic for the entire relationship. Again, you must be able to *hear* the message correctly before you can understand it appropriately.

Perception in Listening

The third component of listening, *perception,* refers to how we understand and interpret the message we have received. This may actually be the most difficult part of the process because we have biases and attitudes that we may not even know exist. These can influence how we perceive what we hear.

Selective perception may occur when our interpretation is biased by self-defensiveness. We think the other person is attacking us and we counter-argue defensively rather than objectively listening to what is said. We're thinking, "How dare you compare me to him . . ." instead of really listening.

A related reason for selective perception occurs when we feel more competent or expert than the person who is talking. We may discount what the person says because we think we know better. For example, we may not objectively consider the words of our parents because we think they simply have no idea what it is like to be a young adult in the twenty-first century. So anything they say is colored in our mind by their lack of expertise about our life. Such selective perception also takes place in classrooms if we don't think our instructor is competent, or at our jobs if we believe our employer doesn't know the task as well as we do. Again, the outcome is that we interpret their words differently based on the fact that we believe we have more knowledge.

Stereotypes we may hold, even if we are not conscious of them, influence how we listen to information. We may hold images of what a certain gender, ethnic group, religious organization, or even occupation is like. Then when we hear messages from someone in that group, we interpret them according to our stereotypic beliefs. ("I didn't know a Catholic priest would find that funny." "I'm surprised a Japanese person would talk like that.")

We often experience selective perception based on the specific words people choose. The words, or their pronunciations, trigger associated attitudes and beliefs. For example, if you hear a speaker use a racial slur in casual language, or hear someone pronounce words a certain way (e.g., saying "tom-ah-toe" rather than "tom-ay-toe"), that may cause you to perceive the message differently. Or, the source might employ sexual innuendoes, suggestive phrasing and words, or visually intense descriptive language about violence. Some sources refer to this as using emotion laden words—words that heighten our emotional responses and disrupt our processing of the information.

We may also selectively perceive messages depending on our liking for the source. If we like the source we may interpret their words positively or as nonoffensive. But if we already have a bad image of them, we tend to perceive almost anything they say in a negative light—as offensive, insulting, deceptive, only for their own purposes. Either strong liking or disliking of the source may color the way we interpret messages when we listen to them.

These are just a few examples of how selective perception may occur in the listening process, how we may *hear what we want to hear*. Distorted interpretations are so common that it is a wonder we ever understand anyone fully. (Maybe we don't!) However, by being aware of potential sources of selective perception you can focus your listening and at least try to hear messages objectively.

Problems with Listening: Barriers We Construct

Listening necessitates active involvement of the receiver. The receiver must do cognitive work to perceive, interpret, and understand the message. We often find that people experience habitual problems with the skill of listening: problems such as pseudolistening, daydreaming, lack of interest, time concerns, and anxiety.

Pseudolistening

If you ask teachers how they know whether their students are listening to them, they'll tell you that the students sit up, look at them, and avoid doing other things (such as talking to others or doing other work). But if you ask students, many will tell you that they can *appear* to be listening to someone even when they are not. This is called *pseudolistening*. It is false listening, giving the appearance of being actively involved—even down to appropriately timed head nods—even when the mind is far away. This illustrates that you must have motivation and decide to listen. Physical elements can help the process, but more is needed.

Information Load

Part of the problem with effective listening is that we can process information so much faster than we typically receive it. Humans are capable of processing anywhere from 400 to 600 words per minute. But the typical speaker talks at only about 150 words per minute, and often much more slowly than that in conversations. So what do we do with the rest of the time/processing space? Hmmmmm. . . . We *daydream,* we "space out," we go somewhere else in our minds to make use of that processing capacity.

Now that might not be so bad, because we do have so much capability to receive and process information. But the problem is that we don't come back and pay attention to the information at hand. As a result, we miss much of the content because we were thinking about something else.

In addition, we can often listen to two things at once. We are capable of processing in multiple channels. Studies have been conducted examining divergent task instructions coming into each ear through a headset (e.g., you're being told to look for errors in a manuscript in the left ear while listening to music and trying to recognize the words in the right ear). The research reveals that people *can* do this. We can listen to two different things at once. Much depends on the difficulty of the two tasks: As the material becomes more difficult and complex, we make more mistakes.

How does this translate to relationships? If you have ever tried to listen to your partner discussing his or her feelings while you are reading the breakfast cereal box and listening to the news at the same time, or listen to your father "lecture about school" while you're wearing a headset and insisting you can hear him through the music . . . , well, you get the picture. As we divert more of our listening attention to other things, we have less capacity to attend to and process information that people are giving to us. Often this may be quite important information, at least to the success of a relationship. So diverting our attention both by listening to multiple sources simultaneously and by daydreaming is a major cause of ineffective listening.

Other Orientation

A significant barrier to effective listening in our society is that the status quo is not listener-oriented. Unlike some other cultures, we tend to strongly value the source, such as an entertainer, more than the effective receiver, or the listener. For example, both Oprah and Larry King are entertainers who supposedly listen actively to the celebrities they have on their shows. But they are actually paid for their interesting comments, questions, and dialogue—that is, their sending ability is perceived as more important than their listening skill. Our society is simply not very listener-oriented.

One of the outcomes of this status quo is that when we listen it is not "our" agenda or stories. We may feel less valued as a listener than as a source. We would rather be the center of attention, the storyteller. If we're in the listening role, we have to focus on the other, which may not be as interesting or pertinent for us. We get bored. When we get bored, we turn off our listening.

Time-Consuming

Listening is *time-consuming*. We may not always listen effectively to our partners because it takes valuable time that we might want to devote to something else (such as watching MTV? reading chapters for class? playing with your dog or cat?).

In fact, finding a receptive listener may be so rare today that when people recognize an effective and willing listener, they really open up. When people find out what a sympathetic attentive listener you are, you may find yourself with friends that you didn't know existed self-disclosing to you. Friends of friends, neighbors in apartment complexes or residence halls, or individuals you meet in the mall may begin opening up to you. In some ways this is great, but it does take time. As a result, some people may essentially train themselves to be poor listeners. They may disregard much of what people try to say to them simply to avoid demands on their time.

Anxiety about Listening

Situational Anxiety. Have you ever been in a social setting where someone is introduced to you, you find the person interesting and talk with him or her for awhile, and then you realize that you cannot remember the person's name? Now what do you do? Weren't you listening when she said her name? Didn't you care? In reality you were probably really trying to listen because getting to know this person *was* important to you. But a certain amount of situation anxiety interfered with your processing of that information and now you cannot recall the name.

Many times when we are introduced to someone, we are actively thinking about how this person will react to us. What will he say? What are we going to say to create a favorable impression? Sometimes we're worried that we may do something and make a fool of ourselves. (Well, calling someone by the wrong name certainly won't create a favorable first impression!) What is really occurring is that we are anticipating the next stage of the interaction rather than focusing on the present stage. This is also common when we are introduced as a speaker or to receive an award. We don't remember listening to any of the information that occurs immediately before we are "on stage"—whether it's a real stage or simply the focus of attention in a one-to-one interaction. We are nervous about our "performance."

Anxiety is incompatible with effective listening because the information-processing capacity that could be devoted to interpretation of information about the other person is diverted to worry about ourselves. One way to counteract this barrier is to focus on the *other person* rather than yourself. We may not get rid of all the nervousness, but it can be alleviated. (Hints about remembering people's names: Repeat the name right after you have been introduced, and then use it regularly in the interaction; if you *do* forget the name, it's better to ask directly what the name is early in your conversation rather than to wait until hours later when you're saying good night. So as soon as you realize you don't know the name, ask the person to repeat it. Of course, this won't help much if you have to ask three times in one conversation.)

High Trait Receiver Anxiety.   All of us have experienced situational nervousness or anxiety about an immediate listening situation as described above. But some people have high levels of *trait receiver anxiety,* which is continuing, enduring apprehension about receiving information. Wheeless initially defined receiver apprehension as "the fear of misinterpreting, inadequately processing, and/or not being able to adjust psychologically to messages sent by others" (1975, p. 263). What this means is that some people regularly worry about their listening to such an extent that they end up not being able to recall information. The anxiety interferes with the information processing either at the time of hearing the information or when they are asked to recall it.

Problems brought on by Receiver Apprehension.   As you can imagine, being anxious when in the listener role brings on problems. Along with the discomfort of apprehension, people may miss information, seem nonresponsive, or even appear to be unmotivated because they cannot remember what was said. Employers don't think highly of receiver-apprehensive employees—although the employer may not realize what is the actual cause of the lower evaluation.

Apprehensive listeners often miss crucial directions for a task, and as a result do more poorly on tests. (It never fails that in large lecture classes, some students fail to write in the correct initial information in the correct boxes, resulting in lost scores and mis-scored tests. Is this because they are stupid? No. They were probably so nervous about getting started with the test that they simply misheard or misperceived directions.)

Apprehension about listening is probably lower with a relational partner or close family member. We tend to be more comfortable in all areas of discussion with close friends, but the apprehension may still be present and work to detract from listening effectiveness. So at this point, you may wonder how can you find out if you are high trait listening anxious. Wheeless (1975) developed the most widely used assessment of receiver apprehension; it is readily available and easy to use.

Behaviors Associated with Listening Competence

Truly effective listening involves both nonverbal and verbal communication behaviors. First we will look at how you can physically get ready to listen more effectively. When you decide you really need to listen to your partner, do these things.

Getting Ready to Listen—SOLER

SOLER is an acronym standing for behaviors you can do that will enhance your readiness to listen to a friend, teacher, or family member.

S = Face the person **squarely**.	Orient your body toward the person; don't look over your shoulder or turn away.
O = Keep an **open** body position.	Remove obstacles and barriers such as tables, piles of books, other work, or whatever might be between you and the other person.
L = **Lean** toward the person.	Close up the space between you by leaning inward. This also reduces the space and minimizes external distractions.
E = Maintain **eye contact**.	Look directly at the person. This also reduces distractions because you aren't processing any other type of visual information.
R = **Relax**.	Anxiety interferes with processing of information, so try to be calm, relaxed, and focused on the interaction.

If you think of being SOLER with someone, this will guide you to specific physical actions that improve the likelihood that you actually *will* pay attention to what the speaker is saying. Now what can you do verbally to enhance listening?

Verbal Backchanneling

This is more than just mindless head-nodding and mumbling "mm-hmm." When you give verbal cues that indicate active listening, you also become more involved yourself, you're processing information more fully, and you heighten your listening effectiveness. Here are some suggestions for more effectively encouraging your partner to talk by using *verbal backchanneling*.

[*Warning!* If you do all of these positive listening behaviors when people are talking to you, they will probably talk to you more often. Be careful! They may actually open up to you. You could develop a close relationship here.]

1. *Ask questions.* As openings come up in the dialogue, ask questions such as "what happened next?" or "what did you do after that?" or "how

did that happen?" This form of backchanneling shows that you are interested in hearing more about whatever topic is being discussed.

2. *Clarify or use illustrations to help the speaker.* Sometimes things become clearer if we add our own brief examples. "You mean like the time we were in Miami and . . ." "Yes, my mother says things like that in front of people all the time."

3. *Vary the verbal response.* Don't just say "uh-huh" or "I see" repeatedly. It makes you sound like a bad psychiatrist from an old movie.

4. *Don't interrupt the speaker, but avoid total silence.* Don't just sit there like a frog, get more involved in the conversation than that.

5. *Give encouragement.* Words of encouragement stated as the speaker is talking show that you are listening. Saying, "What a great idea" or "We could do that" communicates your engagement both with the topic and with the friend.

6. *Check your perception.* This is a very important listening skill because it clarifies what the speaker said, as well as convincing him or her that you are indeed listening. Perception checking basically involves paraphrasing what the other said and restating it in your own words.

Perception Checking

Perception checking is making sure you understand what the other person is trying to communicate. You are also offering understandable feedback on the message you received. Don't jump to the conclusion that you understand, because many times we have totally misperceived the message. This can also save fights, as well as misunderstandings.

Perception checking is *not* simply asking for clarification, nor is it answering the question or responding to the statements. Perception checking slows the conversational process down so that everyone understands the meanings. For example, if a supervisor tells you that you "aren't working hard enough," you might jump into defensiveness and deny it before finding out exactly what he or she means. Maybe what your boss really means is that you are spending too much time on the wrong tasks, but you may have jumped to the conclusion that you're being called "lazy."

Paraphrase what you think the person said back to him or her before going on. Put it in your own words; don't just repeat what was said. Why? Think of it this way: You have just told your significant other "I love you" for the first time. He or she responds, "Oh, you love me?" Might you get ticked and respond, "Isn't that what I just said!"

Or, you tell your parents, "I need more money" and they come back with, "Are you saying you need more money?" Of course! Merely repeating the same words back to someone doesn't get you more information and may get you into an argument.

Sometimes the process of perception checking is called *reflecting* back to the speaker. Reflective listening requires frequent perception checking. For example: A professor says to you, "This paper doesn't look like your usual work." Now you might become defensive, think she is accusing you of cheating, and reply angrily. Then you find out she was trying to compliment you on the exceptionally good work you did on the assignment.

Another example might be when your romantic partner discloses to you and says, "I'm ready for a more serious relationship." You could jump right into it and blurt out, "Me too! I think you're fantastic, the hottest person I've ever known, and I want to spend the rest of my life with you!" And then you find out that your partner was going to conclude by saying, ". . . but not with you." If you perception-check, you might avoid such embarrassing relational moments.

Why Paraphrasing Works

Why can't you just ask people what they mean when they say or do something? For example, why can't you just say, "What do you mean by that?" Well, there are several reasons.

First, that's insulting. When your relational partners say something to you, they think they're being perfectly clear. So if you repeatedly ask them what they mean, they will probably get offended—or think you are a moron.

Second, direct questioning of what people mean to say may provoke anxiety in them. The anxiety or nervousness about speaking with you, or about the topic of conversation, may be why they're not open and clear in the first place. It may be difficult for friends or partners to come right out and tell you that you are smothering them in the relationship, or that they think they are ready for a more committed relationship with you. So they beat around the bush, are nervous and tentative, and are unclear about what they really mean. Perception checking can get at the real meaning without raising their anxiety.

Third, your partner may be unaware of how to better state the message. They are saying it as clearly as they know how. If you just ask directly what they are talking about, they may not be able to say it any more clearly. For example, if your friend says to you she is "feeling rotten," she may not know any more descriptive words to explain her emotions. By perception checking and paraphrasing as a listener, you are helping her frame the message. So when you respond, "you mean you're sick to your stomach?" that helps clarify for both of you.

And finally, while we may hate to think of this aspect, our conversational partner may be lying to us. Perception checking may be a way to find out indirectly whether the individual is being honest, and what the person is actually talking about.

We will return to the skill of perception checking throughout this book because it is such an important feature in self-disclosure, managing conflict, and many other aspects of interpersonal communication.

Nonverbal Sensitivity as a Form of Listening

"Listening" for Nonverbal Cues

In Chapter 4 we discussed nonverbal sensitivity, but it is also important to bring it up here because paying attention and "listening" for nonverbal cues tie in so closely with listening for verbal information. Much of the information transmitted in interpersonal relationships is transmitted through nonverbal channels. Thus, people who are savvy conversationalists look at *how* the message is sent as well as the content of the message. If you look at your partner when he or she is talking, you will pick up a lot of meanings. You might notice her facial expression and whether she is nervous or relaxed. There may be a flush to his face, possibly indicating anger or frustration. When she avoids eye contact, might that mean she is lying to you or could it just be that she is nervous or embarrassed? What is the vocal tone? Confident? Impatient? Sensual?

Other parts of the body offer cues to "listen to" as well. Watch what your partner does with her or his hands. Your partner might have postural cues that can help you interpret what he or she is saying. Does he seem to want to get closer to you by leaning in, or does he appear to want to put distance between the two of you? When people lean away, turn away slightly, or repeatedly step back when you are interacting with them, these are signs that they want to be further away—even though they may not be saying that directly with words.

"Listening" to nonverbal cues can help you avoid mistakes with others. It might help you to distinguish between sexual cues and platonic, friendship cues. It could help you to tell when a topic is really, really important to your partner, and help avoid fights because you don't pay enough attention to him or her. If you have ever heard your partner say, "You haven't been listening to me!" then you need to work on this skill.

Nonverbal Perception Checking

Nonverbal perception checking is a special form of assuring that you understand the conversational partner's meaning. Often nonverbal cues go unchecked and we assume what we see or hear in people's voices is what they really mean. We sort of notice the nonverbal element, but don't bring it into consciousness. In addition, speakers are often totally unaware of how they are coming across to others nonverbally. So, when you nonverbally perception-check, you bring into the discussion how you view them as responding nonverbally. You directly address the nonverbal element of the conversation.

For example, you hear anger and frustration in your roommate's voice as he discusses his romantic partner—even though he isn't openly stating that. You nonverbally perception-check by responding, "You sound angry about that." This gives him an opportunity to examine how he might truly feel about the situation.

Or another type of nonverbal cue could occur when you are disclosing your sexual desires to your partner. Even though she doesn't say anything, you notice her nonverbal cues and say, "You're looking kind of uncomfortable right now." You need to clarify what she is feeling. This too could prevent awkward, embarrassing relational moments later on.

We sometimes hear that "actions speak louder than words." By perception-checking the nonverbal cues we directly examine whether those "actions" we observe are intentional and have meaning for the source. This constitutes another aspect in the entire process of increasing your listening competence.

Conclusions

You *can* improve your listening, but you have to be aware that listening is not a simple, passive activity. It's a skill composed of attention, reception, and perception, as complex as any other communicative activity. (In other words, listening is not a natural ability that some people have and others do not.) To improve your relational listening, *you* need to make the decision.

You may need to adapt your surroundings or your posture so that you can attend more fully to what is being said. You will benefit and gain more information by watching nonverbal expressions and other cues that help you interpret what is really meant in the conversation. Be aware that your listening may be biased, meaning that you tend to distort or twist the perceptions. That is, what you are hearing may not be what the source is intending.

One thing you can be sure of: If you make the effort to become a better relational listener, your friends will notice it, they will appreciate it, and your relationships will improve.

If you are interested in listening as an area of study, you're not alone. There is an organization called the International Listening Association, which is affiliated with the field of communication. They meet annually to present research and discuss issues revolving around the process of effective listening. Look for them on the Web.

R E F E R E N C E S   A N D
R E C O M M E N D E D   R E A D I N G S

Baron, R., David, J., Brunsman, B., & Inman, M. (1997). Why listeners hear less than they are told: Attentional load and the teller-listener extremity effect. *Journal of Personality and Social Psychology, 72,* 826–838.

Bostrom, R. (1990). *Listening behavior: Measurement and application.* New York: Guilford Press.

Buczek, T., (1981). Sex biases in counseling: Counselor retention of the concerns of a female and male client. *Journal of Counseling Psychology, 28,* 13–21.

Cooper, L., & Buchanan, T., (1999). Interrater agreement in judgments of listening competency: An item-based analysis of the Organizational Listening Survey. *Communication Research Reports, 16,* 48–54.

Cross, S., & Madson, L. (1997). Models of the Self: Self-construals and gender. *Psychological Bulletin, 122,* 5–37.

Preiss, R., Wheeless, L., & Allen, M. (1990). Potential cognitive processes and consequences of receiver apprehension: A meta-analytic review. In M. Booth-Butterfield (Ed.), *Communication, cognition, and anxiety* (pp. 155–172). Newbury Park, CA: Sage.

Wheeless, L. (1975). An investigation of receiver apprehension and social context dimensions of communication apprehension. *The Speech Teacher, 24,* 261–268.

STUDENT RECEIVER ANXIETY SCALE

Respond to each of these questions about how much this describes you, using a five-point scale.

Strongly Agree	Agree	Uncertain or Sometimes	Disagree	Strongly Disagree
5	4	3	2	1

_____ 1. When I am listening I feel nervous about missing information.

_____ 2. I worry about being able to keep up with the material presented in lecture classes.

_____ 3. Sometimes I miss information in class because I am writing down the notes.

_____ 4. I feel tense and anxious when listening to important information.

_____ 5. I am concerned that I won't be able to remember information I've heard in lectures or discussions.

_____ 6. Although I try to concentrate, my thoughts sometimes become confused when I'm listening.

_____ 7. I worry that my listening skill isn't very good.

_____ 8. I regularly can't remember things that I have just been told.

Scale Descriptive Statistics:

Mean = 22 SD 6

Reliability = .83

High Classroom Listening Anxiety = 28 or Higher

Low Classroom Listening Anxiety = 16 or Lower

PERCEPTION CHECKING AS A SKILL

Perception checking is when you check your understanding of what someone has said with the intent of the communicator. You compare your perception to the communicator's perception of what he or she was trying to say.

   Perception-check the following statements. In groups, first each person write down a paraphrase about what the sender is saying. Think of it as if someone said this to you. After you have a perception check for each statement, compare what you wrote with that of others in your group.

1. I am so excited about the end of the semester!

   In other words . . .

2. My mother is just sickening.

   In other words . . .

3. I'm feeling stressed out in this relationship.

   In other words . . .

4. Papers can be turned in early but not late.

   In other words . . .

5. I want our relationship to move to another level.

   In other words . . .

6. I think you were cheating on the test.

   In other words . . .

7. You always think you're too good for my friends.

   In other words . . .

13 Understanding and Communicating Emotions

OBJECTIVES

Emotions are key to our well-being. The understanding and communication of emotions is key to our well-being in relationships. Because jealousy can be so destructive in relationships, this chapter provides specific ideas on how to recognize the emotion of jealousy, as well as how to cope with it in yourself or others.

As a first step in dealing with your emotions, you need to understand the following.

1. Describe the components of emotions.

2. Explain five of the seven characteristics of emotions and use examples to illustrate each.

3. The model "own it, name it, locate it" helps us to communicate our feelings. Describe the process and create two emotional communication examples using the model.

4. List at least three alternative descriptive terms for these feelings: (a) afraid, (b) concerned about the relationship, (c) challenged.

5. Describe three different sources of jealousy.

6. Be able to recognize different sources of jealousy when given a depiction of an interaction.

7. Discuss four factors within the individual that tend to increase the experience of jealousy.

8. Explain three ways males and females have been found to differ in their experience of relationship jealousy.

9. Describe why these differences might develop.

10. Use illustrations to explain the three major productive ways of coping with jealousy.

CHAPTER OUTLINE

Components of Emotions

Characteristics of Emotions

Affective Orientation

Effective Communication of
Emotions: Own It, Name It, Locate It
 Assistance in "Naming" Emotions
 Words to Describe Emotions

A Specific Emotion: Jealousy
 Sources of Jealousy
 Individual Factors in the Experience
  of Jealousy
 Differences in Jealousy among Men
  and Women
 Coping with Jealousy

Have you ever been so furious that you couldn't think straight? Or have you ever seen someone crying so hard that they were incoherent? To most of us, emotions may seem to be quite unexplainable and unpredictable phenomena. They may seem to "just happen" to us. Exactly what emotions *are* is still a matter of great debate, but there are several components of the phenomenon that can help us to better understand the process.

Components of Emotions

All emotions involve a *physiological* component. Due to changes in brain activation, our body readies itself to confront some situation—either real or imagined. This often involves increased heart rate, respiration, and blood pressure. Such increases in activation within the body are what may cause us to feel heated, or to become flushed.

The changes in physiological activation lead to *nonverbal manifestations.* Sometimes this may include muscle tension—for example, the rigidity we feel when riding a roller coaster or clenching our fists in anger. Sometimes it is the flushed appearance as blood rises to the surface of the skin, or the pallor as blood vessels constrict and keep blood away from the surface of the skin.

A third component of emotion is the *cognitive interpretation* of events. It is not clear exactly when cognitive labeling of an emotion takes place. In some circumstances we seem to interpret arousal according to situational cues, but at other times the type of brain activation and chemicals emitted lead to the experience of specific feelings. We do know that for the emotion to really occur and have impact, people must have thoughts and cognitive responses to identify the process.

If people only have a cognitive label but are not activated, they will experience "as if" emotions. This has been demonstrated in some stroke patients or patients with brain lesions who have damage to certain parts of the brain. They may recognize a situation as sad, but not *feel* sad. They may note that a certain experience should produce excitement or anger, but report that they don't really feel that way. Conversely, if certain portions of the brain responsible for labeling are damaged, people may find themselves weeping, but not know why. Or they may experience rage but be unable to explain it.

Thus, for people to experience true emotions there must be at least two factors involved. There must be some physiological arousal and there must be a reasonable cognitive interpretation of the event. Either factor by itself will not produce full emotional responding.

From a communication standpoint, we have to recognize and label the emotion before we can communicate it to a relationship partner. Thus, the more we know about our own emotional responding, and that of others, the better communicators we will be in this area of our interpersonal relationships.

Characteristics of Emotions

First, emotions are *transient* and volatile. This means they may change quickly. They arise rapidly, but they also disperse rapidly. People don't stay really angry at a person for very long without repeated cognitive reminders about how unfair, unpleasant, uneducated, and so on, that person is. So if your boyfriend or girlfriend *stays* angry with you, it's because he or she is thinking repeatedly about what you have done.

Emotions are also very *conditionable.* It is extremely easy to cause an emotion to be linked with a set of circumstances and thus be conditioned to occur. For example, the joy toddlers exhibit when they see a birthday cake with candles, or the fear youngsters experience after a dog snarls and lunges at them can be very easily linked to later events and then generalized to other situations. Students and adults who are very nervous with the opposite sex often recall a specific event in which they were humiliated, embarrassed, or even frightened that was the beginning of their anxiety.

When you are experiencing an emotion, you are aware of the *intensity* of the feeling. All emotions have some strength. You could feel slightly irritated or "mad as hell." Students might feel mildly excited about going on a field trip, or they could be out of their minds with ecstasy.

Sometimes when we experience a very low intensity emotion, we think of it as neutral—almost as if there were no emotion at all. Interestingly, some people are quite unaware of their emotions unless the feeling is very strong. They tend to orient to and follow their rational thoughts or facts in interaction, whereas other people who are more affectively oriented are very attuned to their internal experience of emotions even when the emotions are not intense.

Emotions vary in *quality*. That is, we experience some emotions as negative (we'd rather not go through that again, e.g., grief, depression, anger) and some emotions as positive and enjoyable (e.g., contentment, excitement, happiness). Although counselors sometimes tell clients, "There are no good or bad emotions, it all depends on how you act on them," clearly there are some feelings that tend to be more troublesome and counterproductive than others.

Although we may not know precisely what an emotion *is*, we do know that emotions are different from cognitions or thoughts. The internal processes are different. Some people tend to be more emotional, and others tend to be more cognitive. Internally, different parts of the brain are activated when we experience an emotion than when we are having thoughts. So, one of the outcomes is that these processes sometimes interfere with each other. That is, sometimes when you are very emotionally charged up (maybe passionately in love, or maybe bitterly enraged), you don't think very straight. This is very important for relationships. The more emotional you are, the less thoughtful you might be about your decisions.

Although emotions don't always translate directly to behavior, they do *motivate behavior*. You may (although not always) take actions as a result of the feelings you experience. People may break off a useful relationship in the heat of anger. When students cheat on tests, it's probably due to anxiety or fear of poor performance. Individuals of all ages make major life changes such as getting married, having a baby, or quitting a job based on emotional responses. Experiencing the emotion may not *make* you enact a behavior, but it certainly leads to certain behaviors.

It is important to recognize, however, that we don't act on all of our emotions all of the time. We don't run away very time we feel fear. We don't pursue a romantic relationship every time we feel physical attraction toward someone. Therefore, emotions motivate and guide behavior but they don't determine behavior.

Finally, emotions tend to be *perceived as involuntary*. We feel as if we don't have any control over our emotional reactions, that they simply occur and overwhelm us. This is particularly true of negatively valenced or very intense emotions. Otherwise, why would anyone *choose* to experience jealousy, frustration, or extreme sadness? Thus, whether or not it is actually true, our emotions seem to us to be something we cannot do anything about.

Overview and Advice

Because emotions are perceived as involuntary and transient, sometimes we are unaware of them; and because they motivate behavior, emotions can be dangerous. Remember, when you communicate your emotions to someone, you cannot take that message back. Does this mean we should repress our feelings? No. It means that we need to be aware of ourselves and how we are feeling.

We have to communicate our feelings responsibly if we want to build and maintain relationships. When we say to someone, "I feel disgusted by you!" is this what we really mean? Maybe, maybe not. But now that it has been expressed, it's out there and you can't erase that message.

The best advice is taking two steps. First, we need to examine our own emotions and get some practice at understanding what we are feeling before we blurt it out. Second, we need to know the most descriptive cognitive labels (terms) for the specific emotions in order to encode those specific feelings and communicate them to our relationship partners.

Affective Orientation

As mentioned previously, some people are aware of their emotions and consider their emotional feelings when deciding what to do. Other people are more cognitively oriented. They don't trust their emotions, relying instead on facts, statistics, and concrete figures. This predisposition to use emotions as information is termed *affective orientation* (AO), how much we are aware of and use our emotions as information in our lives.

For example, if you are someone who rejects how you feel and persists with the "logical" course of action when you meet people, you are probably lower on affective orientation. People who are highly affectively oriented can recall more emotional episodes and terms. They follow their "gut level" reaction to situations.

But what is the impact of AO on relationships and communication? Well, research in this area is fairly new, but here are some recent findings.

1. Relationships tend to be more satisfactory if at least one person is high in AO.
2. Females tend to be more affectively oriented than males, but not always.
3. There seem to be some family links with AO. That is, parents who are higher in AO tend to foster that trait in their children as well. And vice versa.
4. Affectively oriented people tend to be more flexible in their communication, more able to adapt to changes.
5. Higher AO people tend to be more conversationally sensitive to others, aware of undercurrents in interactions.

This is an area in need of more research. Any ideas? Volunteers?

Effective Communication of Emotions: Own It, Name It, Locate It

If the appropriate disclosure of our emotions is positive for relationships, how do we go about disclosing them? We want to communicate emotions responsibly, so that we don't just blurt out the wrong thing and ruin the relationship. One way to communicate our emotions is a model called *Own It, Name It, Locate It.*

"Owning" an emotion means making it clear that the emotion is yours. You are *taking responsibility for your own emotions*, and not blaming others by saying, "You make me feel. . . ." This communicates that you understand where the emotion comes from. You verbally communicate this ownership by prefacing your emotional statements with "I feel" or "I am feeling," attributing the emotion to yourself.

The second step of the model involves a clear *labeling* of the emotion. You express and label what you are feeling—suspicious, fulfilled, exuberant, discontent, lusty. Now that you are aware that you are feeling the emotions, you need to apply emotion words to communicate more clearly what they are. You need an emotional vocabulary. Some people are very out of practice at this skill. They seem to have an emotional vocabulary of about four words—good, bad, happy, and sad. If they want to communicate anything more complex than that, they don't have the labels to do it. It's like trying to tell someone what color you want your car to be, but you can't describe the color. In relationships, having a limited vocabulary of feeling terms can be a disadvantage when you are trying to communicate how you feel to your partner.

The final step in this model of expressing your feelings is to locate the emotion. At this point you need to describe to your partner *the conditions under which you feel this emotion.* You locate the emotion in time and situation for them. The more specifically you can describe how, when, where, and under what circumstances you feel the emotion, the clearer it will be for your relationship partner. For example, you might say, "I feel disappointed when we make plans and then you change your mind." Or, "I am thrilled (excited, stoked, etc.) because our football team is doing so well!"

As you can see from these examples, effective communication of your emotions depends greatly on how well you understand yourself and your feelings. If you cannot determine how you feel or what you need in the relationship well enough to verbally describe it to your trusted partner, how can you expect this person to read your mind and interact with you as you would like him or her to do? Self-understanding and awareness is a prerequisite for effective communication in relationships. But once you do understand what is going on emotionally within you, then using such models of verbal interaction can help you improve your communication patterns.

Assistance in "Naming" Emotions

Some people are not effective at communicating their emotions because they don't have "enough words" to describe what is going on with them. They have the motivation to express emotions. They want to figure things out with a friend, roommate, lover, or family member, but they need help in finding the specific words (cognitive labeling) that will best communicate how they're feeling to a partner.

The list below gives numerous examples of emotion words that are useful in relational interactions. Of course, you can't carry this book with you and pull these pages out as a reference guide when you get into an emotional situation. However, these examples can help you expand your "emotional vocabulary" and avoid overusing the feelings "good, bad, happy, and sad."

Words to Describe Emotional Feelings

When you are feeling **happy** in the interaction . . . fortunate, elated, joyous, contented, satisfied, ecstatic, pleased, radiant

At times when you are **confused** by circumstances . . . frustrated, wondering, stymied, thwarted, clueless, at a loss, befuddled, turned upside down

When you are **angry** . . . irritated, annoyed, intense, vicious, furious, bitter, resentful, mad, ticked off, frustrated, grumpy, put off, enraged

If you feel **sad** . . . grieving, disappointed, hurt, depressed, down in the dumps, down, morose, pitiful, wretched

Expressing feelings of **contentment** . . . satisfied, fulfilled, hopeful, at ease, restful, relaxed

When you might be feeling **hemmed in** by a relationship . . . smothered, closed in, crowded, constricted, like you can't breathe, overwhelmed, suffocated, stifled, repressed

Someone is **sexy** . . . hot, wanting, lusty, flirtatious, seductive, warm, tingly, loving, sensual, desirable, alluring, provocative, arousing, erotic

Telling someone how much you **love** them or something about them . . . adore, cherish, admire, respect, feel affection for, desire, idolize, appreciate

When you are **lonely** . . . sad, feeling hollow, alone, isolated, far away from you, distanced, can't make connection, solitary, not understood, unconnected

You feel **used** in the relationship . . . stupid, like a fool, abused, taken advantage of, dirty, low, debased, belittled, degraded, demoralized

If you feel **disappointed** . . . let down, disillusioned, sorry, disenchanted, failure

If you are **excited** by something . . . antsy, anxious, hyped, thrilled, elated, turned on, aroused, stimulated

You are **not believing** your partner . . . uncertain, distrustful, leery, unsure, wary, suspicious, doubtful, wondering, skeptical

You think your relationship is **going nowhere** and you feel . . . disillusioned, tired, dissatisfied, frustrated, disappointed, unfulfilled, resentful, at a dead end, lost, bored

You feel **valued** by your partner . . . loved, worthwhile, respected, admired, protected, contented, admired, prized, esteemed

If you are **disgusted** by something . . . sickened, revolted, turned off, repulsed, wretched, nauseated, scornful, repelled

You're feeling **fearful** about something . . . worried, uncertain, afraid, scared, at a loss, nervous, full of dread, alarmed, panicked

You are **hopeful** about the future . . . encouraged, upbeat, optimistic, promising, cheerful, confident, bright, great, inspired

A Specific Emotion: *Jealousy*

Relational jealousy is a phenomenon that can have a very negative impact on communication in all types of relationships. We have all probably experienced the emotion of jealousy at some time or another, but when jealousy is being experienced, it creates negative affect and significant barriers to communication. Sometimes people may realize how negative their jealousy is but feel helpless to change. First we need to understand why people feel jealous.

Sources of Jealousy

Jealousy is a reaction to loss or threat of loss. Notice that the possible loss doesn't have to be real, but only perceived and the person will respond with jealousy. There are three distinct sources of jealousy: time, opportunity, and third person.

The threat of a *third person* breaking up your special relationship is probably the source of jealousy most people think of first. When this type of jealousy occurs the individual resents potential intrusion into the twosome, whether it be "best friends," work partners, or lovers. This source of jealousy is consistent with the old saying "two's company and three's a crowd." Even on the job, employers may observe such jealousy when employees' established friendships develop and change. The attraction or attention to a new person may be the cause of quarrels and bitter feelings that interfere with work performance. It could happen with new roommates, and is a very common source of problems in romantic relationships. The underlying fear here is that the relationship will be lost to someone else.

A different source of negative feelings is jealousy over *time*. In this case, people are upset if their partners spend too much time doing things other than being with them. This may be due to time spent at work, at basketball practice, at home with parents, playing computer games, or even working on a hobby. The jealousy is not over competition with another person for the relationship—for example, the basketball teammates are not the obstacle; it's the activity itself. Time is a finite resource and when you aren't spending it with *me*, it's my loss.

The third source of jealousy concerns the loss of *opportunity*. Here people are jealous that others had the opportunity to *do* something that they didn't. Your friend gets to go to Costa Rica for spring break while you go back to your hometown. A friend may be jealous because you have the opportunity to meet and work with an eminent professional in graduate school. Because of a wide variety of circumstances (socioeconomic status, timing, ability levels, location, etc.) some people will encounter opportunities to do things that others won't. For example, your chances to break into a movie career are certainly greater if you happen to live in southern California than if you live in West Lafayette, Indiana. Thus, jealousy over opportunity may lead to negative interactions.

Individual Factors in the Experience of Jealousy

Everyone isn't equally jealous. Some individuals have a difficult time recalling an incident when they were really jealous, whereas others feel jealous on a regular basis. So what makes some people more jealous than others?

One of the underlying components of jealousy seems to be lower self-esteem. People who have low self-esteem can easily envision loss and cannot conceive of anyone preferring them. In contrast, people with higher self-esteem would figure that even if there were a threat of loss, they could compete successfully whether it be for the relationship, additional time, or opportunities.

In a similar manner, it is easy to understand why lonely people tend to be more jealous. They have fewer or less satisfactory relationships and they tend to have lower self-esteem. Thus it is no wonder that if there is any hint of a threat of loss, the lonely person reacts with jealousy and clings to the relationship.

People who experience more jealousy also ascribe more strongly to an "ownership norm"—meaning that they feel they own or possess the relationship partner. "She's mine!" "He belongs to me!" This ownership norm is often reinforced by musical lyrics that conceptualize relational partners as possessions. On the other hand, if a person does not feel he or she "owns" a partner, and sees the partner as an independent agent capable of making choices, this person is less likely to feel jealous.

Locus of control also plays a role in jealous reactions. People with an external locus of control tend to be more jealous because they feel that interactions and outcomes are out of their control. "If he wants to choose her for the lead in the play, there's nothing I can do." People with an internal locus of control, by comparison, believe they can make things happen, influence the outcomes. If they see that a partner's time is devoted to something or someone else, they'll take action. They will try to make opportunities happen rather than waiting for circumstances or Fate to decide the issue.

People also tend to feel more jealous in a relationship if they feel insecure about the relationship itself. In such cases almost anything could threaten loss. However, if you are secure in the relationship (e.g., you've been partners for years), you will be less likely to respond with jealousy. This is one of the reasons adolescents often experience so much jealousy in relationships. Their relationships are relatively recent and often short-lived. In general, the longer your relationship has lasted, the more solid and secure you feel it is.

Finally, the person who is the most involved and interested in the relationship will be more jealous than the partner who is less interested. For the most interested person, the relationship is more important and central to his or her life. The person who cares less about the relationship will simply not be as upset if there is a chance the relationship may terminate.

Differences in Jealousy among Men and Women

Interestingly, men and women may not react to relational jealousy in the same manner. It isn't that males are more or less jealous than females, but each sex may have learned to react in different ways.

When men feel jealous they tend to react with hostility and aggression toward their partners. They get angry with them. In fact, sexual jealousy is the most frequent cause of wife-battering and killing (Shackelford & Buss, 1997). (It should also be noted that male sexual jealousy often results in harm to men too. At least one study has found that men were killed in self-defense when they accused their mates of infidelity [Daly, Wilson, & Weghorst, 1982]).

When women feel jealous they often try to be more pleasing to the partner, to be nicer to him. Whereas men might shout, "Why did you do that?" women react to the competition and try to make the relationship more rewarding by dressing up more, cooking a great dinner, or buying a little gift. When women feel jealous, they also tend to be more self-blaming and depressed than men do. "It must be some deficiency in *me* that caused him to be attracted to her."

Women also tend to use jealousy as a way of gaining attention more than men do. Rebecca, a high school junior, may feel insecure in her relationship and subsequently create a scene at the school dance to which her boyfriend will respond with jealousy to prove his love for her. Men, whether because they're less likely to feel insecure or because female partners express affection more openly, seem less likely to manipulate a situation to make their partners feel jealous.

A final way men and women react to relational jealousy differently is in their focus of concern. Different behaviors seem more destructive to the relationship. Men are most upset if they believe their partner has been sexually unfaithful ("Did you sleep with him?"), whereas women tend to be most concerned with emotional involvement ("Do you love her?").

This difference may reflect subtle biases and expectations in our culture, as well as evolutionary patterns (Buss, Larsen, Westen, & Semmelroth, 1992). For men, the most dangerous threat to the relationship comes when his partner is so involved with someone else that she has sexual relations with him. ("It must be an extremely serious problem for her to do that.") In contrast, this bias predicts that women may not be totally shocked if their male partners have sex with someone else, as long as the men's emotions are not engaged. ("If he *loves* her, then it's a major threat.") The differences in reaction seem to be traceable to how endangered vital relationship resources are due to the infidelity (see Harris, 2000).

Clearly, jealousy is one emotion that is not productive in life. We waste time being jealous, and it may ruin relationships. (Have you ever noticed how jealous communication tends to drive the other person away?) So we need to examine a few ways people might cope with their own jealousy, or be taught to handle jealous reactions from others.

Coping with Jealousy

Probably the weakest way of coping with jealousy is to do nothing. This response allows emotions or circumstances to control *you;* therefore, better coping responses involve changing something in the process. This might involve changing the self, the partner, or the relationship.

People might deal with jealousy by *changing themselves.* They might alter the way they think about the interactions or cognitively relabel the situations perceived as threatening loss. For instance, you may relabel jealousy-provoking communication as simply task-oriented interactions. The participants must communicate to get their job done. Teachers might help by discussing ownership norms, the involvement of self-concept, and so on.

Changing oneself could also mean taking direct actions. If you are jealous over opportunities that you perceive others are getting, take action to be included in those opportunities. Get to know people, become involved in areas where you see chances arising. Students may be helped in dealing with their jealousy if they can see that opportunities will be open to them in the future if they work toward them.

In some circumstances, coping with jealous reactions may involve *altering the partner's behavior*. If a high school senior thinks his girlfriend "flirts" too much, she could minimize flirtatious behavior. If a boyfriend spends too much time shooting baskets with the guys, perhaps he could agree to reduce this activity. One of the difficulties of this plan, however, is that it necessitates the nonjealous partner's cooperation in dealing with something he or she might think is a silly issue.

The third alternative for coping with jealousy is to *change the relationship*. If the expectancies aren't being met, communicate about those expectations and negotiate with the partner to alter patterns. For example, you might decide not to spend time with certain people or engage in certain jealousy-provoking activities. Often oaths, contracts, or other declarations of fidelity help assuage jealousy by changing the nature of the relationship.

Of course, an ultimate solution to jealousy would be to terminate the relationship altogether. Students could break up, cut class, avoid interaction entirely. But there are other, less drastic relational changes that can be undertaken to prevent such a conclusion. All of the solutions involve communication and the open discussion of feelings and behaviors if positive outcomes are to follow.

Conclusions

To be effective in close relationships we have to both understand our emotions and be able to express them appropriately. The first aspect includes self-awareness and labeling what your emotions feel like. Learn to recognize the feelings. The second step involves creating a vocabulary and verbal structure to describe those feelings to others (own it, name it, locate it).

We've paid special attention to an emotion that people find very difficult to deal with, and yet very frequently feel, in relationships: jealousy. Jealousy can drive people apart. It can create extreme negative affect in other areas, so we need to be aware of circumstances under which jealousy may arise. We also must remember that people tend to respond quite differently to threat of loss (whether it be loss of opportunity, time, or to a third person). Learning to deal with difficult emotions such as jealousy is absolutely necessary for the continued health of any relationship.

REFERENCES AND RECOMMENDED READINGS

Baumeister, R., & Bratslavsky, E. (1999). Passion, intimacy, and time: Passionate love as a function of change in intimacy. *Personality and Social Psychology Review, 3,* 49–67.

Booth-Butterfield, M., & Booth-Butterfield, S. (1990). Conceptualizing affect as information in communication production. *Human Communication Research, 16,* 451–476.

Booth-Butterfield, M., & Booth-Butterfield, S. (1998). Emotionality and Affective Orientation. In J. McCroskey, J. Daly, & M. Martin (Eds.), *Communication and personality: Trait perspectives* (pp. 171–189). Cresskill, NJ: Hampton Press.

Booth-Butterfield, M., & Booth-Butterfield, S. (1997). *Communication Apprehension and avoidance in the classroom.* Acton, MA: Tapestry Press.

Brehm, J. (1999). The intensity of emotion. *Personality and Social Psychology Review, 3,* 2–22.

Bringle, R., & Buunk, B. (1985). Jealousy and social behavior: A review of person, relationship, and situational determinants. In P. Shaver (Ed.), *Self, situations, and social behavior: Review of personality and social psychology* (pp. 241–264). Beverly Hills, CA: Sage.

Buss, D., Larsen, R., Westen, D., & Semmelroth, J. (1992). Sex differences in jealousy: Evolution, physiology, and psychology. *Psychological Science, 3,* 251–255.

Buss, D., & Shackelford, T. (1997). From vigilance to violence: Mate retention tactics in married couples. *Journal of Personality and Social Psychology, 72,* 346–361.

Canary, D., & Emmers-Sommer, T. (1997). *Sex and gender differences in personal relationships.* New York: Guilford Press.

Daly, M., Wilson, M., & Weghorst, S. (1982). Male sexual jealousy. *Ethology and Sociobiology, 3,* 11–27.

Fehr, B., Baldwin, M., Collins, L., Patterson, S., & Benditt, R. (1999). Anger in close relationships: An interpersonal script analysis. *Personality and Social Psychology Bulletin, 25,* 299–312.

Guerrero, L., Elvoy, S., Jorgensen, P., & Andersen, P. (1993). Hers or his? Sex differences in the experience and communication of jealousy in close relationships. In P. Kalbfleisch (Ed.), *Interpersonal communication: Evolving interpersonal relationships* (pp. 109–131). Hillsdale, NJ: Erlbaum.

Harris, C. (2000). Psychophysiological responses to imagined infidelity: The specific innate modular view of jealousy reconsidered. *Journal of Personality and Social Psychology, 78,* 1082–1091.

Salovey, P., Rothman, A., & Rodin, J. (1998). Health behavior. In D. Gilbert, S. Fiske, & G. Lindzey (Eds.), *The handbook of social psychology* (4th ed., pp. 633–683). Boston: McGraw-Hill.

Seidlitz, L., & Diener, E. (1998). Sex differences in the recall of affective experiences. *Journal of Personality and Social Psychology, 74,* 262–271.

Shackelford, T., & Buss, D. (1997). Cues to infidelity. *Personality and Social Psychology Bulletin, 23,* 1034–1045.

COMMUNICATING YOUR EMOTIONS:
Own It, Name It, Locate It

We often do not communicate our emotions responsibly and in the most effective manner. This can end up in fights, profanity, and bad feelings toward each other. As with other communication messages, communicating your emotions is a learned skill.

Using the model, rewrite these emotional messages so they are communicated responsibly. Remember that *feelings* often come out of thoughts and opinions.

I feel _____ when _____.

1. Your employer wants you to work an extra shift. Instead of saying, "No way, you inconsiderate slave-driver!" you say

2. You want to tell your roommate to clean up part of the apartment, because it's making you crazy.

3. You want to tell your romantic partner that you are becoming bored and dissatisfied in the relationship.

4. Your mother or father is very critical of your friends. Instead of "telling them off" you respond with . . .

5. Your instructor seems to be pressuring you for outside-of-class social contact. You are uncomfortable with this and suspicious of his or her motives.

6. A friend has just said some critical and hurtful things to you.

7. You think your dinner partner's eating behavior is "rude" and disgusting.

8. You believe your romantic partner may be cheating on you. You confront him or her with this.

AFFECTIVE ORIENTATION

Directions: The following statements refer to the feelings and emotions people have and how they use their feelings and emotions to guide their behavior. There are no right or wrong answers. Also realize that emotions and feelings can be positive or negative. One person can feel anger; another can feel love and tenderness. Both cases, however, are emotion. Use the following five-point scale to indicate your answer.

Strongly Agree	Agree	Uncertain	Disagree	Strongly Disagree
5	4	3	2	1

_____ 1. I use my feelings to determine what I should do in situations.

_____ 2. I listen to what my "gut" or "heart" says in many situations.

_____ 3. My emotions tell me what to do in many cases.

_____ 4. I try not to let feelings guide my actions.*

_____ 5. I am aware of and use my feelings as a guide more than others do.

_____ 6. I won't let my emotions influence how I act most of the time.*

_____ 7. I follow what my feelings say I should do in most situations.

_____ 8. Most of the time I avoid letting my emotions guide what I do.*

_____ 9. I usually let my internal feelings direct my behavior.

_____10. Usually my emotions are good predictors of how I will act.

_____11. My actions are often influenced by my awareness of my emotions.

_____12. My emotions provide me solid direction in my life.

_____13. How I act often depends on what my feelings tell me to do.

_____14. Even subtle emotions often guide my actions.

_____15. When I am aware of my emotional response, I listen to it to determine what to do.

Scoring:

1. Reverse the score for items with asterisks. (5 = 1, 4 = 2, 2 = 4, 1 = 5)

2. Sum all items.

3. Score should be between 15 and 75. Mean score = 53.

4. Low AO = ≤ 44   Moderate AO = 44–62   High AO = ≥ 62

14 Making Decisions about Relationships

Resources and Social Exchange

OBJECTIVES

Making decisions about staying in or leaving a relationship becomes increasingly difficult as the relationship becomes more integrated. However, understanding the social exchange model can help you analyze your own decisions.

1. List and explain each of six categories of resources people typically exchange in relationships: love, information, goods, services, status, money.

2. Describe the four components of the social exchange model.

3. Apply the social exchange model to explain someone who stays in a hypothetical relationship that is unrewarding.

4. Predict what happens to the value of relational rewards with repetition.

5. Explain the concept of "weighing" costs and rewards in a relationship.

6. Distinguish between exchange and communal orientations and their potential impact on a relationship.

CHAPTER OUTLINE

Resources

Social Exchange
  Rewards
  Costs
  Outcomes

Comparisons
Additional Aspects of Cost/Reward
  Assessment

Exchange versus Communal Orientation

Have you ever wondered why some people seem very content in what you would judge to be a mismatched relationship? Or have you ever shaken your head and thought about a student romance, "What does she see in him?" This chapter is all about what makes people decide to remain in or leave a relationship. We will look at what partners seek in relationships and the conditions under which they tend to be satisfied or dissatisfied, whether they are teachers and students, friends, associates, or lovers. Although the discussion will focus on one-to-one relationships, most of the information holds true for group interactions and even decisions to stay in your job or look elsewhere.

This decision-making process can, and does, occur throughout the relationship. It may be more simple and happen more quickly early in a relationship before the relationship develops and becomes complex. But we make these judgments about whether a relationship is "working" for us, whether it is worthwhile for what we are getting out of it. If the outcome is positive, we stay in the relationship. If the outcome overall is negative, we are more likely to be dissatisfied with the relationship and look for ways to end it.

Resources

Resources are aspects of ourselves or our behavior that we can offer to our relationship partners. We all have various resources. Perhaps we are good-looking and drive a great car. Maybe we are an extremely affectionate and loyal friend. Maybe we work very hard to make the relationship wonderful, exciting, and carefree for our partner. Perhaps we have the power to protect a friend; no one dares to cross us. These are all examples of *resources*. The more resources a person can provide the other in a relationship, the more popular or desirable he or she will be as a relational partner. On the other hand, if people have few valuable resources or will not offer the resources they have at their disposal, those individuals may find that fewer people want to have a relationship with them. Resources make us popular.

Categories of resources provided in relationships include love/affection, goods, services, information, status, and money.

1. *Love/affection.* Love is the least tangible but perhaps the most powerful of all the resources we exchange. Love, as a resource, is when we show others we feel positively toward them, care for them, have affection for them, and generally help them to feel secure and important.

Your relationship partners may offer this resource of love and affection in various ways, from sending notes, to telling you directly, to demonstrating love nonverbally. But we're also showing love and respect when we "stand up for" our friends and defend them to others, or talk positively about them even when they're not around. Loyalty to and respect for others are love resources, as much as the indefinable "chemistry" that occurs when people are romantically attracted to each other.

2. *Goods.* Goods are products, tangible items, that we can give to our partners. They are direct and observable. When one of your little cousins presents you with a vase she has made in class, she is sharing goods with you. When your fiancé sends you flowers or buys you gifts, that's giving you "goods." When you take a pan of brownies to a bake sale, give blood at the Red Cross blood drive, or take a bag of canned goods to a disaster relief center, you are sharing goods.

3. *Services.* Services are a bit less tangible and concrete than goods. The resource of services is *doing* something for someone else. You try to make someone's life easier. You are performing a service when you give someone a back rub, help set up a friend's computer, take out the garbage, iron a shirt, help someone move, proofread and type a paper, cut a friend's hair; the list could go on and on. Anytime you do something so that your relational partner does not have to do it, or do it when he or she cannot do it, you're offering a service.

We tend to be more selective about who we exchange services with than who we exchange goods with. For example, it's easier to convince people to provide toys for needy children at Christmas than it is to convince them to take their time to deliver those toys.

4. *Information.* Information is a very intriguing resource. When we have information as a resource it means we have knowledge or expertise that we can share with other people. The student who can share information about how to solve the biochem problems has a valuable resource. Any information that is valued can be a resource to exchange in relationships. The colleague who is an expert and is proficient in her or his job has information as a resource to share.

In addition, any person in your social network who always seems to know what's going on has the resource of information—for example, the person who talks on the phone to everyone and knows who has broken up with whom. The individual who finds out first that school will be canceled the following day due to a winter storm has the resource of information.

Information may be complex or simple: local customs, where to buy lunch, directions, or where to get your car serviced. But the value of information as a resource also depends on how important that information is perceived to be. If you can give an in-depth explanation of genealogical searches, or how a computer works, or how to select color and fabric for a quilt, but no one cares about such information, it will not be a valuable resource.

Information is also a very transient resource: It is only valuable if it is *new*. Once you know how to solve the problem or have heard the latest news, that information is no longer of value to you. Thus, for a person to maintain the resource of information, he or she must always be able to offer you something you haven't heard before or don't already know.

5. *Status.* Status is also less tangible or concrete than goods and services, because status is so much in the eye of the perceiver. People have status whenever they possess some attribute that makes them important, desirable, or enviable in the eyes of a group. This may involve direct power to grant favors (e.g., the boss). Or status may be very indirect and a function of "reflected glory" (e.g., a friend of the boss). In our society we admire people who are physically attractive, so they have high status for that reason. We may want to be seen interacting with or in a relationship with a good-looking person.

But almost anything might confer status. An excellent dancer or the toughest fighter might have high status in some groups. In most school systems, athletic prowess gives status. Famous people tend to have high status as evidenced by the numbers of people who try to get close to celebrities, regardless of their other attributes. Although money, itself, is a separate resource, in most cultures wealth also indicates high status.

Interestingly, status only tends to be a powerful resource in casual relationships, before you know the person very well. After you're well acquainted with a gorgeous, powerful, or famous person, you tend not to notice that status element. You tend to simply think of him as Ty, your friend, until other people bring it back to your attention.

6. *Money.* Money is a resource that we will exchange with almost anyone, regardless of our relational status with them. One of the reasons money is such an important relational resource is that we can use it to purchase other resources that we would not be able to provide otherwise. If we don't want to wash the car, bake a cake, or build a fence, we can pay someone to do it for us. Indeed, it hasn't been all that long ago that wealthy people could hire others to go to war in their place, or could employ a "whipping boy" who suffered the physical punishment meted out to a wealthy child.

In addition to buying status symbols, the reality is than when people have more money they can often buy better tools to achieve their objectives—everything from the fastest computers with the most memory to top-of-the-line athletic shoes. Sometimes students have more "friends" if they can pay the others' way at the movies or the bars.

In more romantic interpersonal relationships it's always said that "money can't buy love." However, we have to recognize that money can fund leisure time, exciting travel and activities, elegant clothes and gifts, and so on—all things that can enhance positive feelings. Thus, money becomes a very powerful resource because of all the other resources it can provide.

Social Exchange

Discussing provision of resources is only looking at one side of a relationship. When you are involved in a relationship with a friend, colleague, or student, there are costs as well as rewards associated with that relationship. Not only do you receive benefits from the friendship, but you have to expend energy and put up with negative aspects sometimes. You may experience good feelings and a sense of accomplishment when you tutor a student, but certainly there is also effort and work involved, that is, resources are expended. Consequently, relationships are a constant ebb and flow of resources given, resources received, and varying amounts of effort put into maintaining the relationship.

A *model of social exchange* can be quite explanatory in understanding our decisions to stay in or get out of any relationship. Social exchange has four central components that we weigh and consider: rewards, costs, outcomes, and comparison level of alternatives.

Rewards

Rewards are anything in a relationship that makes it positive or that you want repeated. Rewards could be as abstract as the security and feeling of being unique and cared for in an ongoing relationship. Or they could be as specific as those enjoyable Christmas gifts you receive, the service of having laundry done for you, or the benefits of your partner's expertise in figuring income taxes. There is tremendous range to what constitutes a reward in a relationship. Basically, anything that makes you feel good could be considered a reward.

Costs

Relationship *costs* are anything that is negative, effortful, or that you do not want repeated in a relationship. Conflict is a cost in relationships when it causes discomfort and hurt feelings. Sometimes being the provider of services is costly because you are the person who does the laundry or figures the taxes for your partner. Anytime you expend effort in maintaining your patience, explaining information, or doing tasks for others, those represent costs in the relationship. Obviously, as with rewards, some costs are greater than others. The cost of having your significant other cheating on you is no doubt a larger cost than having to wait for him or her after work. So costs and rewards carry different weights in the relationship.

Outcomes

You must consider both rewards and costs to estimate *outcomes*. If relational rewards outweigh costs the outcome is "profitable," overall positive, and more likely to be continued. On the other hand, if the costs in a relationship outweigh the rewards we are operating at a loss, so the relationship is probably dissatisfying and less likely to be continued. To illustrate, the longer a relationship operates at a loss, the more likely it will be that the partners will look to other people for friendship.

Comparisons

The estimation of whether or not a relationship should be continued is also a function of the *comparison level of alternatives*. Relational alternative comparisons may be based on (a) our past experiences with interactions in relationships or (b) our current assessment of relationship alternatives.

Past Experiences.   When we gauge our relational outcomes, we automatically compare them with those of similar relationships we've experienced or have previously observed in others. Thus if all of our other interpersonal relationships have been physically violent, then as we assess our current relationship, which is also violent, it may not seem so negative. This may partially explain why some people remain in abusive or dysfunctional relationships—their past experience is similar to the present state. In contrast, if we've had other relationships that were wonderfully fulfilling, very entertaining, and not personally costly, then our comparison level is very high and it will take a very special partner to live up to that past relationship comparison.

Current Alternatives.   We also assess our current available options when deciding to terminate or maintain a relationship. "What else is out there?" If we don't think our present relationship is rewarding, but don't see any alternatives that look more promising, we'll probably "stick it out" with our current partner. For example, your friend irritates you by frequently borrowing books and materials and giving you unrequested advice. But because there is no one else in your locale you have as much in common with, you'll probably retain that relationship. For many marital partners in rural locations there are few relational alternatives (i.e., single adults), so they are more likely to remain in a relationship even if it is not fulfilling. Similarly, teenagers may cling to their present "steady" date even when the relationship is not rewarding, for fear of not finding another partner.

On the other hand, if there are positive-appearing potential relationship partners, and we're in a nonrewarding relationship, we are more likely to terminate the "nonprofitable" relationship. Thus, if we are in a rewarding, comfortable relationship we won't typically look for something better. But if we're in a nonrewarding relationship and positive alternatives are on the horizon, we are more likely to make the transition. This is one of the reasons for the high "turnover rate" in adolescent friendships and romances.

Adolescents are in an environment where there are numerous other potential relationship partners with similar interests, backgrounds, and availability.

It should also be noted that sometimes being alone or without a partner is a viable and preferable option. If the assessment of costs and rewards is dismal, you may decide that it is more rewarding, or at least less costly, to be out of the relationship altogether—regardless of other relationship alternatives.

Additional Aspects of Cost/Reward Assessment

It would be foolhardy to believe that the social exchange model can precisely predict when a person will decide to terminate a relationship. Human relationships are too complex for that. Although social exchange is a useful tool for examination, it does have limitations.

Individual Assessment.   First, it is very difficult to predict outcomes for another person. What is rewarding or costly to the person in the relationship may not be the same to the observer. In addition, it is almost impossible to quantify or estimate exactly how rewarding a particular resource is. To some individuals security in a relationship is very heavily weighted, but to others security is only a minor aspect. Some people may be very rewarded by interacting with a high-status individual, whereas others don't think it's any big deal.

Personal Bias.   Another consideration in assessing equity or weighing the costs and rewards is biased processing. We may not always be objective and fair when we tally up our inputs and outcomes. We may conveniently forget, or be unaware of and minimize many of the benefits we receive from being in the relationship.

Anticipated Future Outcomes.   In addition, because we don't tally up our cost/reward ratio on a daily (or even weekly) basis, relationships can operate with costs outweighing rewards for quite a while. Some people have a great capacity to forego gratification. In other words, they'll suffer many costs if they perceive that there will be rewards in the future. That's one of the ways partners maintain relationships while they are physically separated. They can project to the time when they will be back together. Another example might be when one partner is in graduate school: Money may be very tight, and the partner may be stressed with little time to spend on the relationship. But they both look forward to the future when graduate school will be over and the relationship more rewarding. Therefore, a relationship that may not be rewarding at present may still be very stable because the partners are looking to the future when costs will decline or the rewards will increase. Thus, social exchange models are best applied to one's own relationships, and only cautiously used in trying to analyze relationships of those around you.

Repetition of Costs and Rewards. The exchange of resources in relationships doesn't occur in a vacuum. In ongoing relationships, various resources tend to be repeated in patterns of behavior. What happens when that irritating little gesture goes on and on? Or what happens to our valuing of a reward like physical attractiveness when it becomes a consistent part of the interaction? We also note that repetition of costs or rewards can affect the ultimate decision.

Costs. When costs are repeated, their value tends to increase—that is, they become more annoying. We may overlook it when a person eats noisily one time, but if it happens all the time that cost becomes greater. We dislike it more if a person is consistently late than if the person is late once.

On the other hand, sometimes repetition of costs is desensitizing. We may dislike someone's language at first, but then get used to it so that it is no longer a cost. If we habituate to a costly behavior (e.g., smoking, rudeness, violence), then that aspect becomes less noticeable to us.

Rewards. The repetition of rewards invariably causes their value to decline. At first it is exciting that our partner listens so closely to us. But as we converse repeatedly, we lose sight of this reward. We come to expect it, and may feel disappointed if it doesn't occur.

Similarly, if a friend sends you thoughtful cards for every occasion, you come to take it for granted. Or, if your partner is extremely attractive, you may get used to it over time, not really notice how good-looking he or she is, and view the physical attractiveness less as a reward.

Exchange versus Communal Orientation

Finally, we recognize that people do not all make decisions in the same way. As a personality characteristic some people tend to be more *exchange-oriented,* whereas others tend to be more *communally oriented.* The social exchange model applies most clearly to exchange-oriented people.

Exchange-oriented people consider quite strongly the costs and benefits of the relationship. But communally oriented people gauge a relationship in terms of what people *need* or the needs of the community. The latter people tend to give benefits without consideration of getting anything back in the relationship. For example, they may give gifts, shower the person with love, and so on, because that person really needs it. Then, they don't feel negative if the partner cannot give those resources back. In addition, communally oriented individuals are less concerned about being in someone's "debt," or putting resources back into the relationship. They worry less about how things balance out in a relationship.

It isn't clear exactly how people would get along in a close relationship if one is communally and the other exchange-oriented. In organizations, the different orientations affect job satisfaction, but research in this area tends to evaluate only one person at a time. Additional research is needed to clarify how well communally oriented and exchange-oriented people interrelate in ongoing relationships.

Conclusions

Everyone doesn't measure relationship satisfaction with the same yardstick. Sometimes you scrutinize the situation, sometimes your own needs, sometimes the capabilities of the other person. But we have developed some models that predict what people tend to consider when deciding whether a relationship is "worth it" and whether to go or stay.

Relationships entail the exchange of diverse resources (i.e., love, services, goods, information, status, money). The more resources we have to offer someone, the more desirable we tend to be in interpersonal interactions. The social exchange model predicts that we will consider four components: costs, rewards, outcomes, and comparisons of alternatives. When we judge that a relationship is more costly than it is rewarding to us, and when we have other alternatives, we'll tend to move toward getting out of the relationship. Conversely, as long as a relationship is more beneficial than costly, or if we don't perceive other alternatives for ourselves, we will tend to maintain and make the best of the relationship we have.

Individuals weigh resources differently depending on their own needs (both physical and interpersonal) and whether they are *exchange- or communally oriented* themselves. These facts make it difficult to predict why someone else would decide to maintain a relationship. But such an understanding of our own decision making is crucial.

Relationships in work settings present some particular benefits and potential costs. The next chapter focuses on these relationships and how to manage communication surrounding them to maximize rewards and minimize costs.

REFERENCES AND RECOMMENDED READINGS

Buunk, B., Doosje, B., Jans, L., & Hopstaken, L. (1993). Perceived reciprocity, social support, and stress at work: The role of exchange and communal orientation. *Journal of Personality and Social Psychology, 65*, 801–811.

Canary, D., & Stafford, L. (1993). Preservation of relational characteristics: Maintenance strategies, equity, and locus of control. In P. Kalbfleisch (Ed.), *Interpersonal communication: Evolving interpersonal relationships* (pp. 237–259). Hillsdale, NJ: Erlbaum.

Clark, M., & Reis, H. (1988). Interpersonal processes in close relationships. *Annual Review of Psychology, 39*, 609–672.

USING SOCIAL EXCHANGE

Think of a specific relationship-of-choice that you are in. Develop a list of the rewards and costs that go along with that relationship. Be as specific as possible.

Rewards for You

Costs for You

Now turn the tables. Taking the perspective of your partner, what are the rewards and costs in the relationship for *him* or *her?*

Partner's Rewards

Partner's Costs

CONSIDER THE RESOURCES

Below is a list of the six main types of resources people exchange in interpersonal relationships. After each category, list several resources that would fall within that category.

Goods

Services

Affection

Status

Information

Money

15 Relationships at Work

Just Friends, Flirting, or Harassment?

OBJECTIVES

Because most of us work outside the home for a major part of our lives, it is important to understand the complexities of interpersonal communication in the workplace. Check your knowledge with these.

1. List three reasons why it is not surprising that interpersonal relationships develop at work.

2. Explain three differences observable in interpersonal communication at work compared to social interactions.

3. Describe how platonic friendships may be positive in the workplace and how they can be negative.

4. Describe how flirting differs from sexual harassment, but how it may be perceived as harassing.

5. Describe five factors that influence whether we perceive communication messages as sexual harassment. Use examples to illustrate.

6. Be able to recognize communication patterns or situations that constitute sexual harassment.

7. Describe three of the five factors that can distinguish flirting from harassment.

8. Explain five distinct communication tactics you could employ to cope with potential harassment—without losing your job.

CHAPTER OUTLINE

Why Interpersonal Relationships
Develop in Work Settings

Differences between Work and
Social Communication

Just Friends: Platonic Relationships
at Work

What Is Flirting?

What Is Sexual Harassment?
  Male and Female Differences

Status

Specificity of Communication
  Messages

Context Expectations

Particularly Difficult Situations

Distinguishing between Flirting and
Harassment

Communication Strategies to Deal
with Harassment

Many adults meet and form strong interpersonal relationships (both platonic and romantic) at the workplace. Interactions with our colleagues may develop into strong personal friendships that carry over outside of the job. That's where we may meet the "love of our life." So it is important to examine (a) how social, potentially relational, communication evolves in organizations, (b) how such interactions may become (or be perceived to be) sexually harassing, and (c) how to communicate in order to avoid major hassles in this area.

Why Interpersonal Relationships Develop in Work Settings

It makes sense that we view coworkers as potential relationship partners. In the workplace, we spend significant amounts of time with these people working on cooperative, or similar, tasks. This relates back to the concept of proximity discussed when we examined predictors of attraction. Very simply, you are more attracted to people you are near and spend time with. This happens on the job.

    In addition, your coworkers may be perceived to be quite admirable, especially if you are less experienced at the job. Coworkers may be experts—other people in your profession look to them for advice and leadership, they have an excellent reputation in the field, they may be very skilled and professional at what they do. Something that seems very difficult, complicated, or intimidating to you, they can do smoothly and easily. You go to them for advice and encouragement. They may be in positions that you aspire to be in at some point; for example, you would like to be a vice president or supervisor in the organization someday, or you would like to own your own business too. So it is not surprising that we are often impressed with and look up to the people who work with us on the job.

There is also often a sense of homophily or similarity with coworkers. You have similar goals, interests, and professional skills. You are working together for some common outcome, so there is a sense of "togetherness." You're a team. At times coworkers may have a better sense of what is going on, the pressures you face, the rewards in your environment, than most other people you know. So you feel understood by them in a way that you don't feel with other people.

All in all, it is not surprising that close interpersonal relationships develop at work. It is only natural given the other predictors of attraction and relationship initiation we have discussed. But there are some important differences between work communication and strictly social or interpersonal relationships too.

Differences between Work and Social Communication

There are three central differences between communication at the workplace and communication for social purposes: (a) goal differences, (b) rules versus laws, and (c) choice.

First, when you are on the job the *goals are different* from when you are just "socializing." Although interpersonal communication may occur at the workplace, it takes a secondary role. The primary role is to do your job well. Further, if the job doesn't get done, you may lose your job. Organizations want employees to be happy, but their main concern is that the organization run efficiently and productively. If interpersonal relationships interfere with that goal, the individuals will suffer. You might miss out on a promotion, receive a reprimand, or even get fired if interpersonal communication creates barriers to effective job performance. By comparison, the goal of interpersonal communication that is outside of work is primarily for the pleasure of the relationship and the fun of interacting. You don't usually get into trouble for having long conversations with a friend on your front steps at home, but you might in the workplace. Sometimes time spent on social relationships gets in the way of accomplishing work goals.

Second, in interpersonal relationships we tend to make up our own *rules*. They are quite loose and flexible, depending on who we are with at the time. This is not true in the workplace. (Recall the discussion in Chapter 10 about interpersonal interactions and verbal language at home versus at work.) *Legal restrictions* apply to how we communicate with coworkers. We can't use language or nonverbal communication that may be idiosyncratic to us but out of place on the job (such as high-fashion clothing, joking, touching, or slang terms). In part, the necessity for objective rules arises because more relationships at work are *unequal*. That is, even social relationships in the workplace may be between people with unequal organizational power. Some organizations (e.g., the federal government) have specific rules against social, romantic, or familial relationships between people who work at the same office. So the rules regarding workplace communication are more formal and direct compared to those for our away-from-work relationships.

The final major distinction between communication in the workplace and social communication is the issue of *choice*. We choose our own friends, but we don't necessarily choose our colleagues. Accordingly, we could choose to *end* a relationship with our friend or lover, but we cannot always end relationships with colleagues.

Interpersonal relationships are primarily ones in which we can make the decisions to begin or to terminate them. But that interaction is decided for us within organizations. Of course, within the organizational setting there are people we may become closer to, go to lunch with, do activities with on weekends. But even if the friendship ends, we may still have to work with them, unless we leave that job.

Thus, for all of these reasons we need to be aware of communicative differences that may occur in workplace interactions. Few of us begin relationships thinking about what it would be like if the relationship ended and we still had to see and interact with the terminated partner every day. It tends to be uncomfortable for both parties. Meetings are difficult. Research projects flounder. In extreme situations, you may find that information you self-disclosed to a coworker when in a close relationship comes back to haunt you. If the person feels burned, he or she may want to strike out at you.

Friendships with our coworkers may be natural and fun, but they can also complicate things. Romantic relationships at the workplace are even more difficult. Complex communication situations arise when one worker feels attracted to another—whether or not it is two-sided. How the communication is handled here may result in the label "flirtation," or it may be interpreted as "sexual harassment." There are very clear differences in the consequences for the work participants and for the organization as a whole.

Just Friends: Platonic Relationships at Work

Both platonic relationships and romantic relationships are likely to develop in the workplace. Platonic relationships are those with people (either male or female) we consider friends, just friends, without sexual or romantic potential. We generally have more platonic than romantic relationships at any given time, because romances in our culture tend to be exclusive. That is, most people maintain romantic relationships one at a time (unless we want a whole lot of trouble!). The same is not true for platonic relationships. We may have a large group of good friends with whom we socialize and spend time.

Platonic friendships develop at work for the same reasons romantic relationships do. We spend significant amounts of time together, often cooperating on the same tasks. We may be united against a similar "enemy"—the supervisor, union, or administration. We often come from similar backgrounds and have similar interests and goals. Thus it is very reasonable that we will form interpersonal relationships on the job.

Can friendships on the job be productive? Of course! We tend to have more positive affect toward the job if we like the people there. It may be easier to be open in discussions and understand others' perspectives if you are among friends. Time goes faster on the job if you're with friends. (Compare this with how quickly you want to get away from the workplace when you dislike your coworkers.) The job generally seems less like "work" when we have friends who are also our coworkers. But these positive relationships can also have their downside.

By their very nature, it's difficult to be objective about your relationship partners. It may be harder to take a stand in opposition to a close friend at work. You may find yourself in the position of having to evaluate your friend's performance, not easy to do especially if the job performance is poor. Or alternatively, you may have to report to a friend as your supervisor for a project. And if you are close friends working together, supervisors may think one of you contributed more than the other, and therefore "carried" that person.

Interpersonal relationships also tend to be more emotionally charged than simple coworker relationships. We may feel resentment if our friend achieves more than we do. Conflict in relationships can carry over to the job, and vice versa. Further, what is appropriate verbal and nonverbal communication in the social friendship context may not be appropriate for the workplace.

Should we outlaw both romantic and platonic relationships with coworkers? Probably not. Such a law is difficult to enforce and may harm productive workplace camaraderie in some circumstances. As mentioned previously, many organizations have specific rules about how relationship partners of various types may work together. But it is best if all relational partners understand and discuss the boundaries, pressures, and difficulties that the workplace environment imposes on interpersonal relationships.

What Is Flirting?

Flirting is a communication signal that a romantic relationship may be forming. It is communication to encourage another to acknowledge sexual interest, in a nonforced open-ended manner. Many people see flirtation as a harmless and fun form of socializing. You can check out another person, see if he or she is attracted to you, in a nonthreatening manner. Flirting is ambiguous, nonconfrontational. For example, a direct proposition would not be flirting (Duck, 1988), but indirect joking around and casual touching would be.

Research by Montgomery (1986) showed that women thought flirting was more to express friendly attraction and less "sexual" than men did. In addition, some people (often in solid relationships of their own) flirt simply to test whether the opposite sex would still be attracted to them. They have no intention of escalating the relationship. When people respond to flirtation with flirtation of their own, it shows a willingness to participate in that type of interaction—assuming both parties know that it is nonforced and more of a "game." Obviously, misunderstandings can occur!

Further, although flirting often takes place in purely social settings such as parties, family gatherings, or bars, people flirt at work too. The distinction of choice may come into play in this case. If you don't want people to communicate with you in a flirtatious manner in a social setting, you can typically leave or cut off interaction with them. At work this may not be possible. Flirtation may be coming from your boss. Flirtatious comments may be coming from the person you share an office with. Even if you do not accept and reciprocate these communication messages, the situation may become too sticky to get out of. In addition, behavior that one person thinks is merely harmless, open-ended flirtation may be viewed by another as harassing.

What Is Sexual Harassment?

Sexual harassment is unwanted sexual communication that (a) interferes with work performance, (b) is a condition or incentive for work performance, and/ or (c) creates a climate at work that is embarrassing, threatening, or intimidating, and hence interferes with job performance.

The problem with this definition is that not everyone may recognize what is "unwanted" communication, or everyone may not agree on what types of communication create a threatening work environment. Current definitions of sexual harassment are clearly based in the receiver of the message. So then you ask, "How can I tell if I'm being harassing?" That's where clear understanding of communication, both verbal and nonverbal, and the differences between flirtation and harassment come in.

Male and Female Differences

Many people (some estimates as high as 50–60 percent depending on the organization) feel they have been sexually harassed in the workplace, and most of the perceived harassers are male. This may mean that women do sexually harassing things less often (watch someone's body, make suggestive comments, touch more than usual). Alternatively, it may mean that when women engage in these behaviors, coworkers are not intimidated, but when men do the same types of things, coworkers are intimidated.

Along those same lines, it appears that women are more likely to label behaviors at work as intimidating and harassing than are men (Booth-Butterfield, 1989). Women may be more sensitive to those subtle indirect messages and pick up on them earlier. Or women may be more easily intimidated by men than men are by women. In either event, if the receivers are women there is a greater chance that they will interpret sexual communication as harassing.

Status

The impact of *status differentials* on perceptions of communication in the workplace cannot be overestimated. The greater the status differential (difference in the work hierarchy between the two coworkers), the more likely that communication messages from the higher-up will be viewed as threatening or coercive (Gutek, 1985).

Take the example of a study by Sharkey and Waldron (1990) that examined how supervisors may intentionally embarrass their subordinates at work. The supervisors thought the embarrassment basically produced benefits, relational teasing, and good feelings. However, the subordinates thought just the opposite. Subordinates resented the embarrassment and became more negative about the work.

The same holds true with harassment. A behavior that may seem innocent or flirtatious when enacted by your colleague at the same level, or by someone who is lower in seniority than you, may seem inappropriate or sexually harassing when communicated by your supervisor. For example, sexual innuendo and joking around may not seem out of place among students. But if your instructor does it, red flags go up.

As you become more senior, you may not even notice that you have gained status in your organization. You may feel as though you talk, joke, and touch in the same ways you always have. But the receivers of your communication may view you differently and interpret what you think is "flirtation" as "sexual harassment." Be on the lookout for subtle, nonverbal signs of discomfort in your receivers.

Specificity of Communication Messages

Several studies have now shown that communication messages that are more specifically sexual, more directly "reward oriented," and more persistently intrusive are more likely to be perceived as sexual harassment (Bingham & Burleson, 1996; Booth-Butterfield, 1989). "You won't get the work schedule you hope for unless you go out with me." Ambiguous or open-ended communication that can be interpreted in multiple ways is less clearly harassing. For example, if someone stands too close and brushes against you, you may be unsure whether it was intentional or unintentional.

Similarly, communication behavior that happens repeatedly rather than just once is more likely to be seen as harassing. For example, instead of leaving you alone after you tell someone you don't like that type of joking, the person keeps on telling sexual jokes or leaving pictures and cartoons in your work area for you to see. Even persistence in asking for a date, which one person views as affinity seeking, can become very annoying and be interpreted as sexual harassment.

Context Expectations

According to court rulings, there are some *contexts* in which the standards of communication interaction are higher than others, especially where sexual communication is concerned. You expect more educated and refined communication from college professors and lawyers than from workers on a road maintenance crew. You probably expect more open, freewheeling communication if you work at a resort bar or dance club than if you work at an upscale department store. Although everyone has a right to work in an atmosphere free of sexual coercion, and even in the most liberal contexts sexual touching or patting is out of bounds, we have to be realistic about some standards of language and the like and consider this when we apply for a job. Legal restrictions can only go so far in stopping objectionable communication.

Perhaps one of the most important things to remember about context is simply that there are different expectations for communication in interpersonal/social contexts versus employment contexts. Blending these contexts can cause problems to arise.

Particularly Difficult Situations

An especially "sticky" situation in determining appropriate communication at work occurs when employees form consenting relationships with each other that later terminate. So you are working with former romantic partners, previous roommates, sorority sisters, and so on. This becomes more complicated if only one person wanted to break off the relationship. Is it harassment when interpersonal problems are carried over to the workplace? Do attempts to try to patch up the relationship and talk things over with your partner constitute sexual harassment? Are negative job evaluations a function of a former friend's anger toward you, or are you simply not doing your job very well? Conversely, did you receive that high grade in class or positive job evaluation because of your close relationship with your instructor or supervisor?

As you can see, these questions carry interpersonal issues and problems over into the workplace, and they cloud the definition of harassment. That is why many organizations frown on employees dating each other, or supervisors and subordinates forming close relationships. (An example is the U.S. military where romantic relationships between officers and enlisted personnel are forbidden by formal rules.)

Distinguishing between Flirting and Harassment

How can you tell if the interaction you're in is flirtatious or sexually harassing? It's important for you to recognize these cues, whether you are the sender or the receiver.

The first checkpoint is knowledge of the *legal definitions* of harassment. It is your responsibility to keep informed. This knowledge can clarify whether you are a target, and may help you stay out of trouble if you are in a supervisory position and therefore more likely to be perceived as intimidating. Again, sexual harassment is formally defined as unwanted sexual communication that (a) interferes with work performance, (b) is a condition or incentive for work performance, and/or (c) creates a work climate that is embarrassing, threatening, or intimidating, and hence interferes with job performance (Gutek, 1985).

A second factor is *mutuality*. Are both people actively engaged in the potentially sexual communication? If both people are communicating in that manner, making jokes, teasing, being nonverbally suggestive, this pattern would probably indicate flirtation. Sexual harassment tends to be one-sided. One person sends sexually oriented messages, but the other is uncomfortable, doesn't participate, and avoids that type of interaction. In other words, in sexually harassing communication there is a lack of reciprocation.

Repetition is a third factor in determining harassment. Low-level potentially harassing actions become more annoying and intimidating when they are repeated. Even a coworker's request to have lunch may become problematic if it is repeated over and over.

This does not mean that extreme actions are not harassing if they only happen once. Certainly if your boss gropes your body, that constitutes harassment even if it only happens one time. But communication that is repeated becomes even more intimidating.

A fourth factor in distinguishing flirtation from harassment is *timing in the context*. Communicative behaviors that are out in public in a purely social environment are much more likely to be taken as flirtation than those same behaviors enacted just before an important business interview. Sexual jokes may be interpreted very differently out at a bar after work than in a task setting at work. In addition, as with many other types of interpersonal messages, knowing when to stop a communicative behavior before it becomes irritating is important.

Finally, as previously mentioned, whether you are a *male or a female* seems to have an impact on whether you tend to perceive a specific act as harassment or flirtation. In general, females tend to be more conscious of potential sexual harassment and therefore more prone to interpret ambiguous actions as harassing. Males are more likely to be flattered, or at least not threatened, by some of the low-level potentially harassing communication. So unless the behavior is quite clear-cut and unambiguous, if you are a female be aware that guys may think they are flirting when you see the behavior as objectionable. And, if you are male, be aware that women may feel harassed by actions that you think are merely playful. Even the courts don't have clear decisions on exactly what should be interpreted as sexual harassment. That is why it is so important to communicate clearly at the time of the communicative act.

Communication Strategies to Deal with Harassment

Let's say that you clearly perceive the communication messages around you to constitute sexual harassment. Now what do you do? Do you drop that class? Quit your job? Avoid all contact with that person? None of these reactions may be realistic, and they punish *you*, rather than the person who is doing something unethical.

First of all, *prevention of sexual harassment is better than punishment.* Head it off at the pass. Always try to communicate in a friendly, yet professional, manner. It is better to avert potentially harassing communication by not letting patterns even get started in that direction. Be clear about your own communication.

Second, if your best efforts to communicate in a strictly professional manner don't work and you receive harassing messages, *don't ignore the communication,* hoping that "it will go away." Although ignoring is the most common reaction reported by people who have experienced sexual harassment, it is not an effective response. Ignoring such behavior, or pretending that it didn't happen, tends to be interpreted as "OK" and leads to escalation of the behavior rather than de-escalation. ("Well she didn't say anything when I put my hand on her waist, so why don't I just slide it over to her butt?")

Also, some people may honestly not recognize that how they are communicating is offensive and borders on sexual harassment. By bringing it to their attention, you may stop the action without further problems.

Further, by not saying anything about the offensive behavior, you are putting yourself in a bad legal position if the interactions become even worse. People who have been harassed (as well as other forms of victimization) report feeling even more upset and self-blaming if they didn't do anything about the negative actions.

Be specific about your negative feelings. Nonverbal cues such as shrugging out of the person's arm, or dirty looks following sexual innuendoes are not sufficient. You need to use your assertive communication skills (not aggressive) to clearly communicate that you don't appreciate or that you feel uncomfortable with that type of interaction. It is important not to play along with the communication pattern in an attempt to fit in with the group. "Playing along" demonstrates the mutuality of behaviors discussed previously.

A *sense of humor* is important in this area. Don't blow things out of proportion if it's not necessary. Sometimes messages can be sent in a humorous manner and still get your idea across. Sometimes things happen that can indeed be laughed off, assuming they aren't part of an ongoing pattern that weakens and undermines your position in the organization.

If sexually harassing communication persists, make sure you *document the actions.* Write down and date what happened, who was there, and your reaction. If you report such incidents to your supervisor, or decide to file a grievance, such documentation can be helpful to your credibility.

Network with others in the organization. It would be helpful if other people can support the effectiveness of your job performance. That way, if a harasser tries to undermine your work because of your response to the harassment, you will have coworkers who can stand up for you. If no one knows you, or knows of your work, they can't be supportive. An interpersonal network can also be helpful in asking advice, for reality checks, or just sharing concerns. So it will be productive to disclose the incidents of sexual harassment to others in your workplace.

Finally, even though you don't want these interactions to get to the "official" level, *know who your contact person is* in case there is trouble. In every organization there are people who are designated as contacts in case of sexual harassment. Sometimes it may be your direct supervisor, sometimes it may be a personnel office, or it may be someone outside the organization.

But to protect yourself, you need to find out who you would go to in order to report problems with sexually harassing communication.

Conclusions

I hope that you never have to encounter sexually harassing communication on the job—either as a potential victim or as the accused harasser. Our society is making progress in educating workers and eliminating such intimidating communication. But just in case, the information in this section should help you to distinguish between flirtatious messages and those that tend to be perceived as harassment. It should also help you to communicate in a manner that will minimize the harm if harassment does happen to you.

REFERENCES AND RECOMMENDED READINGS

Bingham, S., & Burleson, B. (1996). The development of a sexual harassment proclivity scale: Construct validation and relationship to communication competence. *Communication Quarterly, 44,* 308–325.

Booth-Butterfield, M. (1989). Perception of harassing communication as a function of locus of control, workforce participation, and gender. *Communication Quarterly, 37,* 262–275.

Duck, S. (1988). *Relating to others.* Chicago: Dorsey Press.

Dziech, B., & Weiner, L. (1984). *The Lecherous Professor.* Boston: Beacon Press.

Gutek, B. (1985). *Sex and the workplace.* San Francisco: Jossey Bass.

Koeppel, L., Montagne-Miller, Y., O'Hair, D., & Cody, M. (1993). Friendly? Flirting? Wrong? In P. Kalbfleisch (Ed.), *Interpersonal communication: Evolving interpersonal relationships* (pp. 13–32). Hillsdale, NJ: Erlbaum.

McKinney, K., & Maroules, N. 1991. Sexual harassment. In E. Grauerholx & M. Koralewski (Eds.), *Sexual coercion* (pp. 29–44). Lexington, MA: Lexington Books.

Montgomery, B. (1986). Interpersonal attraction as a function of open communication and gender. *Communication Research Reports, 3,* 343–362.

Sandler, B., & Shoop, R. (Eds.) (1997). *Sexual harassment on college campus: A guide for administrators, faculty, and students.* Boston: Allyn & Bacon.

Sharkey, W., & Waldron, V. (1990, Nov.) *The intentional embarrassment of subordinates in the work place.* Paper presented at the annual conference of the Speech Communication Association, Chicago.

Shotland, R. L., & Craig, J. (1988). Can men and women differentiate between friendly and sexually interested behavior? *Social Psychology Quarterly, 51,* 66–73.

FLIRTING OR SEXUAL HARASSMENT? HOW DO *YOU* TELL THE DIFFERENCE?

In Groups . . .

1. How do you know when social communication in the workplace has gone too far and become sexually harassing? What behaviors tip you off? How do you tell the difference?

2. Can you give an example of communication interaction that could be sociable and acceptable, but then turn into harassment?

3. What are some ways to communicate effectively when faced with potentially harassing communication at work?

PERCEPTION OF SEXUAL HARASSMENT SCALE

As you read the following scenes, consider that the person doing the behavior is the opposite sex from you. Respond to each of these situations with a rating of 1–5, with 1 meaning that this situation is not at all harassing and 5 meaning this is extremely sexually harassing.

_____ 1. A prospective employer insists that you spend a weekend with him or her before final hiring.

_____ 2. Your scores on written assignments begin dropping after you refuse to date your graduate student instructor. As far as you can tell your behavior has changed in no other way.

_____ 3. Your boss repeatedly touches your shoulder, arm, or hand when giving you instructions at work.

_____ 4. Your professor smiles at you every time you see him or her on campus.*

_____ 5. Your teacher makes sexual comments and innuendoes about other people when you are present.

_____ 6. Your instructor stands very close to you, often brushing against you whenever you talk in the classroom. The person doesn't do this with others that you can see.

_____ 7. Whenever you work on a task, your professor invites you to continue socializing at a local drinking establishment or elsewhere.

_____ 8. A higher grade is promised if you spend the night with your instructor.

_____ 9. Your teacher sometimes puts sexual cartoons or suggestive pictures on your desk for you to see.

_____ 10. Your professor often calls you sexy "pet names."

_____ 11. Your boss often pats you on the bottom in passing or as a greeting.

_____ 12. Two professors enter the meeting room and come over to sit beside you.*

_____ 13. Your professor's eyes scan your body as you discuss a class assignment.

_____ 14. As you go to work each day, there are workers who whistle, hoot, or make gestures as you go past.

_____ 15. Your teacher consistently cracks sexual jokes around you after you have explained your distaste for this practice.

_____ 16. Your manager puts his or her arms around your waist and tries to kiss you as you're working late one afternoon.

_____ 17. You have just been awarded a departmental honor. Your department head congratulates you with a hug and a kiss.*

_____ 18. While explaining a task your teacher places your hand between his or her legs.

_____ 19. A graduate teaching assistant suggests that you would get better grades if you were physically friendlier with him or her.

_____ 20. Your instructor consistently gazes at your body, looking you up and down as you walk past. This makes you feel uncomfortable.

_____ 21. Your teacher questions you about your weekend plans.*

_____ 22. Your teacher continually pressures you for a date even though you have told him or her you are not interested.

_____ 23. Though you are uncomfortable with the topic, your supervisor regularly discusses sexual matters with you and questions you about your sexual activities.

_____ 24. In an elevator with your professor, he or she starts a conversation.*

Scoring: Add up scores on all the items _except_ the items with an asterisk.

16 Influence and Assertive Communication

OBJECTIVES

Whether we recognize it or not, communication intended to influence or control is ongoing in relationships as we try to get others to see or do things our way. We try to influence others, or perhaps resist their influence attempts. Check your knowledge of these processes with these tests.

1. Define dominance, and discuss the important role of perceived abilities.

2. Explain three principles predicting relational dominance and be able to recognize them when they are operating in an interpersonal situation.

3. Interactional dominance can be observed in the specific communicative behaviors we enact in conversations. Describe six of the eight communication behaviors of dominance.

4. Explain why each of the above behaviors qualifies as a dominant behavior.

5. Give three examples of when you have observed interactional dominance occurring in "real life."

6. Provide the definition of assertive communication, and compare it with nonassertive and aggressive communication.

7. Explain why assertive communication is a tool.

8. Describe two ways males and females may receive different responses in reaction to their assertive communication.

9. Using illustrations, explain four ways assertive communication can be helpful.

10. Explain ERA (empathy, rationale, and action) and create a scenario using ERA to respond to a difficult relationship situation.

11. Describe four aspects of your nonverbal communication that can help you be more assertive when you need to be.

CHAPTER OUTLINE

Dominance as Influence
  Relational Dominance
  Interactional Dominance
  Qualification of Dominance
    Behavior in Communication

Assertive Communication
  Assertive, Aggressive, and
    Nonassertive Communication

Female versus Male Assertiveness

What Assertiveness Can Do for You

Verbal and Nonverbal Components of Assertiveness
  Verbal Components
  Nonverbal Components

Dominance as Influence

In every relationship, dominance or power will inevitably be exhibited. This doesn't mean that one person will be in absolute control, or that one person will direct all aspects of the relationship, but human interactions are characterized by negotiated *dominance,* the perceived ability of one person to shape, control, or direct the feelings or behavior of another.

Dominance can be explained on a broad, relational level (e.g., Mickey is more dominant than Minnie in their relationship), as well as on a situation-by-situation level (in some settings with some people you are quite confident and expert, but in others you're not). It is important to remember that dominance shifts. No one is dominant in all situations and no one is submissive in all situations. Statuses change and dominance patterns alter. To illustrate, your roommate may be quite dominant when talking with you, but very quiet and submissive when talking with his or her parents.

In addition, dominance is *perceived* control. Therefore, you cannot be dominant unless your receiver sees you that way and is willing to enact the reciprocal submissive role. That is why communication is so important in these processes. You want to communicate in such a way that you'll be perceived as dominant when necessary.

Relational Dominance

Three different principles predict who is going to be more dominant in a relationship: the principle of least interest, the principle of most alternatives, and the principle of resource control. The *principle of least interest* predicts that the person who cares the *least* about the relationship will have the greatest amount of control. At first glance this may sound counterintuitive. You might think, "Wait, wouldn't the *most* interested person be most dominant because they care more? They'll work harder." But no. The person who is *most* interested, or who cares the most about maintaining the relationship will do almost anything to keep the relationship alive. In comparison, the individual who is not heavily committed or invested in the relationship will be able to shape the other's behavior, or else he or she will leave.

Take an example where Jeannine is really committed to her friend Charla, but Charla is more independent and doesn't care as much about Jeannine. Thus, when Charla changes plans unexpectedly or slights her friend in some way by not calling or not responding to her e-mail, Jeannine will keep on adapting and try to patch things up. The principle of least interest is also evident in dating relationships. If a student is head over heels in love with another, but the object of this love isn't as interested in having a relationship, then the least-interested party will again be able to control the actions and feelings of the other. In some cases, the least-interested person may take great advantage of the most interested person.

A second principle of relational dominance is the *principle of most alternatives*. Simply put, the individual who has the most relational alternatives will be the most dominant. "If you don't play according to *my* rules, there are plenty of other people who *will*." In contrast, if people are very dependent on that relationship because they don't have many other friends or potential relationship partners, they will be submissive to the opinions of the current partner. We find that popular students can control the activities and attitudes of their friends because they always have others with whom they can socialize. The person who doesn't have a network of friends may find he or she has to give up a great deal of control, or even integrity, in order to remain in the relationship with the partner who has more alternatives.

The third principle of relational dominance is the *principle of resource control*. The person who controls most of the relational resources is dominant. This principle is very straightforward and easily observed. If the basketball belongs to one person, he or she will be able to set schedules and call the shots. Often the person with more money makes the choices—or else chooses to allow the partner decide. If the resource is a service, the person rendering the service is dominant. ("Yes, I'll type your paper for you, but you'd better be nice to me.")

Interactional Dominance

Dominance is also exerted in our everyday interactions with others. Specific communicative behaviors are characteristic of dominant communication and serve to control or change the other participants' behavior. (In Chapter 10 we described powerful and powerless language. These interactional dominance behaviors are consistent with that discussion.) You have probably noticed some of these as you have had conversational interactions with your classmates, or in a totally social climate such as a party. As these communication actions are discussed, you might consider your own behavior and decide whether it's appropriately dominant, overdoes the dominance to become aggressive and domineering, or tends to be weak and submissive.

One characteristic of interactional dominance is *volume*. When people are trying to become more dominant during a conversation, they talk louder so they can be heard. Volume may also serve to talk over and drown out the other communicators' voices. Submissive communicators tend to speak in soft, timid voices and so may not have their ideas heard. As voices in any context raise, it is probably an indication that people are competing for communication dominance.

Getting your ideas across is crucial if you want to shape others' behavior or get them to go along with you. That's why *interruptions* are a second source of interactional dominance. The person who wants control will interrupt others in order to get a point across. Of course, the submissive counterpart to this is to be interrupted, to have your opinions cut off, and to not have the opportunity to finish your message. Note that in classrooms, students may be unlikely to interrupt the professor, but they may be quite likely to interrupt other students or to be interrupted themselves.

When people are in the dominant role (or are trying to be), they also *talk more* compared to others around them. They hold the conversational floor for more of the time, while others listen. This floor-holding is accomplished in part through interruptions but also through the rate of their speaking. Dominant communicators *talk faster with few pauses*. Such a pattern prevents others from initiating messages. There isn't room to get a word into the conversational stream. In comparison, more submissive talk patterns tend to be slower, more hesitant, and allow longer unfilled pauses. This creates ample opportunity for, or even invites, others to participate. Often we see this reciprocal pattern when people are in task or working groups. The emergent leaders will take charge, speak faster, and talk over the less expert group members.

Similarly, it is the more dominant communicators who will *issue instructions*, or tell others what to do. The dominant person gives orders, the submissive person follows them. In a work setting the supervisor gives assignments, sets deadlines, and instructs employees on how to accomplish goals correctly. The workers (who are the less dominant people in this setting) then follow these instructions to comply.

Contradictions or verbal disagreements are also characteristic of interactional dominance. If dominant individuals have a differing opinion, they will state it directly. In contrast, a submissive strategy is to go along with the conversation, to voice verbal agreements. Of course this doesn't mean they *actually* agree, but it means they don't feel confident enough to state their disagreement. When you listen to conversations between two dominant individuals, you will probably hear them contradict each other and disagree numerous times.

Topic shifts are another pattern observed in conversational dominance. The more dominant individual will determine the direction and topic of the interaction, what will and will not be discussed. Whether the subject is talking about themselves, about business, or asking questions about the other, the more dominant communicator leads the conversation. If more submissive communicators attempt to change the subject, their messages will probably be ignored unless a dominant individual lends support.

Topic shifts are an extension of general *interaction control.* The more dominant conversationalist initiates interaction and also decides when it's over. A more dominant person will begin a conversation when he or she thinks the time is right and the more submissive individual will follow along. Topic shifts and interactional control are extremely visible in classrooms where it is usually the teacher who decides topics of study or discussion, when it is time to move on to a more appropriate topic, and when the interaction should be terminated. The same holds true in social interactions. The more dominant person gets to determine when to begin and end.

Qualification of Dominance
Behavior in Communication

There are several important points to remember about interactional dominance overall. First, these conversational behaviors are equally applicable to interactions with family, lovers, coworkers, and friends. Take a minute to notice who sets the agenda, who interrupts whom, who contradicts, and other cues of dominance, because it may give you some clues about the undercurrents in the relationship. You can typically tell who is most powerful or who is challenging power by how people interact in groups.

Second, these characteristics will be most observable when participants are on roughly equal footing or have equal status, so that there can be competition for dominance. If one person in the conversation has extremely high status or authority, he or she will not need to increase volume or interrupt to control the interaction. For instance, if you are in a meeting with the governor of your state, you will no doubt play a more submissive role and not challenge for interactional control.

A third point is that specific dominance behaviors tend to vary across ethnic or cutlural contexts. What is appropriate volume or rate of speaking in Hispanic groups may not be among Asians. African American communicators may have quite different patterns of talking than Caucasions. So we have to interpret interactional dominance communication in its cultural context.

Finally, dominance or power is most effective if it is not flaunted. People may react against you if you make it obvious that you are in complete control and they must submit to your decisions. This can cause big fights! Therefore, effective communicators use dominance wisely and sparingly, choose their spots carefully, and are not overtly controlling in every situation.

Assertive Communication

Tina sees an attractive classmate across the room and would like to suggest studying together. But she can't bring herself to go over and initiate that conversation.

You and your partner get into a heated quarrel over plans for the holidays. You snap some sarcastic comments about family background and your partner stalks out of the room.

Nonassertive communicators are not likely to be effective. It's as simple as that. Assertive communication enhances your competence in interpersonal interactions. Yet "assertiveness" has gained a bad reputation with many people. The main reason for this negative image is that people often do not understand what assertive communication really is, how it differs from aggressive and nonassertive communication, and how assertiveness can be put to use effectively in communicative interactions.

One thing to remember about assertiveness is that it's a tool. People choose to use assertive communication in some situations but not others. For example, you may find that you are very persuasive and assertive when making decisions at school, but you don't take a stand with friends about what movie to see, or with your family about plans for moving to a different town. Sometimes this is because you don't have strong attitudes about an issue and it simply doesn't matter to you what movie you see. No one needs to be assertive all the time. But if you are aware that you sometimes overdo attempts to dominate, or at the other extreme, if you regularly feel frustrated that people take advantage of you or don't consider your opinions, then you need to know more about assertiveness.

Assertive, Aggressive, and Nonassertive Communication

The very word, assertiveness, sometimes conjures up images of harsh-faced people saying blunt and often hurtful things to each other. Perhaps an acquaintance of yours has attended a short assertiveness workshop, thought he or she understood the concepts, and returned home to "dump" on you.

People are sometimes extremely rude to others but excuse it by saying, "I was just being assertive." No, this is *not* assertiveness but rather aggressive communication. *Assertive communication* is when you directly communicate your opinions, thoughts, or feelings directly but at the same time respect the opinions, thoughts, and feelings of the other person. It is always a balanced action. You stand up for your rights, but you also fully respect the rights of others.

Aggressive communication, by comparison, communicates your own thoughts and feelings but it may be at the expense of the other person's rights. People are often aggressive when they lose their tempers, as in a tense situation at school. They aren't thinking of how others feel. When people use aggressive communication, it may be because they don't know any other ways of communicating (many families only provide aggressive, abrupt, or hostile models), or it may be that the person knows how, but decides to "win at any cost."

People often experience a *reactance effect* when confronted with aggressive communication. They feel their rights or freedom are threatened and defiantly move in the opposite direction. An example is when universities tell students they *must* sit in certain sections at athletic events, or *must* attend certain convocation ceremonies. Because the statement seems arbitrary and an infringement on students' rights, the students may ignore it and adopt extreme attitudes. People also experience reactance when told they should not date or even spend time with a particular person. Suddenly that person becomes even more attractive. In situations such as these, where reactance occurs, aggressive communication is clearly counterproductive.

Can aggressive communication ever be effective in getting your way? Certainly. We often comply or give in to aggressive communicators out of fear or distaste. ("Let's get this quarrel over with!") But aggression probably does not result in long-term attitude change, and it tends to be damaging to both classroom and personal relationships. Simply put, we do not like people who communicate aggressively with us. So although aggressive communication may *seem* to be effective in the short run, if you want to maintain positive relationships it is not the best strategy to use.

Nonassertive communication is just the opposite of aggressiveness. Nonassertive people are so concerned about other peoples' feelings and opinions that their own feelings get trampled. These people will sit through a movie they dislike rather than saying they would rather go to a different movie.

Nonassertive communicators are experts at "beating around the bush," "dropping hints," or attempting to get their ideas across solely nonverbally, as in "the evil eye." As a result, people who communicate in a nonassertive manner are less effective. They might not even bring up the topic of concern, or if they do bring it up it is in such an indirect manner that the target overlooks the point.

Nonassertive people may also be overcompliant with other people's requests. In an effort to be nice and not upset anyone, nonassertive communicators are often taken advantage of. They may be described as "nice" but also as "wishy-washy" or "weak" and not be especially respected by people around them. In comparison, the assertive communicator is saying, "I respect your right to think or act as you do, but you must respect my rights and consider my perspective too."

Female versus Male Assertiveness

Your past experience as a communicator also influences both use of assertive communication and others' perceptions of you as an assertive communicator. Cultural expectations have led to differing uses and perceptions of assertive communication for females and males in the United States, as well as in other societies.

In our society, women have been reinforced for being nonassertive and indirect in their communication. Often females are punished for attempting to communicate assertively, and instead they learn to be passive or manipulative. Just watch old situation comedies such as *I Love Lucy, The Donna Reed Show,* or *Leave It to Beaver* to see examples of manipulative communication by women.

However, males in our society are not taught to be assertive either. Rather, they often learn that aggression is acceptable and that "real men" may get their way by bulldozing aside other peoples' rights. Note Clint Eastwood of Dirty Harry fame, television's Ralph Kramden on *The Honeymooners,* or Stanley Kowalski from the play *A Streetcar Named Desire.* These are not positive models of assertive communication.

What this means in terms of real-life assertive communication is that women may be expected to communicate nonassertively and men may be expected to communicate more aggressively in many situations. Subsequently, when men or women break out of that pattern, they may have difficulty due to (1) a lack of experience and (2) other people's perceptions. In fact, women who enact assertive messages are often perceived as aggressive because of the contrast with stereotypic submissive communication. Men who enact assertive messages may not be taken seriously and be viewed as nonassertive in contrast to societal models of aggressiveness and dominance.

A change in any habitual communication pattern may be received with surprise and resistance. If Charles has typically communicated in a nonassertive manner, people come to expect that and the first time he employs an assertive response friends may perceive it as aggressive. They may wonder, "What's wrong with him today?" An aggressive pattern followed by assertion may make the source seem unusually mellow or good-natured. It's not that communicators are doing anything wrong, but the contrast between what receivers are accustomed to and the new assertive messages may seem odd.

What Assertiveness Can Do for You

What are the benefits of being assertive? In many ways, assertive communication involves more work or takes longer than other communication styles. But the advantages of communicating assertively are clear and undeniable.

Assuring Fair Treatment.   First, assertive communication can help assure fair treatment of yourself and others. A nonassertive person may put up with rude or unfair communication and not do anything about it. Aggressive communication, on the other hand, may only make the situation worse by alienating the receiver. A good example is in classroom communication.

If you believe your grade is incorrect or that a supervisor is not treating you fairly, then using assertive communication can help you to receive equitable treatment. ("I understand that you have many grades to record, but I received a C when my test scores averaged a B. Could you please recheck my grade?") Other situations in which communicating assertively can help might include convincing your partner that it's not fair to make weekend plans and then not show up, returning faulty merchandise to a store where it was purchased, or informing an employer of your work record as you request a pay raise comparable to other employees. In each of these cases, assertive communication will be helpful in gaining the behavior change that you want.

Social Interactions.   Assertive communication facilitates the initiation or termination of social interactions. Many conversations would never get started if one person didn't act assertively and take the first step. People need to communicate assertively to ask others to dance, go to a basketball game, or just to have coffee with them. However, sometimes getting *out* of a social interaction is more difficult than getting into one.

Someone who wants to terminate a conversation could always just abruptly walk away, or tell the person to "drop dead." However, such aggressive communication is not particularly good for the relationship. In contrast, nonassertive people regularly find themselves trapped in conversations without knowing how to gracefully exit. The assertive person considers the other's feelings; after all, that person is evidently having a good time, needs to talk, or doesn't have anything else pressing to do. But assertive communicators also directly communicate their own needs to end the interaction.

A situation you may experience is when a stranger or acquaintance inappropriately self-discloses with you. Although you don't want to hurt the person's feelings, you may feel uncomfortable with such intimacy and want to terminate the interaction. ("I know you want to talk about how she treated you, but I don't think I'm a good person to discuss this with. Maybe you should talk about it with someone closer to you.") A similar experience might occur when you want to terminate a relationship. You don't want to hurt the person or cause him or her embarrassment, but you also don't want to continue an unproductive relationship. In these situations, you are persuading the receiver to end the interaction without hard feelings.

Expressing Feelings.   Assertive communication can also help you to directly and responsibly express your feelings in an interaction. Nonassertive communicators tend to avoid talking about their emotions or try to indirectly communicate how they feel—hoping the receiver will pick up on their emotional "vibrations." ("Well, if they really loved me, they would know how I feel.")

Aggressive communicators, on the other side, may get their emotions out in the open, but employ such an abrupt or hot-tempered manner that the outcome is negative. This often happens because they bottle up feelings and then explode later at some provocation. For example, a roommate who never expresses feelings of frustration with the way you leave the kitchen after cooking, may erupt and ventilate intense emotions on a particular occasion when something else happens to trigger the situation. Certainly this unpredicted outburst will not be good for roommate relations. It would have been far better if the roommate had expressed the feelings in an assertive, responsible manner when the problem occurred rather than waiting until he or she could no longer hold it in. ("I understand that you have a busy schedule, but I feel embarrassed about the way the kitchen looks, and think we ought to keep it clean.")

Expression of emotions in romantic relationships can also benefit from assertiveness. If you like someone, tell the person. If you want to keep your emotional distance a bit more, express that too. Many nonassertive communicators get swept along on someone else's emotions because they can't bring themselves to tell their partners that they don't feel as loving as the partner does. At the other end of the continuum, some potentially romantic relationships may stagnate because the nonassertive communicator won't express how he or she feels.

Handling Requests.   Responding to requests for favors from friends or acquaintances is always a delicate matter. Many favors that seem unreasonable to you may not seem so to them because they don't have all the background information. Perhaps they are not aware of how limited your time is, or they don't realize you have strong personal beliefs against the issue they are advocating. Maybe they don't realize how often they have made the same request previously. Although the aggressive response may needlessly offend and hurt the well-intentioned requester, people who use nonassertive responses end up doing all sorts of unreasonable "favors" because they cannot bring themselves to say "no." They loan money or personal belongings when they would rather not, they do tasks that aren't part of the job, they let others copy their homework, or they canvas the neighborhood in support of a cause they don't even advocate themselves.

The best solution to unreasonable requests is a direct assertive response: "I understand that you may need money, but you've asked to borrow a few dollars several times without paying it back. I can't loan you more money until you return some you've borrowed." The assertive response in turning down unreasonable requests should terminate the request so you are not repeatedly harassed, and at the same time should not alienate the requester. You are, in a sense, persuading the requester to see things your way.

There is a fine line, however, between what someone views as an unreasonable request when they are being asked, and what they view as unreasonable if they themselves are initiating the request. In other words, if *I* ask *you* to take care of my Labrador retriever for the weekend, I'm thinking that's a reasonable request. However, if *you* ask *me* to take care of your Labrador retriever for the weekend, I might not think it's so reasonable.

Nonassertive communicators avoid initiating even highly justified requests such as asking for a ride home when it's right on the driver's route, asking for the delay of a deadline in an emergency situation, or requesting additional explanation from an instructor. In such cases, nonassertive communicators do not get the assistance they need (and deserve) because they are overly concerned about the other person's response. They argue to themselves, "I don't want to impose," or "They'll probably say no anyway, so why ask?"

Therefore, just as assertive communication can help you turn down unreasonable requests, using assertiveness can also help you when you need to initiate requests of your own. ("I know you covered the model of self-disclosure in class, but I'm not sure I completely understand it. Could you explain it a bit more?")

Verbal and Nonverbal Components of Assertiveness

Both verbal and nonverbal aspects of your communication are important in determining whether your message will be perceived as assertive, aggressive, or nonassertive. The verbal components are the words and language you choose for your messages. The nonverbal aspects are all the ways you communicate beyond your words, including your posture, eye contact, tone of voice, and gestures.

Verbal Components

A good assertive statement contains three verbal components: empathy, rationale, and action (ERA). *Empathy* is when you communicate to other people that you understand their position or how they feel. For example, "I know you must be worried about . . ." or "I understand that you're very excited right now . . ." or "I can see that you're in a difficult situation with this. . . ." An empathy statement shows that you are considering receivers' thoughts and rights, while using assertive communication. By indicating your concern you are more likely to get the receiver on your side and open to your persuasive appeal.

The second essential part of an assertive statement is the rationale. The *rationale* is the issue at hand, or the reason you have for bringing something to another's attention. Examples of rationale statements might include "I think you need to study differently for tests" or "People all over the auditorium are looking at us," or "We planned on going to the computer show all semester." The rationale is actually the thesis or the main concern in assertive communication because you, as the source, state your feelings or ideas directly. Without this step, people either are left guessing about what you want or may overlook your position altogether.

The third verbal component of an assertive statement is the *action* step. The action statement communicates specifically what you want *done* as a result of your rationale statement. It may be that you want your receiver to think differently, to reconsider something, or to behave in a different manner. It may also include action that you will take as a result of your concern. Examples include ". . . so I'm willing to study with you to help," ". . . if you don't stop we'll have to leave," ". . . and call this number if you need help," and ". . . so please quiet down."

Without the action step, you may be expressing your ideas in an assertive manner but the process is not complete. The source needs to provide specific directions for accomplishing the expected change. Thus the action step provides direction for reducing fear, focusing and redirecting arousal, and accomplishing goals.

If you put the three verbal components just discussed into one assertive statement, you get messages like these:

"I realize you're in a difficult situation with all the different group activities happening on campus (empathy), but we've planned to go on this trip all semester and the arrangements are made (rationale), so I think you need to stick to your word and go on the trip (action)."

"I know you're probably upset about your grades (empathy), but I am not the cause of your problem and yelling at me won't help (rationale). Why don't we just talk about this. (action)."

Nonverbal Components

The way you communicate nonverbally is also very important for an assertive image. The verbal model using empathy, rationale, and action will be more effective if the nonverbal communication is assertive as well. In fact, if either nonassertive or aggressive nonverbal cues accompany the verbal message, it is likely that the three-part assertive model will be undermined. So what are nonverbal cues of assertiveness?

Eye contact is one of the most important nonverbal cues in assertive communication. It is more assertive to look receivers in the eye while talking to them than to look down or avert your eyes. Think of situations you have noticed with nonassertive, submissive, and timid people—the hesitant clerk asking the boss for a raise, a child explaining torn clothes to Mom, or even Bashful of Snow White's seven dwarves. One of the most obvious features of these nonassertive characters is a lack of eye contact. Direct eye contact communicates confidence and sincerity, and makes people appear more sure of their position.

On the other side of the coin is the aggressive stare. Prolonged, intense eye contact tends to produce discomfort in receivers, to signify a challenge, or to appear intimidating. Assertive communicators use steady, direct eye contact but don't hold it so long that it becomes aggressive.

Along similar lines, the rest of your face needs to appear assertive as well. If your *facial expression* looks unsure or apologetic (pursed or pouting lips), this will communicate nonassertiveness even though you may not *feel* unsure. Similarly, if you look hostile or angry (gritting your teeth and clenching your jaw), you are likely to be perceived as aggressive. Some individuals' facial features almost naturally appear either nonassertive or aggressive. For example, eyebrows placed high on the forehead give the appearance of surprise or innocence, whereas prominent bone structure in the forehead and large eyebrows often seem scowling and angry. Thus, these features may determine the interpretation, even when the source does not intend such messages. Some facial features, like the habitual set of your mouth or chin, can be modified. However, other aspects may not be easily changed and the best advice here is to know what you look like, what messages your features suggest, and work within that knowledge to create a consistent and intentional image.

Posture and gestures also contribute to an overall assertive image. Assertive posture is erect but not stiff, with head and shoulders directly facing the receiver and weight evenly distributed on both feet. Firm, well-formed gestures help complete the picture of the direct, straightforward communicator.

Compare this nonverbally assertive image with a nonassertive posture in which the head may be tilted to one side or bowed down, shoulders hunched defensively forward, gestures small and incomplete, and feet tucked tightly together. Aggressive gestures and posture by comparison often appear out of control with arms waving wildly, pounding motions, and a suggestion of threat. In the latter description the movements may be *too* large and the posture *too* intense to be labeled assertive. Thus, the assertive posture suggests a person more self-confident and in control than does either nonassertive or aggressive body movements.

Tone of voice is another important nonverbal cue when determining whether a message will be understood as assertive, aggressive, or nonassertive. Even a verbally complete assertive statement may seem nonassertive and weak if delivered in a mousey little voice accompanied by many pauses and hesitations. Or it may sound very hostile and aggressive if spoken in harsh or threatening tones. Therefore, your tone of voice needs to be consistent with the assertive words you say. This is especially important in classroom communication where students are quick to pick up on vocal cues.

Vocal tones are particularly difficult to monitor and be aware of because we don't hear ourselves accurately unless we audiotape our voices. Although we can practice eye contact, posture, or facial expression in a mirror in order to look more assertive, it is less convenient to monitor vocal cues. Many people habitually talk in tentative tones or use a childlike voice or, at the other extreme, sound belligerent without being aware of that perception. Therefore, it is a good idea to practice with a tape recorder (or a good friend) to get feedback in determining how you *sound* when attempting to communicate assertively.

Will assertive communication always work to achieve the outcome you desire? No. Assertiveness doesn't result in perfect communication. It doesn't mean you will win every argument. At times, receivers will be resistant and you will have to increase the strength and persistence of your assertive message. Sometimes you will decide that this particular issue is not important enough to battle over and then look for alternatives.

Conclusions

Some people contend that whenever we are communicating, an underlying goal is to influence others. Although this may not be our conscious goal, clearly some styles and forms of communication are perceived as more dominant and powerful than others. For example, contradicting or talking loudly tend to be interpreted as dominance moves. But relationally we also observe dominance patterns (principle of least interest, principle of resource control, principle of most alternatives) that predict which partner will be able to exert more control and influence over the other.

One of the most direct forms of communication intended to influence others in interpersonal communication is assertive communication.

Appropriate assertive messages both directly express and defend your own ideas, and simultaneously respect the ideas of your partner. (Compare this productive message pattern to that of aggressive and nonassertive messages.) The most effective assertive messages will use congruent nonverbal cues such as direct eye contact and confident tone of voice to reinforce the verbal components of empathy, rationale, and action (ERA).

Although assertive communication won't guarantee that you'll get your way, it's the best chance you have without ruining friendships with aggressive communication. It is also extremely important to understand dominance and influence in communicating when dealing with conflict in your relationships—as we will see in the next chapter.

RESOURCES AND RECOMMENDED READINGS

Alberti, R., & Emmons, M. (1970). *Your perfect right: A guide to assertive behavior*. San Luis Obispo, CA: Impact.

Bradac, J., & Mulac, A. (1984). A molecular view of powerful and powerless speech styles: Attributional consequences of specific language features and communicator intentions. *Communication Monographs, 51,* 307–319.

Duck, S. (1988). *Relating to others*. Chicago: Dorsey Press.

Serber, M. (1972). Teaching the nonverbal components of assertiveness training. *Journal of Behavior Therapy and Experimental Psychiatry, 3,* 179–183.

Tusing, K., & Dillard, J. (2000). The sounds of dominance. Vocal precursors of perceived dominance during interpersonal influence. *Human Communication Research, 26,* 148–171.

ASSERTIVENESS ANALYSIS

Think about the cultural background in which you have been raised. How has that affected whether you tend to communicate in an assertive, aggressive, or non-assertive style?

Some areas to consider include the following:

Parents

Country of origin

Ethnic background

Gender

Religious upbringing

Age

Family occupation

Other

FRAMING A FULLY ASSERTIVE RESPONSE

The following are scenarios that you might encounter in your interpersonal relationships. Your task is to respond to them *assertively* using the ERA model. Even if these are very difficult, anger-provoking situations, you need to communicate assertively not aggressively. Write your fully assertive response in the space provided.

Example: Your new roommate begins telling you intimate details about his or her love life, which you don't want to hear.

EMPATHY STATEMENT: I understand that you might want to talk about this, but

RATIONALE: I really feel uncomfortable hearing those details, so

ACTION: can we talk about something else.

1. Your boyfriend or girlfriend is acting very flirtatious with others out in public.

   EMPATHY:

   RATIONALE:

   ACTION:

2. You believe your good friend is lying to you about his or her weekend.

   EMPATHY:

   RATIONALE:

   ACTION:

3. Your family is criticizing you for not spending more time at home with them.

   EMPATHY:

   RATIONALE:

   ACTION:

4. Someone at your workplace keeps calling you objectionable pet names ("Big Boy" or "Sweet Cheeks") even though this person knows it irritates you.

   EMPATHY:

   RATIONALE:

   ACTION:

5. A person you are in the beginning stages of a romantic relationship with wants to move faster in the relationship than you do.

   EMPATHY:

   RATIONALE:

   ACTION:

6. You think your instructor has given you a lower grade on a class project than you deserve.

   EMPATHY:

   RATIONALE:

   ACTION:

17 Conflict Management

How to "Fight Fair"

OBJECTIVES

Fighting in relationships is one of the most agonizing and difficult communication skills to do effectively. Yet, how we choose to handle our conflict strongly predicts our satisfaction and stability in the relationship. If you can do all of the following, you're on your way to improving conflict communication.

1. Give the definition of interpersonal conflict and explain how it differs from philosophical discussion.

2. List the four major sources of conflict in relationships and give an example of each.

3. Distinguish between the two major patterns of unproductive interpersonal conflict management. Be able to recognize these patterns in illustrations.

4. Describe at least five of the "toxic" conflict strategies people sometimes use.

5. Explain why each of these conflict strategies is toxic for the relationship.

6. Discuss three major attitudes or orientations partners need to keep in mind about conflict in relationships.

7. Describe eight productive conflict strategies.

8. Be able to apply these productive conflict strategies in interpersonal scenarios.

CHAPTER OUTLINE

What Constitutes Conflict?
  Sources of Interpersonal Conflict
Toxic Conflict Strategies

Interpersonal Problem Solving: Attitudes

"Rules" for Fair Fighting: Communication Skills

What Constitutes Conflict?

Conflict occurs any time the actions or attitudes of one person interfere with or create obstacles for the actions of another person. Often this will be accompanied by a negative emotional tone in the interaction. Thus, not only is someone's action an obstacle for us, but it typically causes us anger as well. By this definition, then, we wouldn't define a philosophical discussion of politics as a conflict situation until what one person believed or how he or she acted got in the way of another person's ability to engage in free choice about actions.

For example, the fact that your roommate believes strongly in a different religion than you do doesn't necessarily result in conflict unless the roommate expects you to follow those religious practices too.

Also note that the more closely you are entwined, or interdependent, in a relationship, the greater is your potential for conflict. If you live with someone, that person's actions are more likely to cause obstacles for you, and vice versa. Because relationships are communicative systems, actions by one person often cause reactions in others. Thus, disagreement is a normal part of any relational system.

The problem most people have is that they don't handle the conflict-related communication very effectively. Therefore the conflict issue, as well as the communication surrounding it, can cause severe relational distress. Remember, conflict is a normal (although not necessarily pleasant) part of all relationships. It will always be there. You have to learn how to manage it.

Sources of Interpersonal Conflict

When you ask married people what they fight about, one of the most common answers is "Money." Money and how to manage it tends to be a major conflict area for almost anyone who is pooling resources—whether they are married, roommates, or in some other partnership arrangement. But the list of what people have conflict over can be almost endless: sex, families, jobs, vacations, housecleaning, friends, activities, meals, pets, past history, and on and on. So it is useful to categorize sources of conflict and narrow the list.

There are four major *sources of interpersonal conflict*. People in relationships (including family members, coworkers, lovers, other students) can have conflict emerging from (1) differing goals, (2) differing ways of achieving those goals, (3) differing interpersonal needs, and (4) behavioral expectations.

Conflict over *differing goals* occurs when people have different ends they want to achieve. They differ on the outcomes or goals they view as important. For example, you might be ready for a serious relationship, but your dating partner just wants to have fun for now and not really look to the future. Sometimes there is conflict in schools because custodians have different goals concerning the gym or auditorium than students do. The custodians' job is to keep the floors and facility neat, clean, and in good repair, but the students may just want to *use* it.

We may also experience conflict when we agree with someone about the goals but *disagree on how to achieve those goals*. We want to have a relatively neat, clean apartment. But how do we achieve that? One roommate might want to pick up and clean on a weekly basis, whereas another thinks you should only clean for special occasions or when the apartment gets to the point where fungus is growing in the kitchen and the living room has to be shoveled out. And a third roommate might think you ought to hire someone to clean the apartment. The goals are identical—a quality appearance to the apartment—but people don't agree on how this should be done. Thus, we can have real conflict with someone even though we are in complete agreement on the goals we'd like to see accomplished.

A third source of conflict is *differing interpersonal needs.* You have low affection needs, but your boyfriend or girlfriend has high needs. You might end up fighting over how you are (or are not) getting those needs met. Open conflict often occurs when two or more people try to be the leader of a task group—trying to meet their control needs. People regularly argue over inclusion needs, as in when you want to have people around you and over at your living area, but your roommate wants more alone time.

Conflict over interpersonal needs is made more difficult by the fact that we are not usually good at empathizing with others' needs if we don't experience similar levels of that need. For example, it is very difficult for a person who has low inclusion needs to understand and cooperate with the drive to socialize that his or her partner feels.

The fourth source of conflict, and one that is particularly salient for teachers and parents, is *expectations of behavior.* We may quarrel with people if they don't act the way we want them to—or conversely, if we don't do what they want us to do. The range of behaviors that may cause conflict is endless: everything from "appropriate" apparel to "appropriate" language, what is the correct way to squeeze the toothpaste tube, "wild" behavior at a party, amounts of affection displayed, or how males should act compared to how females should act in various situations.

Conflict over behavioral expectations can occur over small, relatively inconsequential actions such as chewing food with your mouth open or who opens a door, or it can occur over actions with major consequences such as cheating on exams, driving while intoxicated, or breaking fidelity contracts in a relationship. Sometimes the conflict happens because one person didn't understand what was expected (this is not uncommon with small children), but often someone knows exactly what the other expects and decides that the expectation is unreasonable, or simply not important.

Conflict can occur for all of these reasons, but the important point here is that how you *communicate* about the issue will affect the relationship. Accept that your interactions are going to have conflict—it's a part of life—and decide to be effective in handling the conflict to improve the relationship.

Toxic Conflict Strategies

Some of the ways we "fight" are very destructive for the relationships. Sometimes our communication poisons the relationship slowly, killing off the positive feelings, or sometimes our communication is so "toxic" that it ruins the relationship quickly and completely. In addition, these toxic strategies seem to contaminate the partner as well. When one person is using unfair, destructive conflict strategies in communicating, it is common to retaliate in kind. This creates a vicious cycle of escalating hostility.

There are two major communicative patterns of ineffective conflict: avoiding and erupting. *Avoiders* are people who hate arguing and will avoid discussing conflict issues at all costs. They may become silent and refuse to talk when you mention a touchy issue. Or they may agree that discussion of that problem is needed "sometime," but that sometime never comes.

Avoiders may also be adept at changing the subject. If you bring up an issue, they may use humor to get you laughing or introduce another interesting topic to get you sidetracked so that they won't have to face the relational conflict point. The danger with avoiders is that in trying to keep the peace in a relationship, serious problems may go unattended. As with most physical ailments, minor symptoms of trouble in a relationship should not be left unattended until they present a major threat to the system.

The second major pattern of unproductive conflict is erupting. *Erupters* are people who lose their temper and become very emotional and overt when angry. This can be particularly unpleasant for the people around them who experience this aggressive communication. An eruption may be a brief outburst, such as when someone shouts, "Just leave me alone!" Or it may be an extended venting, a tirade accompanied by physical actions such as furious pacing, slamming doors, or throwing objects. In extreme cases, erupters may physically strike out at someone.

One of the toxic tactics erupters use in conflict situations is "belt-lining," saying things that will intentionally hurt the other. Everyone has an emotional belt line, below which are topics that are too sensitive or hurtful for them to talk about. People who know us well are likely to know, because of our self-disclosure with them, what is below our emotional belt line. When people "belt-line," they bring up these hurtful types of information and hit below the belt of the partner. For example, if someone felt guilty about driving the car that injured a child and the partner brought up that incident during a fight, that would be "belt-lining." Belt-lining is extremely dirty fighting because the goal is always to hurt the partner and thereby "win" the argument.

Belt-lining often deals with physical appearance or past history. Name-calling is a special form of belt-lining. When you hear students on the playground call a kid "Fatty" or "Stinky," or when more "adult" people call someone a "loser," a "slut," or a racial slur, this is a form of belt-lining and is meant to cause psychological harm to the victim.

Another very ineffective form of communication during conflict incorporates both avoiding and erupting and is called "gunny-sacking." When people gunny-sack, they avoid dealing with minor problems and try to ignore them. They hide those small problems away in a mental "gunny sack" where they won't have to communicate about them. Then one day the gunny sack gets full, or because of external stresses is weakened, and it bursts open. The person tries to stuff one more little irritant into the sack and it rips apart, pouring all those complaints and old problems out onto whoever happens to be in the area—hence the "erupting" part of gunny-sacking.

One of the detrimental aspects of gunny-sacking is that the extent of the eruption is usually totally out of proportion to the action that caused it. The person who is the target of the eruption may have done something very minor that he or she has done before. The outburst, when it comes, seems very confusing and irrational, and nothing constructive is accomplished.

Another negative aspect of gunny-sacking is that it is a cyclical pattern. After the eruption, the person starts filling the sack again rather than learning to deal with problems. Thus, in a relationship with a gunny-sacker you see a period of apparent calm while the gunny sack is filling, followed by an outburst, and then a return to apparent calm. This pattern of behavior is often found in cases of domestic violence.

Kitchen-sink fighting is a form of generalized erupting. Whenever partners get into an argument, they throw everything but the kitchen sink at each other—old hurts, behavior from last New Year's eve, an unbalanced checkbook two years ago. One reason this is dysfunctional and doesn't really "clear the air" as some people might contend, is that there are so many issues and complaints that the conversational partner feels overwhelmed and cannot deal effectively with any of them.

An unfair strategy that is more avoidant is "hit and run." You bring up a point of contention, and then leave the field so that it can't be discussed. You might mention how disappointed you are with your partner just as you're walking out the door for work, leaving him or her to worry about it without being able to find out more information.

To summarize, the problem with all of these toxic conflict patterns (you can probably think of many more that aren't mentioned here) is that they don't address the actual issue in the relationship or between partners.

Whether because they cause negative affect, hide or avoid real problems, or cloud issues with extraneous detail and old complaints, these techniques divert attention from the cause of the problem. When they are used in communication, nothing gets solved and the relationship deteriorates.

Interpersonal Problem Solving: Attitudes

There is hope. Just because we aren't using good communication in our interpersonal relationships now doesn't mean we can't *learn* to be better at it. Further, the basic ideas of handling disagreement constructively can be taught to young children, so they don't have to grow up engaging in toxic conflict patterns.

We begin with some attitudinal aspects of communicating effectively in conflict situations. Sometimes people simply have the wrong ideas about what conflict is and how it should be handled—perhaps because they have had poor models. A first step, then, is to change the thinking and attitudes to more productive ways of dealing with interpersonal differences.

First, when you think of experiencing conflict in a relationship, assume that you *want to maintain that relationship.* You probably don't have the luxury of throwing away a relationship with your roommate unless you want to find someone else to take his or her place immediately. (Although I do think that many university students avoid working on conflict at the end of a semester if they don't plan on sharing an apartment with that person again.)

Similarly, with people we care about outside of school, we want to maintain those friendships and positive affect, so we should undertake these more constructive (although at times difficult) communication strategies.

A second attitudinal feature of effective communication in handling interpersonal differences is *eliminating any win–lose orientation.* Many people feel that they *must* win an argument, come out on top, prove they're right. A win–lose orientation means there can be only one winner, and for every winner there must be a loser, just as in a basketball game. But relationships aren't supposed to be competitive events, and this dominance orientation is very unproductive in conflict. A better way to look at a potential conflict situation is to try to think how it could be a "win–win" situation. How can both parties win? How can they both gain something and feel good about themselves and the relationship?

Part of this win–win orientation is a *willingness to consider alternative solutions* to the problem. Your way doesn't have to be the "right" way. It is often difficult for us to envision a better solution to an issue than the one we've thought of. Then we become defensive and dig in to maintain our positions without keeping an open mind about the other's ideas, perspectives, or proposals.

Fear of having conflict is yet another dysfunctional attitude that many people hold concerning interpersonal dissension. We may think, "If I have a sharp disagreement with my partner, there's something terribly wrong with the relationship." Not necessarily true. Remember, all relationships experience interpersonal disagreement and dissension. What people often fear is the damaging effects of poorly handled conflict communication. Sometimes individuals become avoiders because of previous experience with an erupter in their life. If a child sees parents in repeated ugly eruptive conflict interactions, he or she may decide "I'm never going to be like that," and subsequently try to avoid communication about problems entirely. Thus, a more productive orientation is to not fear experiencing differences with someone, and to learn how to communicate in such a way as to solve the problem and improve the relationship as a result.

"Rules" for Fair Fighting: Communication Skills

There are several specific communication skills and patterns you can adopt that will improve your communication about interpersonal differences within a relationship. These are often referred to as "rules" for fair fighting and can serve as guidelines for you.

1. *Both parties need to agree to follow the "rules" and try to use positive communicative strategies.* It may be very difficult, if not impossible, to manage conflict productively if one person persists in using toxic strategies.

2. *Set a time for the interaction (the "fight").* No, this is not so that one person can think up "ammunition" to use against the other. That would represent a win–lose orientation. Setting a time accomplishes two purposes. First, it allows you to cool down from any initial anger or frustration. The worst time to discuss a problem is when you're emotionally upset. For example, don't discuss your friend's drunken behavior at a party when you're angry about it. Or, don't discuss the fact that your roommate forgot to pay a bill when you have just found out that the service was disconnected and you are angry about it. When you are angry, or emotionally aroused, you're not thinking clearly and may say things you will regret. So set a time to discuss the issue.

The second benefit of setting a time for the discussion is that it helps get avoiders to actually sit down and discuss the issue. Although specifying a time doesn't guarantee that a true avoider will engage in conflict management, it's certainly preferable to the ambiguity of discussing the problem "sometime."

3. *Make sure the time you set aside for discussion is sufficient and appropriate for both parties.* Allow enough time to really work through problems, to really talk about what is occurring. That is, don't agree with your spouse that "we'll discuss our problems at 6:30 P.M. Thursday," when you have company coming over at seven. It's probably best to allow at least an hour or so for discussion.

In addition, don't set a time when either person would be disadvantaged due to fatigue, stress, and so on. For example, Friday nights after a hectic, tiring week at school are probably not the best times to interact about relational problems. Similarly, it would be best to avoid major conflict sessions and relational decisions during periods that are extrastressful: finals week, the week before Christmas, or in the middle of a series of potential job interviews.

4. *Consider one issue at a time and then move on.* Focus on one problem or irritant in your discussion, come to some agreements, and then go do something else. Don't try to solve all of your problems in one sitting. If you develop a pattern of regular discussions about problem areas, you can continue to work on them little by little. Problem solving and managing conflict is hard work and costly in the relationship even when people do it effectively. So don't overload your interaction with additional major issues by saying, "While we're talking about this . . ." or "That reminds me. . . ."

5. *Describe the issue or problematic behavior.* Try to avoid evaluative terms and describe the action that creates obstacles for you so the other person has a clear picture. Rather than griping about someone's "bad manners," explain and describe what the person does (e.g., consistently late to meet you, interrupting other speakers, taking care of bodily functions in public). What constitutes "bad manners" for one person might not for another. Similarly, it might not be the behavior itself but the situation in which the behavior is displayed that causes the problem. By describing the behavior and the situation, that issue becomes clearer.

6. *Take responsibility for your emotions.* In other words, don't blame others for the way you feel. Statements such as "You make me so angry" or "Don't ever embarrass me again in front of my friends" are blaming and may invoke defensiveness. Recognize that your emotional reactions are *yours*. A better way to think about and state your feelings is to "own" them. "I feel angry when you just drop your clothes on the floor and leave them there." "I feel left out when you don't discuss important things with me." Notice that these statements incorporate both taking responsibility for feelings and descriptions of problematic behavior.

7. *Check perception.* Don't assume you know what other people are thinking or feeling, or even that you've understood what they are saying. Paraphrase in your own words what you think they mean. "You're saying you think you work too hard in this relationship." "You mean you want me to spend more time with you." "You're saying you don't have time to get this done." You can also do perception checks on nonverbal communication, on how the other appears or sounds. You might say, "You look like you're really bored. Are you?" Or, "You have sort of a confused look on your face." Perception checks help get thoughts out in the open and hopefully avoid more misunderstandings.

8. *Try to keep the pace of the interaction slow rather than rapid.* Another benefit of perception checks is that they slow down the pace of the interaction. Hostile, angry, and sometimes aggressive episodes seem to be characterized by a fast pace. Words are out before you even realize it. By slowing down the rate of interaction, by checking others' meanings, you give yourself time to think and react more rationally than you would in the "heat" of the moment.

9. *Express positive affect.* This is a person you care about, even though you might be having some interpersonal problems with her or him right now. Show that affection both verbally and nonverbally. Problem-solving sessions can be relationally scary, and we need reassurance that the relationship and the partner are still valued. So restate how much you care for or respect the person.

10. *A major goal of effective interpersonal problem solving is always to lower the emotional belt line of yourself and your partner.* This is accomplished by avoiding the negative conflict strategies, by disclosing yourself, and by remaining provisional, that is, not assuming your perspective is the only correct perspective. A lower emotional belt line means that the person feels safer and more secure in the relationship. The lower the emotional belt line goes, the more area there is above the belt that can be discussed and dealt with constructively.

Conclusions

Constructive problem solving involves self-disclosure, understanding attributional processes and interpersonal needs, assertiveness, role-taking ability, self-discipline, awareness of relational stages and expectations, effective utilization of feedback, and just about any other feature of communicative interactions that we have discussed. It's very complex. But good conflict skills are also very important if you don't want to see a valuable relationship head toward termination.

REFERENCES AND RECOMMENDED READINGS

Folger, J., Poole, M. S., & Stutman, R. (1997). *Working through conflict: Strategies for relationships, groups, and organizations* (3rd ed.). New York: Longman.

Cupach, W., & Canary, D. (1997). *Competence in interpersonal conflict.* New York: McGraw-Hill.

Dindia, K, & Baxter, L. (1987). Strategies for maintaining and repairing romantic relationships. *Journal of Social and Personal Relationships, 4,* 143–158.

Emmers-Sommer, T., (1999). Negative relational events and event responses across relationship-type: Examining and comparing the impact of conflict strategy use on intimacy in same-sex friendships, opposite-sex friendships, and romantic relationships. *Communication Research Reports, 16,* 286–295.

IDENTIFYING YOUR CONFLICT SOURCES

For each of the four sources of conflict, write two or three examples.

Conflict over differing goals

Conflict over differing ways of achieving the same goals

Conflict over different levels of interpersonal needs

Conflict over expectations of behavior

CONFLICT MANAGEMENT STRATEGIES: THE GOOD, THE BAD, AND THE UGLY

Communication Patterns That Drive Our Partners Crazy: Things *Not* to Do in Conflict

See if you can identify yourself, your partners (either platonic or romantic), or your family in any of the strategies listed here. In the margin put an *S* if you have done it, a *P* if your partners have, and an *F* if your family has used any of these strategies.

1. *Overmirroring:* Whatever the other person says, you say the same words back.

2. *Reversing the attack:* What started out as their issue, becomes yours. You were late for a meeting with them, but then you start justifying it by mentioning all the negative things they have done.

3. *Name-calling:* You think of any gross, hurtful label you can to fling at your partner: "loser," "slut," "slob," "freak." These are all particularly "helpful" in solving relationship problems.

4. *Belt-lining:* Saying things that "hit below the belt" emotionally. These are messages intended to directly hurt the other person. They are typically aspects that people can't easily change about themselves.

5. *Trivial-tyrannizing:* Starting an argument about a small matter because you are irritated about something else. Examples would be leaving dirty dishes in the sink, driving recklessly, playing music too loud. The intent is to get back at the partner, but not really bring up the issue you're upset about.

6. *Subject-switching:* Whenever the partner tries to bring up a topic of conflict, you change the topic. TV may be used as a barrier. Sometimes humor is used to distract the person.

7. *The "silent" treatment:* Obviously an avoiding tactic. Refusing to speak to the person, but slamming doors to get attention. You won't talk even if the person asks you what's wrong?

8. *Gunny-sacking:* Storing up old irritations until you can't hold it in anymore and the "gunny sack" explodes. You lose your temper and dump on your partner. The behavior that triggered the explosion may be totally out of proportion to the size of the explosion.

9. *Kitchen-sink fighting:* Letting them have it with everything you can think of. Bringing up old topics, every slight you have felt, every little thing they have ever done.

10. *Leaving the field:* Bringing up an issue and then leaving. Mentioning a problem in the relationship just as you are going out the door. In other words, you get the "fight" started and then leave.

11. *Overreacting:* You blow up over a minor matter. Your romantic partner is merely talking with someone else and you threaten to break up. The reaction makes a huge issue out of a minor matter; also called "making a mountain out of a mole hill."

AVOIDING AND ERUPTING CONFLICT PATTERNS

1. What are some strategies you have seen people use to *avoid* conflict in relationships? Describe what they did.

2. What are some *erupting* strategies you have seen people use? Describe.

3. How were each of these examples unproductive for the relationship?

18 When All Else Fails

Making the Best of Termination

OBJECTIVES

Relationships grow and change. They ebb and flow. But relationships don't stay the same over time because people and situations change. Sometimes termination is inevitable and may be the most positive outcome. But going through it can be tough. By being able to complete the following objectives you can come to understand your own terminations more fully.

1. Explain four forms of dissatisfaction that often lead to relationship termination. Use examples to complete your explanations.

2. List six specific reasons that relationships terminate.

3. Contrast the direct versus indirect and the other- versus self-oriented forms of communicating during termination phases.

4. Discuss how the tactics people tend to use for distancing themselves at the end of a relationship relate to the stages of coming apart discussed previously.

5. Give an example of each form of communication used in breaking up: positive tone, negative identity management, justification, behavioral de-escalation, de-escalation.

6. Give three suggestions for communication during breakup that may allow us to "still be friends."

7. List three or four common problems people experience after a termination they did not choose.

8. Give three suggestions for handling communication *after* relationship termination, when you were *not* the initiator of the breakup.

CHAPTER OUTLINE

Dissatisfaction Phase

Reasons for Relational Termination

Communication during the Relational
Termination Stage

Distancing Ourselves
Termination

Terminating So We "Can Still Be
Friends"

You've Been Terminated . . .

Honest, But Probably Not the Best,
Reactions

What Tends to Work in Coping with
a Lost Relationship

Summary of Response to Relational
Termination

Putting It All Together

Not all relationships are meant to go on forever. Sometimes the most productive and beneficial outcome to a relationship is for it to end. But we also need to be aware of the reasons why a relationship that was formerly so positive can go down hill. We will discuss these reasons, as well as how to communicate at the end of a relationship so as not to ruin all the good times that have gone on before, to preserve feelings, and so as not to alienate the other person in case he or she ends up being your boss some day. Don't burn your bridges.

Dissatisfaction Phase

How do we get the first inkling that our friendship is starting to fray? The dissatisfaction phase is when you realize that the relationship is not all that it could (or should) be. It's not working out very well. This phase may happen when you start to become aware that the positivity of social exchange is lacking. At this point, you realize that the relationship is not meeting your needs, but you may not be ready to actually terminate. There are four general categories of dissatisfaction leading to the potential ending of a relationship.

One of the most common categories is *dissatisfaction with your partner*. This happens when you realize that you don't care for your boyfriend or girlfriend anymore. He just doesn't seem as attractive. Her annoying habits, which you thought you could overlook, become unbearable. (It used to be kind of cute that she snapped her gum, but now you really hate it.) Even your partner's positive traits, such as being affectionate, begin to wear on your nerves. Or, it could be that your best friend has changed his behavior.

He used to be so much fun and now all he wants to do is hang out and watch TV. Maybe you're growing in different directions due to career paths, other friends, or other opportunities. What is occurring is that your rewards from being with this person are decreasing, or they are being relabeled as costs.

On the other hand, you may be quite happy with your partner but experience *dissatisfaction with the relationship*. You want to move toward more intimacy, whereas your partner does not. Or maybe your partner is "pressuring" *you* for a closer relationship, but you want to keep it more casual and not so serious. Sometimes people experience this form of dissatisfaction when they are platonic friends with someone and want to change the relationship to a romantic one. Or you might have a platonic relationship, but the other person keeps calling and wanting more frequent and extended interactions with you. You can't seem to get away from this person. You feel hemmed in. For whatever reason, the basic structure of the relationship creates negative feelings and dissatisfaction.

A third form of dissatisfaction has to do with *others who form the relationship network*. You like your partner, you like the relationship you have together, but you can't stand her friends. People outside the immediate relationship cause interference. Sometimes it might be your partner's parents or siblings. Couples may have arguments over "how you act when you're around your friends." Sometimes people external to the relationship actively try to create problems in your relationship, such as stating they dislike your partner or telling you negative things they have heard about your partner. It may come down to a choice between keeping the relationship or keeping the friends. Either way, these outside people put stress on your relationship.

Finally, you may experience dissatisfaction due to an *inability to deal with strain imposed by circumstances*. Some relationships are more difficult to maintain than others, because of situations out of control of the partners such as poverty, long-term illnesses, or crime. Long distances put a strain on relationships. Extremely long working hours are hard on a relationship. For example, if one of you travels a great deal—someone in the military, a salesperson, a long-distance truck driver—these circumstances make maintenance of the relationship challenging. People who work odd time shifts in high-stress jobs, such as law enforcement or the medical profession, often report having difficulties keeping relationships together. So external circumstances may increase costs in the relationship, and may thereby also increase dissatisfaction.

But remember: Dissatisfaction doesn't always lead to termination. Recall that a final step discussed in the social exchange model is the comparison of alternatives. If you don't perceive reasonable alternatives to this relationship, you may remain in it but still be dissatisfied or unhappy.

Reasons for Relational Termination

After a relationship has ended, partners are often able to explain why they thought it happened. There tend to be six major reasons given for why the relationship ended.

Often relationships end due to *poor relationship skill levels* of partners. Perhaps they don't know they have to work on a relationship to keep it alive. Perhaps they don't understand the need for self-disclosure or sharing emotions. Perhaps they don't handle conflict well and are either major avoiders or major erupters. Any kind of communication skill deficiency could cause a decline in the interpersonal relationship.

Some relationships seem to just "wear out." The partners experience *boredom and disinterest*. You simply tire of a relationship that does not change or stay exciting. Sometimes this is due to normal individual growth and is to be expected in many relationships. But if you are committed to the relationship and it is central to your life, you need to take steps to make sure that it does not become stagnant and boring.

Many relations end when a *major expectation is violated*. A good example is fidelity. A romance may terminate if you find that your partner has been "romancing" someone else at the same time. This often includes lying and deception too. Many people report that they could no longer remain in a relationship after their partner told others personal information they had disclosed in confidence. The breaking of any major expectation or vow in the relationship may cause immediate termination.

Difficulty of maintenance, as mentioned above, is also a cause of break-ups. Having a work situation that is stressful, long distances separating the partners, and so on, may lead to more than just dissatisfaction. If the dissatisfaction becomes extreme, termination often follows.

Many times people don't plan to end the relationship, but they experience *conflict that gets out of control*. This could be an argument that gets out of hand and partners say things in heat that they may not really mean. "OK, if that's the way you feel, GET OUT." Conflict may escalate to saying or doing hurtful things—and communication cannot be taken back. So before you know it, you have terminated the relationship.

Finally, people may terminate their relationships, not because they are dissatisfied or rules are broken, but simply because *better "alternatives" come onto the scene*. You were quite happy with your girlfriend or boyfriend when you were in high school, but now at college there are so many more attractive alternatives. You often see this happening when one person in the relationship becomes "famous" for some reason—she is an acclaimed athlete, his musical group hits the big time, a major book gets published. Other people may suddenly find them more desirable and seek them out—providing many more relational alternatives than they had before.

Alternatives do not necessarily mean a relationship will terminate, but they may destabilize it and be part of the social exchange determination.

Communication during the Relational Termination Stage

The actual strategies we use when we decide to break up with someone differ on whether they are *direct or indirect* and *other-oriented or self-oriented.* Direct strategies deal in a straightforward manner with the partner and don't beat around the bush. The termination is assertively discussed. Other-oriented versus self-oriented strategies refer to who you are concerned about when you communicate during the termination stage. If you use other-oriented strategies, you show concern for your partner's feelings and allow the person to save face. In contrast, if you employ self-oriented communication you are concerned primarily with yourself, just getting out of the relationship no matter what the cost to the other person.

For example, terminating a relationship with someone by telling him or her to "drop dead" would be a direct, self-oriented tactic. It gets the job done quickly, but may hurt the feelings of the partner. On the other hand, if you try to end the relationship by waiting and waiting until the other person decides to terminate, that would be more indirect and other-oriented.

Distancing Ourselves

Prior to the actual terminating interaction, we often begin distancing ourselves from the other person. This can be done both physically and psychologically.

Physically we try to put space between ourselves and our relational partner. We try to "disassociate" with him or her. We talk less frequently and are less immediate when we do talk. We may become less physically intimate, sit further away on the couch, and engage in less kissing. On weekends we may find ourselves spending more time with others than with our friend, and making excuses to *not* be together. Such avoidant communication patterns also exemplify the "behavioral de-escalation" category described below.

Psychologically or emotionally we start to perceive this person differently. We may envision life or activities without him or her. We may start to notice more of the person's negative points and fewer of the positive attributes. We probably will have less positive affect toward the person and find ourselves being irritated or disgusted by him or her. This doesn't necessaarily mean that the person is *behaving* any differently than he or she has all the time in our relationship, but we are *seeing and interpreting* the actions differently. Emotionally our exchange model shifts from perceiving more rewards to perceiving more costs.

Our communication patterns with our partner tend to change as we distance ourselves. Our conversations may become vague, general, non-specific. We don't talk about anything intimate or detailed or new. We may find ourselves becoming cautious about what we tell the partner, anticipating the end of the relationship. Instead of acting like our natural self, we fall back onto roles more frequently. We may also find ourselves in boring, repetitious patterns of interaction in which we talk about the "same old thing."

Communication patterns in distancing also become more *nonimmediate*. That is, whereas we used to smile at the person and lean toward him or her as we talked, we now are more neutral and nonimmediate. We may make less eye contact, lean away rather than toward the person, touch the person less, and all of the other signs of immediacy may lessen. This pattern indicates that we are disengaging from our partner, rather than becoming closer in the relationship.

The Termination

Terminations tend to differ depending on whether the relationship is romantic or platonic. If you think about it, we don't usually say that we "broke up" with our best friend. We may do the distancing behaviors, but termination of platonic relationships is usually less dramatic and the end points are more ambiguous compared to romantic relationships. This is due in part to two factors. First, romantic relationships tend to be more emotion-based, built on more intense affect than are friendships. So termination is a hotter, more memorable and intense occurrence.

The second factor differentiating romantic from platonic terminations is that in our society we tend to participate in only one romance at a time. We're more heavily invested in that one romance. Even if this is sequential (you have first one romantic relationship, break up, and then have another), we tend to intensify with one person, focusing time and resources on this person. (Exceptions, as with polygamous Mormons, tend to be rare or hidden.) Thus, if this romantic relationship ends, there is a clearer break.

But how do people actually go about ending their relationships? What communication messages do they use? Five specific categories of breaking up or terminating relationships have been identified.

Positive Tone.   This is where the individual tries to end on a good note, keeping things pleasant. "I'm very sorry. I don't want to hurt you in breaking up. You're a great person and I want to stay friends."

Negative Identity Management.   This type focuses on what might be harmed or lost if the couple stayed together. It suggests that staying together could actually ruin the relationship or cause the partners to miss out on too many things. "I've got this great opportunity to study abroad, but you want to finish your degree here." "Life is too short and we should both date around."

Justification.   The justification category usually involves a full explanation of why the termination is happening. Conversation is quite direct and honest. "Here's why I feel dissatisfied in our relationship. It's too serious, too soon. I don't want to be focusing on a serious relationship when I'm trying to get my business off the ground."

Behavioral De-escalation.   This type of communication is very indirect and avoidant, just letting the relationship trail off, interacting less and less frequently. " I didn't say anything to my partner. I just avoided seeing them, or being around where I knew they'd be." This would probably include not returning phone calls, or having your roommate say you aren't there when you are. Behavioral de-escalation may be more likely to be used in less committed relationships.

De-escalation.   This strategy directly communicates an intent to see less of the other person, although it is often only temporarily or partial termination. "We're becoming too dependent on each other and should let it rest for a while." "Maybe we shouldn't see each other over the summer, give ourselves some time apart." "We'll each find new roommates next semester."

Do you recognize yourself or people you know in any of these strategies? Keep in mind that the particular strategy might change once you get into the conversation, depending on the response of your terminated partner. You might start out with a positive tone, but deteriorate to a shouting, name-calling event if the other person is verbally aggressive.

Even though we recognize that it is impossible to remain close and involved with every friend and relationship partner we have ever had in our lives, we still don't want to "burn our bridges." Can we terminate relationships in ways so that we could go on with the person in a different type of relationship without animosity? Ask yourself, could you work with a former close friend or lover? Would it be embarrassing or downright ugly to have to talk with them every day? There are communication patterns that tend to ease the distress.

Terminating So We "Can Still Be Friends"

There is a recognizable structure in the communication interaction that terminates a relationship. It is sort of like putting a period at the end of a sentence. You know the relationship is finished. Many people have compared such interactions to actually saying good-bye to the partner—and not just for the weekend.

In relationships that have progressed through several stages of coming together, positive terminal interactions accomplish several goals. First, they tend to *summarize the substance of the relationship*. "You've been my best friend since junior high and we've been through a lot together." "We've been together for a long time." This aspect goes over the history of the relationship with statements such as "We've had our ups and downs, but a lot of good times." Such messages in terminating conversations recognize that this has been a substantial, important, or fun relationship.

But such "breakup" conversations also directly *signal impending decreased access* to the other person. That is, they tell the other that you won't be around as much, or you won't be seeing as much of each other. "I think we need to see other people." "We can still do things together, but we just won't be living together." Such messages are a part of that separation process, and can be observed when someone takes a new job, as well as when a relationship terminates.

Positive messages in terminating also communicate a *supportiveness for what has transpired* in the relationship. People often tell the other how much he or she means to them. They may reaffirm how important the relationship has been in their lives, or what a great time they have had, or how much they still care for the partner. This communicates that the relationship hasn't been a "waste," in part so the other partner doesn't feel as though he or she has been "used" or was deceived and a fool. It was worthwhile, but may not be a good experience now. It may also tell the other how you have grown to be different than you were when the relationship began.

Certainly, terminating a relationship competently also involves all of the positive communication skills we have discussed throughout this book. It takes nonverbal sensitivity to know when the best time will be. Terminating requires effective adaptation to changes that occur in the conversation (is your partner really upset, does your partner seem understanding?). Good listening skills are a must. In addition, effective terminating demands self-disclosure and assertive communication strategies, so that a problematic or unproductive relationship doesn't drag on and on.

When relationships end, partners do not have to become enemies. It is possible to terminate without hurting the other's feelings too much. (Remember it may be very understandable for the person who is "terminated" to have negative feelings if he or she wanted to remain in the relationship.)

However, if you communicate competently (that means you have the knowledge, skill, and motivation to do it), you can remain friends with people who you used to be close with. Yes, the relationship will change. But the termination doesn't have to ruin all the positive experiences and feelings that went on before. You can learn about yourself from this, and both of you can go on to other productive interpersonal relationships.

You've Been Terminated . . .

The termination of a relationship can be difficult for both people involved. But it's not quite so hard to end a committed relationship when *you* initiated the breakup, is it? It may be a very different matter if you are the person who wanted to keep the relationship, rather than end it. But your partner wanted out. In other words, how do you deal with relationship loss when you are "let go" rather than being the partner who did the "letting go"? You may feel out of control, depressed, angry, at a loss, dazed, and confused. For many people losing a close relationship is one of their worst life events, and we won't minimize the hurt felt. But the relationship has terminated. The specialness is over, so now what do you do?

In this final portion we will first take a look at typical feelings and problems people face when they have had a relationship terminated against their wishes. Then we'll explore some methods researchers and clinicians have found to help ex-partners cope with relational loss. (These factors may apply both to relationships that end because of individual choice and even to those that end by the death of the partner.)

Honest, But Probably Not the Best, Reactions

Hoping and Praying.   Sitting around hoping you can "get them back" probably won't be productive. *Escapist* coping strategies include activities such as daydreaming about the person, fantasizing about getting back together, and hoping for a miracle. Although some long-term terminated relationships do rekindle, most do not. If romantic partners go back together, it is typically only short term. If friends rekindle the relationship it is usually because some external barrier has been removed. That might mean that they move geographically closer, they are no longer under the influence of drugs or alcohol, their parents change their minds about you, and so on. In the meantime, a positive approach would be to consider this relationship a learning experience, take a step forward, and to try to move on.

Emotional Upheaval.   Dealing with the intense negative feelings can be a huge obstacle. We feel that our emotions are out of our control, and we may feel overwhelmed with feelings of anger ("I can't believe he did that to me!"), sadness ("I don't think I can go on without her"), jealousy ("That sleaze is enjoying the relationship now"), self-doubt ("What did I do wrong?"), or confusion ("I don't know what to do now, how to regain my life").

Alone and Lonely.   Loneliness is often a major problem after a breakup. You have become very accustomed to having a partner to share a spaghetti dinner with, go to the movies, take walks, play racquetball, and a wide variety of other activities. This person knew and understood you so well. So it is understandable that when this companion is gone, you feel lonely and adrift.

Social support from friends and family is great and useful, but it cannot entirely compensate for the loss of your significant other. Friends help. They are there for you. They listen. But they can't replace your significant other and erase your emotional loneliness. Nevertheless, social support *can* help with loneliness of social isolation. Your friends and family can open new avenues, introduce new acquaintances and activities that can help keep you busy, both emotionally and physically, so that you don't ruminate and "obsess" about the terminated relationship (Stroebe et al., 1996).

Intrusive Negative Thoughts. Often after a romantic relationship breaks up, we can't stop thinking about our ex-partner and what happened. We may be unable to sleep because of such intrusive thoughts. This is termed rumination. *Rumination* is when we passively and repetitively focus on our symptoms of distress and the circumstances surrounding those symptoms. "Why am I in such a mess?" "Will it ever get better?"

People who engage in this form of unproductive rumination don't try to problem-solve. Instead they just think about or talk about how unmotivated, sad, devastated, or lethargic they feel. This is not productive.

Rumination also makes negative thoughts, feelings, and memories more cognitively accessible and actually interferes with positive coping (Nolen-Hoeksema, McBride, & Larson, 1997). If all your mental resources are taken up with thinking over and over again about what you could have done differently, how wonderful that former relationship was, and so on, there is little mental capacity left for more productive, forward-looking thoughts.

What Tends to Work in Coping with a Lost Relationship

We feel devastated by the fact that our significant other dumped us. We are lonely and bereft because our best friend just moved to Australia. There is no denying the loss of the close relationship. But what can we do to try to handle it productively, rather than destroy other parts of our lives.

Keep Busy. Activity engages the mind, it distracts you, and it tires out the body. If you sit around doing nothing, it is harder to move on. Some people feel so distraught that they lack energy and feel totally weak. So force yourself if necessary. But do something active. The loneliness literature indicates that people who remain busy are less likely to feel lonely. This may be a good time to begin a new hobby, because many of your usual activities may include memories of your ex.

Think Future.   Try to orient to the future rather than the past. Don't look back; there's nothing you can change there. People who experience traumatic loss sometimes get "stuck" in the past—reliving the negative event over and over and not moving on (Holman & Silver, 1998). Focusing excessively on the past has been found to have negative consequences for identity formation, self-satisfaction, and achievement. Try to look ahead productively. Make plans for the future—even if the "future" is next week's class assignment or tomorrow's community meeting.

Bolster Your Self-Esteem.   High self-esteem people tend to deal more productively with failure events than low self-esteem people do. This is in part because they search for the positive aspects in their self and behavior and focus on those plusses. Low self-esteem people tend to focus on the negative features (Dodgson & Wood, 1998). So do something to try to build your self-esteem. Focus on your strengths (everyone has them!). Perhaps make lists of your positive features. This is much more productive than wallowing in thoughts about "what a loser I am!"

Focus Outward Rather Than Inward.   Engaging in thoughts and feelings about ourselves following a relationship termination doesn't tend to help and often exacerbates the intensity of our negative feelings. Certain coping strategies have been found to be more productive than others. *Problem appraisal strategies* are directed at management of the problem; but rather than deal directly with the event, they deal with managing one's appraisal of its stressfulness. For many situations, the problem appraisal style of coping is found to be the best for minimizing distress following a situation that was out of your control (Terry & Hynes, 1998). For example, you might try to step back and be more objective, try to see the positive side of the relationship ending, accept it, and make the best of the situation.

An additional aspect of this outward focus is paying attention to others rather than our own problems. Volunteer to help out at a homeless shelter, with disaster relief, or at a humane society if you want to see significant problems. It may make your own personal issues pale in comparison.

Get Help If You Need It.   Remember, if you can't handle the feelings of loss on your own, there are external sources of help. Use them. You may try the ideas discussed here but still feel terrible months later. The negative thoughts and feelings are affecting your academic standing, your work, relationships with other people, and even your health. Call a counselor. Phone numbers are in every phone book. Work with someone who is an expert in these issues of relational loss and can guide you through them, rather than going on and potentially endangering your future.

An important note to remember: *Time does heal.* As time passes, the sadness you feel will decline, but it certainly may not feel that way at the time. In the same way that an injured knee takes time to heal, so does the pain from an ended relationship. It's important not to do anything dangerous to yourself in the meantime: quit a good job, move away from a positive situation, engage in substance abuse, risky sex, or activities with suicidal intent. Men in our society tend to engage in more self-destructive activities, such as drinking too much or driving too fast, following the loss of a relationship than do women. This may be due to their social network, or because they report more intense emotional responses immediately after the fact than women report (Seidlitz & Diener, 1998). So men need to be especially mindful of the pitfalls they face after relationships break up.

Summary of Response to Relational Termination

These ideas take conscious effort. They don't happen magically, and they don't happen overnight. *You* are taking charge of how you feel and dealing with the situation. Even deciding to call on a professional to guide you through this time is your own initiative. These efforts can pay off by helping you to regain control, get back to "normalcy," and have a productive outlook on life, even following negative relational events.

Remember, there is not just one "perfect mate" or "perfect friend" for each of us. There really are other individuals who can make great partners for you. But you'll have to find them. Relationships are processes, which means they ebb and flow and go through cycles. In some ways, the ending of one relationship prepares you for a better beginning of the next one.

Putting It All Together

As you can see from all the previous chapters in this book, interpersonal communication is a complex, ongoing process requiring both cognitive knowledge and information about what to do as well as behavioral skills to enact the appropriate communication. Is it worth all the effort? Without a doubt! Interpersonal relationships are central to our life satisfaction and functioning. We want to be happily connected in a relationship.

The first chapters in the book deal with understanding yourself and the basic interpersonal communication process. You have to understand yourself so you can be a better partner. This information should also help with empathy as you look at things from the other person's perspective.

Insight into your self-concept helps bring out areas you may need to think about and explore. You need to be aware of the ways and times you feel good about yourself. You need to be clear about how a relationship may be affected when you don't feel good about yourself. It is also important to understand your own and your partner's interpersonal needs for inclusion, affection, and control. How do these fit together in your relationship? How can you both get your needs met and enhance your relationship? Many interpersonal relationships have been destroyed because people couldn't understand and adapt to each other's interpersonal needs. You don't want yours to end like that.

Understanding components of personality is crucial to relationships. You need to comprehend a variety of individual traits that may be operating to influence your interpersonal communication. This book has discussed a few central communication-related traits, but there are others that may be salient for you. Especially at the extremes, traits strongly influence how we communicate and react to others.

A central component in the development and maintenance of relationships is understanding and building the communication skills necessary. For example, we have to realize the impact of various forms of verbal and nonverbal messages. We need to be able to encode our own nonverbal cues clearly and to respond appropriately to others'—whether the messages have to do with how one looks, differential interpretations depending on cultural background, or meanings of touch.

Disclosing and expressing emotions are also crucial skills. Done poorly they can wreck a relationship. But communicated effectively they can enrich and deepen all kinds of relationships, from friends to family to romantic partners. The complement of expression is listening. All too often, we focus little attention on this skill. Listening doesn't just happen naturally. We do have to put some effort into listening well and understanding the barriers to good listening that most people face. As with all skills, communication skills improve with practice. You have to *do* it to get better.

Relationship decisions, especially under trying or potentially negative circumstances, are complex and demand our attention. The third portion of this book focuses on more difficult interactions. How we go about making the tough decisions in relationships (such as whether to continue or not, getting our partner to view the relationship differently) will be important across our life span, no matter what our cultural background.

Sometimes we face problems, such as complicated conflicts between social and task needs in relationships at work. Other times, the complication is primarily within our personal relationships and relates to how we handle disagreements and fighting. No one said relationships were easy. And when we have conflicts or when termination occurs, we face major challenges to our well-being. All of the concepts and skills discussed are integrated into our interactions. In real life, communication components don't come through as discrete chapters. How we develop and communicate in our interpersonal relationships will affect our happiness and quality of life, so it's important that we learn to do it well.

The Beginning

Consider this book a start. A first step. An introduction to the huge world of study in communication in interpersonal relationships. Many people stumble through their lives using trial and error or "common sense" to try to make their relationships function effectively. That means there will be numerous foul-ups. Many people mistakenly believe that good relationships "just happen," and therefore they don't pay much attention to them until the relationship is really in trouble. We all want to "live happily ever after," and we certainly struggle to do it. Our struggles are often ineffective because we can't step back and get perspective, and understand the benefits of others' experience when we are so close and involved.

What most people don't realize, however, is that there is an entire field of study with large volumes of solid research examining what tends to work and what doesn't in interpersonal relationships. You don't have to begin at square one every time you consider a relationship. Use the information and insights already gathered over the years by high-quality researchers to help you develop your own relationship. Will this research answer all the questions that arise in your individual and unique situation? Probably not. But it could be a good beginning.

Take the information discussed here and go look for more. There are entire books written, journals published, and courses built around conflict skills, understanding how self-concept works, nonverbal messages, outcomes related to personality, relational decision making, and all sorts of relational communication concepts. The list is long and the information in-depth. If any of these address your area of interest, go find them.

You've reached the initiating and experimenting stages within the field of interpersonal communication. Now you are ready to go on to the deeper levels. Relationships are worth it!

REFERENCES AND RECOMMENDED READINGS

Banks, S., Altendorf, D., Greene, J., & Cody, M. (1987). An examination of relationship disengagement: Perceptions, breakup strategies and outcomes. *Western Journal of Speech Communication, 51,* 19–41.

Buss, D., & Shackelford, T. (1997). From vigilance to violence: Mate retention tactics in married couples. *Journal of Personality and Social Psychology, 72*, 346–361.

Cody, M. (1982). A typology of disengagement strategies and an examination of the role intimacy reactions to inequity and relational problems play in strategy selection. *Communication Monographs, 49*, 148–170.

Dodgson, P., & Wood, J. (1998). Self-esteem and the cognitive accessibility of strengths and weaknesses after failure. *Journal of Personality and Social Psychology, 75*, 178–197.

Downey, G., Freitas, A., Michaelis, B., & Khouri, H. (1998). The self-fulfilling prophecy in close relationships: Rejection sensitivity and rejection by romantic partners. *Journal of Personality and Social Psychology, 75*, 545–560.

Drigotas, S., Safstrom, A., & Gentilia, T. (1999). An investment model prediction of dating infidelity. *Journal of Personality and Social Psychology, 77*, 509–524.

Emmers-Sommer, T., (1999). Negative relational events and event responses across relationship-type: Examining and comparing the impact of conflict strategy use on intimacy in same-sex friendships, opposite-sex friendships, and romantic relationships. *Communication Research Reports, 16*, 286–295.

Harvey, J., & Omarzu, J. (1997). Minding the close relationship. *Personality and Social Psychology Review, 1*, 224–240.

Holman, E., & Silver, R. (1998). Getting "stuck" in the past: Temporal orientation and coping with trauma. *Journal of Personality and Social Psychology, 74*, 1146–1163.

Nolen-Hoeksema, S., McBride, A., & Larson, J. (1997). Rumination and psychological distress among bereaved partners. *Journal of Personality and Social Psychology, 72*, 855–862.

Owen, W. (1993). Metaphors in accounts of romantic relationship terminations. In P. Kalbfleisch (Ed.), *Interpersonal communication: Evolving interpersonal relationships* (pp. 261–278). Hillsdale, NJ: Erlbaum.

Seidlitz, L., & Diener, E. (1998). Sex differences in the recall of affective experiences. *Journal of Personality and Social Psychology, 74*, 262–271.

Stroebe, W., Stroebe, M., Abakoumkin, G., & Schut, H. (1996). The role of loneliness and social support in adjustment to loss: A test of attachment versus stress theory. *Journal of Personality and Social Psychology, 70*, 1241–1249.

Terry, D., & Hynes, G. (1998). Adjustment to a low-control situation: Reexamining the role of coping responses. *Journal of Personality and Social Psychology, 74*, 1078–1092.

INDEX

Affective orientation, 59, 174–175
Affinity-seeking, 96
  as a skill, 98, 100
  compared to affinity maintenance,
    101
  list of strategies, 99–100
Androgyny/versatility, 64
Argumentativeness, 59
Assertive communication, 217 ff.
  vs. aggressive and nonassertive
    communication, 217–218
  female vs. male, 219
  nonverbal, 224–225
  verbal, 223
  what assertiveness can accomplish,
    220–222
Attractiveness, 28 ff.
  physical, 29, 95
  social, 29
  task, 30

Backchanneling, 163

Composure, 28
Communication apprehension, 72 ff.
  avoidance, 73
  cognitive interference, 74
  disruption, 74
  minimization, 73
  and listening, 161
Communication competence, 7–8, 28,
    78–79
  and cultural background, 9
Computer-mediated communication,
    129
Conflict management, 228–237
  attitudes toward, 234
  defined, 230
  fair fighting, 235–237
  sources of, 230–231
  toxic conflict strategies, 232–234
    belt-lining, 233
    gunny-sacking, 233

Conscientiousness, 27, 61
Cultural divergence, 77

Dominance, 213 ff.
  interactional, 214–216
  relational, 213–214

Emotions, 171 ff.
  characteristics, 173–174
  communication of, 176–177
  components of, 172
  descriptions of, 177–178
Expectations, 96
  short-term, 96–97
Extraversion/introversion, 64, 78

First impressions, 25–27
Flirting, 203. *See also* Sexual
    harassment

Humor orientation, 62

Immediacy, 102
  disadvantages, 103–104
  nonverbal, 102
  positive outcomes, 103
  verbal, 102
Impression management, 34–35
Interdependent/independent
    self-images, 18
Interpersonal communication, 3 ff.
  cultural implications of, 9
  defined, 4
  principles of, 5
Interpersonal needs, 40, 231
  affection, 42
  complementary vs. symmetrical,
    44–45
  control, 42–43
  inclusion, 42
  vs. physical needs, 40
  receiving and giving, 43

Jealousy, 178–182
  coping with, 181–182
  individual factors in, 179–80
  male/female differences, 180–81
  sources of, 178–179

Language intensity, 131–132
Listening, 153 ff.
  attention, 156–157
  functions of, 154–156
  information load, 159–160
  other orientation, 160
  perception, 158
    selective, 158
  problems with, 159
    anxiety, 161–162
  pseudolistening, 159
  SOLER, 163
  time, 160
Locus of control, 63

Machiavellianism, 60

Nonverbal communication, 109 ff.
  eye behavior, 114
  facial expression, 114
    facial management techniques, 115
  interpretation of, 110
  kinesics, 113
  nonverbal perception checking, 166
  nonverbal sensitivity, 123, 124, 166
  paralanguage, 115
  physical appearance, 111–112
  time, 121
    circadian rhythms, 121
    punctuality, 122
    timing, 122
  touch, 116
    interpretation of, 118–121
    meanings in relationships, 117, 118

Nonverbal perception checking, 166
Nonverbal sensitivity, 123–124, 166

Personality traits, 57ff
  affective orientation, 59
  androgyny/versatility, 64

argumentativeness, 59
conscientiousness, 27, 61
development of, 57–58
extraversion/introversion, 64–65
humor orientation, 62
link to communication, 58
locus of control, 63
machiavellianism, 60
tolerance for ambiguity, 61
verbal aggression, 59
Perception checking, 164, 170, 237
  nonverbal, 166

Receiver apprehension, 162
Relational maintenance, 101, 135
  assurances, 135
Resources in relationships, 187–189
Rules and roles, 4

Self-concept, 14, 16–19
Self disclosure, 141 ff.
  appropriateness of, 146
    reciprocation, 146
    trust, 146
  defined, 142
  functions of, 142–143
  levels of, 144
  male-female differences, 147–148
  risk, 145
  valence, 144–145
Self-esteem, 15, 15, 75
  and attributions, 16
Self-monitoring, 35
Self-serving bias, 15
Sexual harassment, 203–207
  context expectations, 205
  dealing with, 207
  distinguishing between flirting and
    harassment, 206
  male-female differences, 204
  specificity, 205
  status, 204
Shyness, 70
  love-shyness, 71
Similarity, 30
  attractiveness of, 32–34
  in perceptions, 30–32

Social exchange, 186, 190–193
  comparisons, 191
  exchange vs. communal orientations,
    193–194
SOLER, 163
Stages of relationships, 82 ff.
  diagram, 91
  stages of coming together, 83–86
    bonding, 86
    experimenting, 84
    initiating, 83, 95
    intensifying, 84
    integrating, 85
  stages of falling apart, 87–90
    avoiding, 89
    circumscribing, 88
    differentiating, 87
    stagnating, 88
    terminating, 89–90

Termination, 89–90, 242 ff.
  communication during, 246
    distancing, 246
    positive messages in, 248–249
    the termination interaction, 247
  coping with, 251–253
  reasons for termination, 245
  sources of dissatisfaction, 243–244
  unproductive reactions to, 250–251
Tolerance for ambiguity, 61

Trust, 46 ff.
  components of, 47–49
  defined, 47
  vs. gullibility, 50
  reciprocation wariness, 50
  and self-disclosure, 146

Verbal aggression, 59
Verbal communication, 127 ff.
  accusatory language, 130
  assurances, 135
  connotative meanings, 128
  denotative meanings, 128
  euphemisms, 132
  hate speech, 130
  idiosyncratic, 136–137
  intensity, 131
  powerful/powerless language,
    132–133
  and situations, 134–135
  and stages, 136–137
  vocabulary development, 136

Willingness to communicate, 74
  predictors of willingness
    to communicate, 75–77
Work relationships, 199 ff.
  differences between work and social,
    200